Control Culture

Control Culture
Foucault and Deleuze after Discipline

Edited by Frida Beckman

Edinburgh University Press is one of the leading university presses in the UK. We publish academic books and journals in our selected subject areas across the humanities and social sciences, combining cutting-edge scholarship with high editorial and production values to produce academic works of lasting importance. For more information visit our website: edinburghuniversitypress.com

© editorial matter and organisation Frida Beckman, 2018, 2020
© the chapters their several authors, 2018, 2020

First published in hardback by Edinburgh University Press 2018

Edinburgh University Press Ltd
The Tun – Holyrood Road
12(2f) Jackson's Entry
Edinburgh EH8 8PJ

Typeset in Monotype Ehrhardt by
Servis Filmsetting Ltd, Stockport, Cheshire

A CIP record for this book is available from the British Library

ISBN 978 1 4744 3675 5 (hardback)
ISBN 978 1 4744 3676 2 (paperback)
ISBN 978 1 4744 3677 9 (webready PDF)
ISBN 978 1 4744 3678 6 (epub)

The right of Frida Beckman to be identified as the editor of this work has been asserted in accordance with the Copyright, Designs and Patents Act 1988, and the Copyright and Related Rights Regulations 2003 (SI No. 2498).

Contents

Acknowledgements		vii
Notes on Contributors		ix
	Introduction. Control of What? Frida Beckman	1
1	Notes from an Investigation of 'Control Society' Gregg Lambert	20
2	Post-Mortem on Race and Control Neel Ahuja	34
3	Periodising (with) Control Seb Franklin	44
4	Subjects of Sovereign Control and the Art of Critique in the Early Modern Period Carin Franzén	63
5	Posthumanism, Social Complexity and the Political: A Genealogy for Foucault's *The Birth of Biopolitics* Cary Wolfe	82
6	'That Path is for Your Steps Alone': Popular Music, Neoliberalism and Biopolitics Jeffrey T. Nealon	101
7	Cinema in the Age of Control Gregory Flaxman	121

8 Towards a 'Minor' Fascism: Panoptic Control and Resistant
    Multiplicity in TV's *Spooks*   141
    Colin Gardner

 9 Species States: Animal Control in Phil Klay's 'Redeployment'   166
    Colleen Glenney Boggs

10 Control and a Minor Literature   180
    Frida Beckman

11 Philosophy and Control   193
    Paul Patton

Index   211

Acknowledgements

This book has been a long time coming and has had various potential shapes along the way. I know the idea of producing an edited collection on the topic of control existed before me, but I guess I was born to embody it. This, I realised at the inaugural meeting of the Society for the Study of Biopolitical Futures (SSBF) at Syracuse University in 2013 and I want to thank Gregg Lambert for inviting me, and him and Cary Wolfe for continuing to keep me in the loop. The collection is part of the larger and collective endeavour of this society to analyse the status of biopolitics in our present moment and also and more specifically part of my own affiliated project on control.

This project on control – entitled Cultures of Control – developed into a research network with that name, a speaker series at Stockholm University called 'Dialogues on the Cultures of Control', at which several of the chapters of the volume have been presented as work-in-progress papers, a larger conference on control (SLSAeu: Control) in Stockholm in 2016, and the monograph *Culture Control Critique: Allegories of Reading the Present* (2016). These various activities have been possible thanks to generous research and network grants from the Swedish Research Council, The Swedish Foundation for Humanities and Social Sciences, and Literature as a Leading Research Area at Stockholm University. The collection has benefited enormously from all the many encounters and conversations had within these frames. I want to extend a great thanks everyone involved in one way or another: to the contributors who came to Stockholm for the dialogues – Neel Ahuja, Colleen Glenney Boggs, Gregory Flaxman, Gregg Lambert, Jeffrey T. Nealon, Paul Patton and Cary Wolfe – to the others who participated in these dialogues – Roberto del Valle Alcalá, Ron Broglio, Brad Evans, Jairus Grove, Ulf Olsson, Jakob Nilsson, Lauren Wilcox and David Watson – and to the contributors who have joined the collection directly – Seb Franklin, Carin Franzén and Colin Gardner. This book is truly a collective effort.

Many thanks also to Carol Macdonald – it has been a great pleasure working with her and the team at EUP again.

As with most efforts, the completion of this book has also demanded patience and support from family and friends. Some of the travelling and symposia connected to this project happened while my mother, Yvonne, stayed with my children. Some of the final editing of the volume took place while Tomas cooked a Christmas dinner for my family.

For all of you, and of course, and encore, for Julia and Logan.

Notes on the Contributors

Neel Ahuja is Associate Professor of Feminist Studies at the University of California-Santa Cruz. Among other works on race, posthumanism and security, he is the author of the book *Bioinsecurities: Disease Interventions, Empire, and the Government of Species* (Duke University Press, 2016) and the article 'Abu Zubaydah and the Caterpillar', *Social Text* 29:1 (2011).

Frida Beckman is Associate Professor in Comparative Literature at the Department of Culture and Aesthetics at Stockholm University, Sweden. She is the author of *Between Desire and Pleasure: A Deleuzian Theory of Sexuality* (Edinburgh University Press, 2013), *Control Culture Critique: Allegories of Reading the Present* (Rowman & Littlefield International, 2016) and *Gilles Deleuze: A Critical Life* (Reaktion Books, 2017), and she has authored many articles and book chapters on literature and film.

Colleen Glenney Boggs is a scholar of nineteenth-century American literature. The recipient of fellowships from the National Endowment for the Humanities, the American Philosophical Society and the Mellon Foundation, she has published two books: *Animalia Americana: Animal Representations and Biopolitical Subjectivity* (Columbia University Press, 2013) and *Transnationalism and American Literature: Literary Translation 1773–1892* (Taylor & Francis, 2007). Her work has appeared in *American Literature*, *PMLA*, *Cultural Critique* and *J19*. She co-edits the book series Edinburgh Critical Studies in Atlantic Literatures and Cultures, serves on the PMLA editorial board, and has edited the volume *Options for Teaching the Literatures of the American Civil War* (MLA, 2016).

Gregory Flaxman is Associate Professor and Director of Global Cinema Studies at the University of North Carolina, Chapel Hill. He is the author of *Gilles Deleuze and the Fabulation of Philosophy* (2011) and the editor of *The Brain is the Screen* (2000; both from University of Minnesota Press), and he is the co-author of a forthcoming book on film, faith, and philosophy (from Edinburgh University Press).

Seb Franklin is Lecturer in Contemporary Literature at King's College, London. He has published on contemporary literature, digital technology, cybernetics and critical theory in journals such as *Grey Room*, *Novel: A Forum on Fiction* and *Camera Obscura*. In 2015 he published the monograph *Control: Digitality as Cultural Logic* with MIT Press. He is currently working on a monograph entitled *Forms of Disposal*.

Carin Franzén is Professor in Language and Culture at the Department of Culture and Communication at Linköping University, Sweden. She specialises in relations between the early modern period and our contemporary world, with a particular focus on literary representations of subjectivity in relation to love, passion and desire. She has published many books and articles including, recently and in English, 'Joi d'amor as Discursive Practice' (2017), 'Love and Desire in French Moralist Discourse' (2017) and 'Duras and the Art of the Impossible' (2016). In her most current project she explores the way early modern libertinism was involved in the questioning of established dogmas, thus contributing to a mode of critical thought.

Colin Gardner is Professor of Critical Theory and Integrative Studies at the University of California, Santa Barbara, where he teaches in the Departments of Art, Film & Media Studies, Comparative Literature, and the History of Art and Architecture. Gardner has published two books in Manchester University Press's 'British Film Makers' series: *Joseph Losey* (2004) and *Karel Reisz* (2006), as well as *Beckett, Deleuze and the Televisual Event: Peephole Art*, a critical analysis of Samuel Beckett's experimental work for film and television and its relation to the philosophical writings of Deleuze and Guattari (Palgrave Macmillan, 2012). His most recent books are *Deleuze and the Animal* (Edinburgh University Press, 2017) and *Ecosophical Aesthetics: Art, Ethics and Ecology with Guattari* (Bloomsbury, forthcoming), both co-edited with Patricia MacCormack.

Gregg Lambert is Dean's Professor of the Humanities at Syracuse University, Founding Director and Principal Investigator of the Central New York Humanities Corridor. He is also a Senior Fellow in Continental Philosophy at Western Sydney University and Distinguished International Scholar at

Kyung Hee University, Seoul. He has published widely on critical theory, literature, film, and especially on the philosophies of Gilles Deleuze and Jacques Derrida. Among his books are *Return Statements: The Return of Religion in Contemporary Philosophy* (2016) and *Deleuze and Space* (co-editor, 2006), both published by Edinburgh University Press.

Jeffrey T. Nealon is Edwin Erle Sparks Professor of English and Philosophy at Penn State University. His publications centre on contemporary literary and cultural theory and recent books include *Foucault Beyond Foucault* (2008), *Post-Postmodernism; or, the Cultural Logic of Just-in-Time Capitalism* (2012) and *Biopower and Vegetable Life* (2016, all three published with Stanford University Press). His latest book – *I'm not Like Everybody Else: Biopolitics, Neoliberalism and American Popular Music* – is due for publication in 2018.

Paul Patton is Scientia Professor of Philosophy at The University of New South Wales in Sydney, Australia. He is the author of *Deleuze and the Political* (Routledge, 2000) and *Deleuzian Concepts: Philosophy, Colonization, Politics* (Stanford University Press, 2010), and of numerous articles and book chapters on Deleuze, Foucault and a variety of topics in contemporary social and political philosophy.

Cary Wolfe is Bruce and Elizabeth Dunlevie Professor of English at Rice University, Director of 3CT: Center for Critical and Cultural Theory, and series editor of *Posthumanities* at the University of Minnesota Press. He has published numerous book and articles especially within the field of the posthumanities and animal studies. Published books include *What is Posthumanism?* (Minnesota University Press, 2010) and *Before the Law: Humans and Other Animals in a Biopolitical Frame* (University of Chicago Press, 2012).

Introduction: Control of What?

Frida Beckman

'The world', Gilles Deleuze says in a conversation with Antonio Negri in the spring of 1990, has 'been taken from us'. It has been taken from us because we have lost our belief in it and without belief, we have closed down the potential to spawn 'new space–times', to make space for even the most modest events that evade control (Deleuze 1995: 176). Strikingly, but not unusually within the framework of Deleuze's oeuvre and in particular within his more political writings, this statement is at once bleak and constructive. In the same breath as it states that we have lost belief and thus the world, it offers at least the beginning of a suggestion of how to regain it. Deleuze notes the loss of belief but also reminds us that if we could only summon up the tiniest bit of it, this would enable us to 'precipitate events' and engender 'new space–times, however small their surface or volume' (Deleuze 1995: 176). Art plays a crucial part in such claims to hope. As he writes in his second cinema book; exactly because the world has turned into 'a bad cinema, in which we no longer believe', true cinema may be able to help us restore 'our belief in the world' (Deleuze 2013: 187). It is now three decades since Deleuze started flagging questions of control – in presentations such as 'Having an Idea in Cinema/What is a Creative Act?' in 1987 and 'What is a Dispositif?' in 1988, the conversation between Deleuze and Antonio Negri entitled 'Control and Becoming', published in *Futur Antérieur* in 1990, which is also the same year in which Deleuze's short but seminal article 'Postscript on Control Societies' was first published in *L'Autre Journal*. During the decades that have passed since then, the shifts away from disciplinary society that Michel Foucault had already predicted and that Deleuze articulated in these brief engagements have escalated in ways and on a scale that neither of them could have possibly imagined. So what is the status of our belief today? And what is the role of artistic and cultural expression in relation to it?

When Foucault stated in one of his lectures at Collège de France in 1979 that 'control is no longer just the counterweight to freedom, as in the case of panopticism: it becomes its mainspring' (Foucault 2008: 67) and Deleuze pointed to 'the widespread progressive introduction of a new system of domination' based on continuous modulations and codes in 1990 (Deleuze 1995: 182), few would have imagined that it would be possible, and, indeed, common practice to trace people's movements with the help of their smartphones, or that people would voluntarily wear watches that monitor the nature of their physical activities during the day and every minute of their sleep during the night, or that social media would use algorithms to individualise not only advertisements but also information and political messages. Perhaps few would also have been able to imagine a speed of technological development which makes you realise that even as you write down the most recent examples in a book manuscript, they will most likely already seem out of date once the book is published. But even if they could not, of course, foresee the details or speed of this development, Foucault and Deleuze, did, it seems, in some sense pre-empt the conditions that would enable such technologies to flourish, the transformative effects this would have on disciplinary modes of power, the accelerating consequences on the continued development of biopolitics, and the ensuing emergence of the complexities of control society.

There will be reason, in this introduction as well as in the various chapters of this book, to revisit and revaluate Foucault's and Deleuze's theories of discipline and control in the light of these more recent developments. Indeed, and while Deleuze's conception of control constitutes a key starting point for this volume, this conception should be considered as a necessarily specific and historical attempt to map an emerging dispositif. A dispositif, in brief, and as Deleuze traces it via Foucault, is 'a tangle', a composition of lines of different nature, lines that 'do not just make up the social apparatus but run through it and pull at it' (Deleuze 1992b: 159). A dispositif shapes visibility, enunciation, knowledge, subjects, a dispositif is made up of concrete, if always potentially transformable components, a dispositif constitutes a machine 'which make[s] one see and speak' (Deleuze 1992b: 160). Working with the notion of the dispositif is a way of acknowledging the specific components and coordinates of power at any one time while simultaneously recognising how such components and coordinates are variable and also invariably under transformation. 'In each apparatus [*dispositif*]', as Deleuze puts it, 'it is necessary to distinguish what we are (what we are already no longer), and what we are in the process of becoming' (Deleuze 1992b: 164). Underlined here, and this takes us back to the 'new space–times' that Deleuze hopes we will summon up in the face of control, each dispositif should be assessed also in its ability to 'break down' and make way for 'a future apparatus'. It may be possible to trace 'paths of creation, which are continually aborting, but then restarting, in a modified way, until the former apparatus is broken' (Deleuze 1992b: 163–4).

However, and while a dispositif necessarily builds on variable lines and coordinates, these lines and coordinates may be hard, rigid and solid and thus difficult to break (Deleuze 1992b: 164). And at the moment, control, in all its suppleness, seems increasingly hard, rigid and solid. Perhaps it is because of its all-encompassing tendencies that we are struggling to envision its breaking point, perhaps it is because neither Foucault nor Deleuze lived long enough to develop their theories or to respond to the conditions they pre-empted, but it may also be because we are too close to it – because we are as yet unable to 'distinguish what we are (what we are already no longer), and what we are in the process of becoming'. But exactly because of these concerns, is seems important to map and interrogate some of those lines and paths. 'Our ability to resist control, or our submission to it', Deleuze writes in his 'Postscript', 'has to be assessed at the level of our every move' (Deleuze 1995: 176). This is what this volume hopes to do, or at least aspires towards. It aims high as it hopes to contribute to ways of assessing our submission to control as well as our ability to resist it across a large number of discourses and modes of expression. It hopes to be able to do so, not just by discussing and identifying control mechanisms more generally but also, and more specifically, by examining the specificities of a broad range of cultural expression and the ways in which control functions or is resisted in different modes and media.

The chapters in this volume explore control in relation to philosophy, music, cinema, television, contemporary fiction, the history of the novel, early modern essayist traditions, poetry and digital technologies, and they offer a number of unique takes on what the various modulations of control might look like as actualised through differing formal, generic and contextual conditions. On the one hand they look at how in control society 'nothing's left alone for long', and on the other at how different modes of expression construct what Deleuze calls 'war-machines', that is 'a particular way of occupying, taking up, space–time, or inventing new space–times' (Deleuze 1995: 175, 172). This way, the chapters simultaneously contribute to more area-specific studies pertaining to the particular status of different disciplines in the present and to analyses that broaden, deepen, historicise, actualise and problematise conceptions of control. Control can and has been conceptualised in many ways and the different contributors will interrogate or expand on different facets of this concept. The conception of control that is most central to the book as a whole is that which emerges from Foucault and Deleuze so, first, let me just briefly outline these core ideas.

Deleuze begins his 'Postscript' with Foucault and an outline of the way the latter theorises the logic of disciplinary societies. Succeeding sovereign societies, discipline as a mode of political control relies on spaces of enclosure, that is on institutions such as the prison, the hospital, the asylum, the factory, the school and the family. The individual passes from one to the other and is claimed and moulded by their laws and regulations. This logic dominated during the eighteenth and nineteenth centuries, it peaked at the beginning of the twentieth century, and its demise accelerated after World War II. After this point, Deleuze suggests, institutions like these have come into crisis. Indeed, they are finished, he suggests, 'whatever the length of their expiration periods' (Deleuze 1992a: 4). In their place has emerged a different order of power – that which he calls 'societies of control'. William Burroughs is identified as the one naming this 'new monster' control and Paul Virilio is recognised as an early theorist of its free-floating nature. One of the key features of control society as Deleuze theorises it is the instant but continuous adjustment and manipulation of affect that makes the arduous disciplining of the subject moving from one institution to the next increasingly redundant:

> In disciplinary societies you were always starting all over again (as you went from school to barracks, from barracks to factory), while in control societies you never finish anything – business, training, and military service being coexisting metastable states of a single modulation, a sort of universal transmutation. (Deleuze 1995: 179)

This form of power is faster and freer – it does not depend on institutions and on moulding individuals according to their norms, but on the constant modulation and coding of affects and desires.

What emerges in the place of the long-term training of the individual body in disciplinary society is, Deleuze suggests, the 'dividual' of control society, that is parts of selves, affects, desires, which are identified, addressed and controlled by means of samples and data. Deleuze illuminates the differences between different types of power with the help of machines. Sovereign societies relied on simple machines such as levers and clocks, disciplinary society on machines of energy and production, and control societies on computers. This most recent stage is largely a move from the analogical to the digital. 'The family, the school, the army, the factory are no longer the distinct analogical spaces that converge towards an owner – state or private power – but coded figures – deformable and transformable – of a single corporation that now has only stockholders' (Deleuze 1992a: 6). This is also intimately related to geopolitical developments and globalisation as the machines of production have largely been relegated to the Third World. It is in the West, then, that the crisis of institutions has paved way for 'a new system of domination' (Deleuze 1992a: 7).

Several of the chapters in this volume quarrel with or extend Deleuze's conception of control. Concerns include its historical or conceptual relation to

Foucault's understanding of discipline, ways in which either or both of these concepts have been deployed by later critics, or dimensions of control that have remained un- or underexplored. This includes Gregg Lambert – who questions the usefulness of Deleuze's concept and its powerful influence on theories of biopolitics, Seb Franklin – who suggests that our understanding of the relation between discipline and control needs to be broadened beyond its common historical and Western applications, Carin Franzén – who discovers links between the control and the libertine art practices of sovereign societies, Neel Ahuja – who provides a conceptualisation of control and race, and Cary Wolfe – who questions not so much Foucault as Wendy Brown's recent and influential critique of his work. Other chapters explore or deploy the concepts of discipline and control in trying to understand recent developments in different cultural modes of expression. Thus, Jeffrey T. Nealon analyses the changing function of popular music in relation to control over the decades since the 1960s, Paul Patton explores the fate of philosophy as a discipline in an increasingly neoliberal university, Gregory Flaxman investigates contemporary cinematic dreams of escaping 'off the grid', Colin Gardner looks at surveillance and control strategies in television, Colleen Glenney Boggs explores how control is increasingly control without an object, and my own chapter investigates ways in which the novel form may be challenged by control mechanisms.

But, and possibly with Lambert as an exception, these contributors ultimately want to develop rather than dismiss Deleuze's concept. None of them takes the stronger stance of Mark G. E. Kelly, who argues that Deleuze misinterprets Foucault's conception of discipline (Kelly 2015: 151). While acknowledging that the power structures of society have continued to develop and that Foucault himself identified a 'shift in forms of power from repression of bodies to a looser control', Kelly insists that such a shift does not fundamentally change the nature or essence of the regime of discipline (Kelly 2015: 151–3). Contemporary neoliberalism may be 'less disciplinary' in the sense that direct state interventions have decreased but the governing of human behaviour that is more prominent is still about discipline, be it 'at the level of enterprises' (Kelly 2015: 154). For Kelly, then, the shifts that Deleuze discusses must be understood in terms of a shift in intensity rather than in type (Kelly 2015: 154) – it is not a matter of a new power technology but of changing relations 'within disciplinary, biopolitical capitalism' (Kelly 2015: 162). I'm not sure, however, that Deleuze or most of those taking on his control concept insist that the transition does imply the former. Indeed, Deleuze speaks of 'modulations' of forms of power for a very specific reason. An alternative here may be to, like Lambert, see Deleuze's conception of control as a 'mutation' of Foucauldian theory.

Some contributors to this volume make use of the notion of the diagram as it has been developed by Foucault and Deleuze as it is helpful when discussing whether the shift between discipline and control should be understood in terms of essences or intensification. The Foucauldian notion of the diagram, which recurs in Deleuze's work, not least in his book on Foucault, outlines generalisable, abstract functions and is useful when outlining transitions and distinctions between different dispositifs. More specifically, the diagram helps us map, abstractly, the specific functions of different societies. Thus, and as we have already learned above, in the diagram of disciplinary society we can include spatiotemporal stability, institutions, individuals and analogical machines, while the diagram of control comprises abstract fluidity, codes, dividuals and digitality. Many more dimensions can be included in these diagrams, of course, and the different chapters of this book will help identify also the more discreet dimensions of the diagram of control society or, as is the case of Lambert's chapter, help us problematise the distinction that Deleuze makes between disciplinary- and control society in the first place. Another of the contributors to this volume, Gregory Flaxman, has argued, although not in his chapter here, that a crucial difference between the diagrams of discipline and control is that while the former still seems to include the possibility for interpretation to retrieve hidden meanings, the latter offers no such possibility because 'its diagram is never concealed' (Flaxman 2012: 283). To do something more than to illuminate the workings of the diagram itself, Deleuze thus needs to introduce an element that, while immanent to the logic, offers the potential for change. In this light, Deleuze's reliance on an element from science fiction, namely the feature of the future, or the outside, which Lambert quarrels with, is arguably an element that emerges with Deleuze's ambition to incorporate, in the diagram of control, a potential for resistance.

However, and although Deleuze suggests in his 'Postscript' that we need not fear or hope, 'but only to look for new weapons' (Deleuze 1992a: 4) and he does end this essay with the question of resistance, the piece ultimately does little more than outline what he sees as some key differences between discipline and control. In his conversation with Negri, several of these key points are rehearsed but here is developed at least a little more concretely what he sees as essential to a political analysis of the present. Referring back to his and Félix Guattari's *A Thousand Plateaus*, he points to the three main directions it takes when thinking about the analysis of capitalism: the mapping and analysis of the lines of flight that characterise any society, the consideration of minorities, that is being – or rather becoming – without a model, and the characterisation of 'war machines', which 'have nothing to do with war but to do with a particular way of occupying, taking up, space–time, or inventing new space–times: revolutionary movements' (Deleuze 1995: 171–2). In the conversation with Negri, he also picks up Henri Bergson's conception of fabulation and suggests that we ought to 'give it political meaning' (Deleuze 1995: 174). Furthermore, he develops his attention to the relation between communication and control that he mentions in the 'Postscript' and states that we need to 'highjack speech'. Creating, he goes on to argue in a truly Burroughsian vein, 'has always been something different from communicating. The key may be to create vacuoles of noncommunication, circuit breakers, so we can elude control' (Deleuze 1995: 175). What matters, he says towards the end, is the 'real rebellious spontaneity' that may only emerge for a moment and then become part of new forms of knowledge and power, but that engender new space–times that keep us thinking and believing (Deleuze 1995: 176).

Art, Deleuze indicates in 'Having an Idea in Cinema' (1998) – that is, in the third piece in which he explicitly talks about control society – provides such spaces. In this essay, he articulates more directly his understanding of the relation between control, communication and art. Art is not about communication, he argues, in fact, he suggests, it has 'nothing to do with' and 'does not contain the least bit of information'. As such, the work of art has fundamental affinities with the act of resistance, which also needs to be something different from information. Defining information as 'the controlled system of order-words that are used in a given society', Deleuze links this to an emerging control society in which confinement as a control mechanism will be replaced with information that enables a 'free' but nonetheless 'perfectly controlled' movement (Deleuze 1998: 18). In a society where 'information is precisely the system of control' (Deleuze 1998: 17), art harbours resistance and, apart from again referring to the literary example of Burroughs, he also gives examples from music (Schoenberg) and cinema (Straub and Huillet). As these very brief examples suggest – it is a pity that Deleuze never had the chance to explore in more detail how literature, music, cinema, as well as the other arts harbour the power to resist control, although, arguably, he does perform such analysis implicitly in much of his later work – there are many facets to control to be explored in relation to many art forms, a task that the present collection will try to pursue. Such a project is especially important since, and despite Deleuze's pointers to art as a mode of resistance to control, art has not constituted a very common angle in studies of control after Deleuze. There are exceptions, of course. For example, Steven Shaviro uses control as one of the key diagrams of his study of post-cinematic affect (see Shaviro 2010), and Simon O'Sullivan has pursued the question of art practice and resistance and argued that Deleuze's brief control texts offer up 'a veritable arsenal for any practice that might pitch itself against control' (O'Sullivan 2016: 206).

But specific studies of control and cultural expression are far outnumbered by studies of control as related to technology and digitisation. And of course, technology does play a fundamental role in developments in and concepts of control. Deleuze, as we have seen, recognises this in the 'Postscript'. And, as Eugene Thacker puts it, if 'one is to foster an understanding and awareness of how the social and the political are not external to technology', then 'it is important to understand how the technological is in some sense isomorphic to the social and political' (Thacker 2004: xii). Thus, we can see how James R. Beniger identifies a 'Control Revolution' taking place around the turn from the nineteenth to the twentieth century and growing quickly in the US, England, France and Germany. Beniger refers to Max Weber as one of the first theorists to recognise and theorise the need for societal control emerging with the effects of the Industrial Revolution. Weber, of course, and as Beniger notes, analysed bureaucracy, the key technology of control at this time. After World War II, however, computer technology gradually began to take over as the key mode of control (Beniger 1986: 6). Norbert Wiener's 1948 *Cybernetics: Control and Communication in the Animal and the Machine* constituted a key starting point for discussions of control in relation to self-regulated systems. Both the systems and the theories have advanced exponentially since Weiner's study and also since Beniger's study from 1986. But they continue to point to the fundamental link that control has to technological developments and in particular to the emergence of cybernetics and digital communications. Studies of control since then have continued to be related to technology and the most common angle on the subject of control in contemporary research is still the interrelation between control, the materiality of technology, and, increasingly, network systems.

'The network', Alexander R. Galloway and Thacker observe in 2007, 'has emerged as a dominant form describing the nature of control today' (Galloway and Thacker 2007: 4). Exploring the materiality of control in network environments, Galloway questions the freedom associated with digital communication and points to hidden control mechanisms and the codes and protocol that enable them. 'Protocol', he argues, 'is to control societies as the panopticon is to disciplinary societies' (Galloway 2004: 13). While Galloway thus underlines Deleuze's prediction of the centrality of computers to the development of control society, Mark Poster points out that although Deleuze refers repeatedly to the importance of computer technology to this development, he is never very specific and clear about this relation. His reliance on Burroughs when discussing information and counter-information illuminates, Poster argues, this lack of grounding in new technologies as these were hardly prevalent in Burroughs' time (Poster 2006: 59–60). Poster therefore finds the term control society as it has or has not been developed after Deleuze unable to fully account for new technologies of power.

Antoinette Rouvroy proposes the concept of 'algorithmic governmentality' to illuminate the workings of contemporary technology and control. Algorithmic governmentality is not reliant on a process of subjectivation; it does not 'need to tame the wilderness of facts and behaviours; nor does it aim at producing docile subjects', in fact it 'carefully avoids any direct confrontation with and impact on flesh and blood persons' (Rouvroy 2013: 157). Instead, the target of control is 'a unique, supra-individual, constantly reconfigured "statistical body" made of the infra-individual digital traces of impersonal, disparate, heterogeneous, dividualized facets of daily life and interactions' (Rouvroy 2013: 157). Similarly, Benjamin H. Bratton argues that the mode of governance emerging with the technologies of the present is increasingly disinterested in human subjects. We no longer deal primarily with 'the 'state as a machine' (Weber) or the 'state machine' (Althusser) or really even (only) the technologies of governance (Foucault) as much as it is *the machine as the state*' (Bratton 2015: 8). Instead, he suggests, we are dealing with a new mode of governance altogether, one whose 'primary means and interests are not human discourse and human bodies but, rather, the calculation of all the world's information and of the world itself *as* information' (Bratton 2015: 8). This means that what is called for, according to Bratton, is no longer only ways of identifying and theorising new functions of the state or the ways new technologies should be governed, but a recognition and theorisation of how technology today comes to 'absorb functions of the state and the work of governance' (Bratton 2015: 7). This, of course, has implications for global politics. Closely analysing the processes of network society, Tiziana Terranova sees how it is characterised by information overload, an overload moving across multiple communication channels, while it also moves global culture 'within a single informational milieu' (Terranova 2004: 1). While it is possible to see this as a homogenisation of culture additionally under siege by the white noise of continuous information, Terranova argues that the 'annihilation of distances within an informational milieu' brings a 'creative destruction' and '*productive* movement' that releases rather than inhibits the potential for transformation (Terranova 2004: 2–3).

In the light of such radical developments in technology, some of the projections Deleuze makes (with the help of Guattari), such as the continuous computational tracking and control of city-dwellers, may seem, as Bratton puts it, 'quaint'. This is not because Deleuze and Guattari were wrong about the continuous modulation enabled by such technologies – indeed Deleuze does identify the increasing importance and role of computational information technology to societies of control – but because such modes are perfectly commonplace today (Bratton 2015: 158). However, Deleuze did, as Luciana Parisi points out, anticipate the convergence between power and the operative realm of control 'as it constantly works to glue together spatiotemporalities into extended apparatuses of uninterrupted relationality' (Parisi 2013: 102). As such, Parisi shows, his work can also be quite useful in developing a postcybernetic theory of control. Galloway, Poster, Rouvroy, Bratton and Parisi thus in different ways recognise the importance of, but also the need to continue developing, Deleuze's control theories in the field of technology.

At the same time, Foucault's and Deleuze's concepts are used and elaborated in attempts to theorise contemporary developments in biopolitics. In an essay published in 1995, that is in the same year as Deleuze's control essays were translated into English, Michael Hardt traces the concept of civil society from Hegel to Gramsci to Foucault. Foucault's disciplinary society, he argues, can be described as civil society seen from below, describing the same society but pointing out the normalisation procedures that inevitably inflect its democratic potentials (Hardt 1995: 33). While thus bringing to this concept a problematised and problematising perspective on democracy, the disciplinary model continues to rely on the constructions of subjects and identities. What makes control society 'postcivil' is, essentially, the new techniques in which the citizen has become rather 'an infinitely flexible placeholder for identity' (Hardt 1995: 40). Control, he argues, 'functions on the plane of the simulacra of society' and the 'whateverness of the societies of control is precisely what gives them their smooth surfaces' (Hardt 1995: 37). In other words, while the diagram of discipline is similar to civil society in that it relies on fixed positions and identities (albeit as its dark underbelly, as I argue in my chapter contribution to this volume), the diagram of control, relying rather on mobility and flexibility, takes us into a postcivil era.

Where Hardt thus employs Deleuze's concept of control to articulate a theory of 'postcivil society', Brian Massumi uses it to theorise a 'capitalist supersystem'. By outlining the relation between command and control, he provides a picture of specificities, interrelations and developments of and between discipline and control. Command and control, Massumi argues, are reciprocal and can never be separated, but the dynamics between them differ depending on the power structures at hand. Thus, the institutions that constitute a central function in disciplinary society can be discussed as 'normative command centers radiating control' whereas control society relies on a 'fine-meshing of command and control', that is its distribution is increasingly independent of such 'centers' (Massumi 1998: 56–7). Here, Massumi also contributes to developing Deleuze's brief pointer to the shift between discipline and control by showing how this shift entails the deregulation of 'normal'. Normality, as a central dimension of the command of a disciplinary system, relies to a large extent on creating a binary normative system positioning deviant elements as oppositional. In control society, however, normality is liberated from such fixed values and becomes free-standing. 'Normativity', he suggests, 'becomes synonymous with collective visibility and social operativity – with living itself' (Massumi 1998: 57). In fact, this is a key characteristic of this developed capitalist system – normality is not coded but is constantly modulated and emerges in effect – the system is 'formally undetermined but gives rise to determinations', it is 'ungrounded yet grounds' (Massumi 1998: 59). In this post-ideological, posthuman era, command and control 'reciprocally generate each other and disappear and reappear into each other following a complicated and fundamentally unpredictable rhythm covering the totality of social space' (Massumi 1998: 58).

Foucault's and Deleuze's theories also constitute an important starting point for Hardt's and Negri's theorisation of empire during the first decade of the twenty-first century. Through their theories, Hardt and Negri gain the tools to explore 'the material functioning of imperial rule' and develop their analysis of the mechanisms of biopolitical production on a geopolitical scale. Analysing the decline in the power of institutions and autonomy of nation states that has occurred as a result of an increasingly globalised capitalist production, they integrate and develop theories of the transition between discipline and control to account for what they see as 'a new global form of sovereignty' – empire (Hardt and Negri 2000: xii). Biopolitical production is key to this new paradigm, and they understand it as 'the production of social life itself, in which the economic, the political, and the cultural increasingly overlap and invest one another' (Hardt and Negri 2000: xiii). Hardt and Negri make a useful comparison between theories of discipline and control and the better-known Marxist theory of the transition between formal and real subsumption and the Frankfurt School development of these theories in relation to culture and social relations. This comparison – which Franklin picks up on in his chapter in the present volume – points to the similarity between the theories, while also emphasising a crucial difference that exists already with Foucault but that becomes more explicit in Deleuze. While the Marxist and Frankfurt School theories of real subsumption rely on unidimensional processes, Foucault and Deleuze bring out the plurality and multiplicity of subsumption. This is an extension of real subsumption beyond its economic and social dimensions to include also 'the social *bios* itself', that is, all dimensions of living and of life itself.

Increasingly also, and here we approach the more direct context of the present collection, control is being theorised or used as a way of understanding the cultural logic of the present. Franklin argues, in his book-length study on the matter, that while the link between digital technologies and control continues to account for a significant amount of its 'conceptual and explanatory power' (Franklin 2015: xiv), it is crucial that we explore control also as a cultural logic. By proposing control as the cultural logic of the present, Franklin finds a Jamesonian way of addressing the problem of periodisation. Jameson, we may recall, resolved the problem of periodising and thereby potentially obliterating the many differences inherent in postmodernism by positioning it as a cultural dominant 'a conception which allows for the presence and coexistence of a range of very different, yet subordinate, features' (Jameson 1991: 4). True to Jameson, Franklin notes that understanding the political implications of a cultural object requires looking not only at the explicitly political in terms of content but also at 'the specific technical objects, economic practices, industrial formations, political ideals, and organizational diagrams' surrounding it (Franklin 2015: xxii). Thus, for example, he addresses Jameson's classic elaboration on the concept of cognitive mapping in the 1980s as well as Galloway's and Wendy Hui Kyong Chun's problematisation of this method in relation to network culture in the twenty-first century. Franklin wants to develop a model capable also of teasing out the material implications – 'the socioeconomic and cultural costs' – of representation under control. 'The mode of cultural analysis that control necessitates', he writes, 'is thus one that takes the monolithic historical dimension of algorithmic or networked logic [. . .] as inseparable from the formations of sense and subjectivity that produce cultural forms' (Franklin 2015: 99).

Paying close attention to the cultural forms and the cultural logic of control is crucial as what is repeated and underlined in writings on contemporary control is the way in which it implicates itself into every aspect of life and on all levels of being. If disciplinary control still comes with at least some degree of possibility of identifying the locus of power, control has become so subtle and pervasive and so integral to our every move that it has become hard even to identify it. Bernard E. Harcourt suggests that control has become so integrated into our pleasures and desires that we accept it with open arms. Although we are at least vaguely aware of the ways in which our increasingly, and increasingly inescapable, digital existence makes it possible to monitor, mine and profile our behaviour and desires everywhere and all the time, that very immediacy itself – 'the stimulating distractions and sensual pleasures of the new digital age' – sidetracks us from this fact (Harcourt 2015: 3). But it is not the dulling and distracting and forgetting which are the most central mechanisms but rather the ways in which the workings and constituents of our digital life speak to, encourage and manipulate our desires that constitute the key element of contemporary power structures. These power structures, he argues, are different from those of disciplinary society exactly in that there is no real need to enforce discipline or to make a distinction between our regular lives and correctional facilities. Because 'coercive surveillance technology is now woven into the very fabric of our pleasure and fantasies', it has become impossible, today, to separate between pleasure and punish (Harcourt 2015: 21).

Many concepts have been proposed to understand the structure of this new logic. Mentioned here have been Galloway's 'protocol', Rouvroy's 'algorithmic governmentality', Hardt's 'postcivil society', Massumi's 'capitalist supersystem', Hardt and Negri's 'empire', and there are also what Harcourt calls 'expository society', Poster the 'superpanopticon', and Bratton 'the Stack'. What these concepts have in common is the sense of the all-encompassing nature of contemporary control. However, they all to a differing extent also stress the importance as well as the possibility of resistance. And importantly, this resistance is necessarily located within control society itself. Massumi proposes 'productive interference patterns' that introduce excess, deficiency, humour – anything that does not resonate with this system. For Hardt, it is essential that we investigate the ways in which the form as well as the very nature of labour but also of social practices has changed, in order to identify 'the germs for a new movement, with new forms of contestation and new conceptions of liberation' (Hardt 1995: 41). Galloway sees how the regime of control through protocol requires abandoning any ambition to transcend the immanent workings of control but also that 'it is *through* protocol that one must guide one's efforts, not against it' (Galloway 2004: 17). In the face of the power of the 'superpanopticon' to fix the self, Poster suggests, we 'might search for new configurations of selfhood that keep open spaces of resistance', spaces that we will find 'especially in the human–machine mediascapes of networked computing' (Poster 2006: 115). Bratton's Stack model 'is global but not immutable'. The intrinsic modularity that gives it its power is the same modularity that makes it 'a platform, and an interface event, for the redesign and replacement of the Stack-we-have with a Stack-we-want (or perhaps with the Stack-we-want-the-least)' (Bratton 2015: xviii). The potential for change via the multitude in Hardt and Negri's *Empire* has been highlighted by them as well as other theorists of control such as Terranova, who underlines how her understanding of information comes with 'a specific reorientation of forms of power *and* modes of resistance' (Terranova 2004: 37). And the final task that Harcourt sets himself in his analysis of 'expository society', is 'To explore how to resist and disobey' (Harcourt 2015: 26).

So what about art and culture and their role in understanding or resisting control culture? As I underlined at the beginning of this Introduction, Deleuze identifies art as key to such projects. The present collection builds on the work that has already been done in the field of biopolitics while marking the grounds for a variable but sustained engagement with the relation between different art forms, modes of cultural expression and control. Beginning with an approach from a sceptical perspective, the first chapter, by Gregg Lambert, offers a report of an investigation into Deleuze's conception of control and what Lambert argues to be its all too prevailing and mythic influence in discussions of biopolitics. In his 'Notes from an Investigation of "Control Society"', he argues that Deleuze's observations – which he regards as a mutation of Foucault's analysis of the dispositif of discipline – include an element of science fiction that spoils its capacity to function as the teleology of contemporary political and social transformations. Reading Deleuze's piece alongside Ray Bradbury's short story 'The Pedestrian', linking it to Deleuze and Guattari's *Anti-Oedipus* and *A Thousand Plateaus*, as well as comparing the latter to Foucault's notes in *The Birth of Biopolitics*, Lambert's investigation not only questions philosophy as a tool of prognostication more generally but also points to an 'inflationary and paranoid style' shaping this part of Deleuze and Guattari's work. Situating the control essays in the context of the historical as well as personal turbulence from which they were conceived, Lambert does suggest that some aspects of Deleuze's mutation can and should be pursued while ultimately putting Deleuze out of a job.

Lambert's chapter opens up a critical intuition that begins to define a perspective further illuminated in the following set of chapters, which is that Deleuze's elaboration on Foucault is useful in some ways but that it needs to be problematised or expanded to be of much help. Lambert stresses the importance of beginning the work of developing 'different conventions for establishing our contemporary relationship between power and knowledge', and in Chapter 2 Neel Ahuja pursues race accordingly as a severely underexplored potential of Deleuze's work on control. Such missing explorations are, perhaps, unsurprising considering the missing articulation of race in Deleuze's own work, but in 'Post-Mortem on Race and Control', Ahuja investigates the usefulness of Deleuzian control theory for critical race studies. Apart from the lack of an explicit relation to race in Deleuze's own work on control, the understanding of the development of control as a devaluation of the institutions of Foucauldian discipline and especially the prison marks another reason why the interest in Deleuze's conception of control has been limited within the field of critical race studies, which has strongly disputed claims that state violence, including incarceration and torture, has declined. However, Ahuja shows, there are ways in which Deleuzian theories of control can be used productively within this field, especially as a means of elucidating the relation between the long history of racial violence and the plasticity of contemporary biopolitics of race. Indeed, and as he notes, these theories have already been put to use by key scholars in the field, such as Jasbir Puar. Control theories, he concludes, do need to be rethought 'from the inside out', but if and when they are, they can be of importance to understanding race in a context of a contemporary, posthuman landscape.

In Chapter 3, 'Periodising (with) Control', Seb Franklin notes that while Deleuze's different writings on control are often seen to provide us with a relatively linear and historically determinable distinction between discipline and control, taking on longer-term formations such as race, class, gender, sex and disability quickly problematises any clear successive relation between the two. Addressing the role of cultural production, he insists that 'a cultural logic of control' must extend beyond its more obvious applications such as computer technology, post-industrial labour forms and science fictional projections of high-tech futures. To exemplify this, Franklin reads M. NourbeSe Philip's cycle of poems – *ZONG!* – from 2008, which is based on the massacre of enslaved Africans to collect insurance money in 1783. This poem, he argues, illuminates several mechanisms customarily associated with societies of control and it thereby reminds us not to be too near-sighted when it comes to periodising control. Such a wider focus as regards the periodising of control is pursued also by Carin Franzén in Chapter 4, 'Subjects of Sovereign Control and the Art of Critique in the Early Modern Period', where she suggests that contemporary societies of control share similarities with societies of sovereignty. Reminding us of Deleuze's suggestion that modes of control from sovereign societies may indeed reappear, Franzén identifies, explores and excavates such similarities in terms of the ambiguity of control as simultaneously enslaving and liberating. Following Foucault while conducting a careful reading of the form and function of genres developed in the wake of Montaigne, such as fables, letter writing and maxims, Franzén points to ways in which such discursive and aesthetic practices functioned as a subtle but integral mode of critique of contemporary sovereign modes of control. Style is crucial to such practices as they constitute the means of negotiating sovereign modes of power, including docility as well as human sovereignty. Adding to Foucault's thinking of stylisation and critique, Judith Butler's notion of 'virtue' and Catherine Malabou's conception of plasticity, she shows how libertine subjects made cultural practices into an 'art of critique'. Perhaps, she argues, we can learn something from them in encountering and negotiating control society; perhaps a contemporary critique of neoliberal rationality can find use of such 'potential of artistry'.

Another type of near-sightedness is identified and interrogated in Cary Wolfe's chapter, 'Posthumanism, Social Complexity, and the Political: A Genealogy for Foucault's *The Birth of Biopolitics*', in which he explores the possibilities for a posthumanist conception of control. Critically interrogating Wendy Brown's recent suggestion that Foucault's antagonism towards Marxist theories renders his work unable to take on board the mechanisms of a contemporary neoliberal society, Wolfe argues that Foucault does have a relation to Marxism – but one that is less humanist than that sought by Brown. Wolfe thereby sheds light on a conception of the political that he sees as better suited to the political mechanisms of the present. By bringing out theories of social complexity articulated by Foucault in his analyses of transitions between disciplinary societies and governmentality, by Deleuze in his essays on control society, and by Niklas Luhmann, Wolfe argues that the sphere of the political is not on the wane, as Brown insists, but, quite on the contrary, that we in a true Foucauldian fashion need to challenge our assumptions about 'what the political is and how it operates' and then to recognise that everything has become more political.

Where the first set of chapters thus interrogates conceptions of discipline and control from different perspectives, the second set of chapters puts these conceptions to work looking specifically at different modes of cultural expression – music, cinema, television, literature and philosophy – and also more directly at the intensification of control after the post-World War II period that Deleuze describes. Thus, in Chapter 6, '"That Path is for Your Steps Alone": Popular Music, Neoliberalism and Biopolitics', Jeffrey T. Nealon argues that popular music constitutes a prime 'operating system' of biopower in the present. Naturally, other art forms too are implicated in biopower, but unlike say poetry, novels, or art, the ever-presence of music in our contemporary everyday lives makes it a privileged example of what Guattari calls 'machinic enslavement'. As such, Nealon underlines, it constitutes an ideal target for mapping the development of biopolitics and control as well as a supreme place to look for Deleuze's 'new weapons'. Tracing the function of popular music from the counterculture to the present, he shows how notions of the individual and authenticity as well as of freedom and resistance have to be rethought. A clear shift during these decades is that the ideas of self-realisation that were intended to position subjects outside societal institutions and norms in the 1960s have become an imperative in a present that thrives exactly on constant updates and modulations. As such, we can no longer neither rely on Adornian rejections of popular music as meaningless distraction from more authentic concerns nor on countercultural celebrations of music's potential for transgressive authenticity, but we have to find alternative ways of understanding the role of music as well as its potential for resistance.

In Chapter 7, Gregory Flaxman explores control and cinema. Deleuze's work on control emerges around the same time as his two cinema books and in the latter, Flaxman notes, we can find an investigation of control society *avant la lettre*. In 'Cinema in the Age of Control', Flaxman takes off from ways in which the critical and cartographic dimensions of cinema carry a correspondence to disciplinary society and compares this to what he observes as contemporary Hollywood cinema's preoccupation with the notion of being 'off the grid'. Exploring *The Bourne Identity* and its successors as paradigmatic of this preoccupation – which may be traced exactly to its current and seeming vanishing point – he notes that such films repeatedly return to the fantasy of escaping off the grid. Being both symptomatic as well as diagnostic, the film evinces a set of elaborations of the grid that also can be seen as aspects of control society and thus as useful to understandings of control. At the same time, and as the hero of these films repeatedly succeeds by tricking an increasingly digitalised and all-encompassing control system by means of old-school tactics, thus seemingly suggesting that the weapons are to be found in the lingering elements of disciplinary society, Bourne's preternaturally gifted character also makes clear that only those who are more than human may succeed in such endeavours.

Control and contemporary television programming is investigated in Chapter 8, Colin Gardner's 'Towards a "Minor" Fascism: Panoptic Control and Resistant Multiplicity in TV's *Spooks*'. Gardner takes a look at the television series *Spooks* and the way it both thematically and formally presents the fluidity of a surveillance culture that includes MI5 and the CIA as well as their Russian counterparts and traditional enemies. Elucidating the fluid relationships between these supposedly very different agencies and showing how the series uses the television medium to parallel this fluidity and make the viewer complicit in this modulatory surveillance culture, Gardner maps the dispositif of what he calls a 'velvet fascism'. This concept he arrives at by adapting Deleuze and Guattari's concept of a minor literature to account for what, through the series, emerges as a 'minor fascism', which becomes a useful way for him to account for the connecting non-hierarchal and deterritorialising lines of the control culture portrayed in the series. Like Flaxman, Gardner draws up connections with Deleuze's *Cinema II: The Time-Image* and in particular with Deleuze's analysis of false movements. In *Spooks*, however, such movements do not open towards a 'people yet to come', but rather – and as the progressive or revolutionary is replaced by the multiplicity, and this multiplicity becomes the driving force of the dispositif of surveillance culture – *Spooks* makes us part of an abstract machine in which a minor fascism is the only mode of negotiation.

A short story is in focus in Chapter 9, 'Species States: Animal Control in Phil Klay's 'Redeployment', where Colleen Glenney Boggs shows how Klay's eponymous story opens up for a way of theorising control as an object in and of itself. This key feature of the intensification of control, she notes, is difficult to theorise and Klay's story is therefore useful in that it provides concrete ways of reading this recession of a separation between control and the objects of control. Boggs' analysis, which positions Foucauldian theories of biopower in relation to contemporary cartoons as well as Locke's conception of education, shows how the redeployed soldier in Klay's story finds himself simultaneously unable to maintain or break species borders, and is also unable to distinguish himself from the control structures of which he is part. As control becomes its own object, conceptions of subjects and objects, humans and animals, home and war are put at stake.

Chapter 10, 'Control and a Minor Literature', explores potential implications of theories and mechanisms of control on our reading of the novel as a literary form. As I note in this chapter, the modern Western novel is shaped largely alongside the emergence of modern industrialisation and thus with the consolidation of disciplinary society in the late eighteenth and early nineteenth centuries. The novel, as well as theories thereof, has been strongly influenced by the centrality of the individual subject to such power structures. If it is correct that the intensification of control comes with a shift from the individual to the dividual, I ponder, will this mean that the novel changes or that our readings of it will? Picking up on Deleuze's brief reference to Kafka in his 'Postscript', I take this back to Deleuze and Guattari's analysis of the particularities of the novel form in their study of Kafka and suggest that this can help us think about the relation between literature and control.

In the eleventh and final chapter, simply titled 'Philosophy and Control', we return to philosophy with Paul Patton who maps out how transitions between discipline and control are visible in the changing role of universities in general, and in the discipline of philosophy in particular. Patton traces the disciplinary moulds shaping an earlier history of philosophy both in terms of institutional mechanisms and in terms of what Deleuze calls the Image of Thought and sees how this assemblage, in Deleuzian terms, or apparatus in a Foucauldian sense, has shaped philosophical thinking. In societies of control, he notes, such assemblages are challenged by the neoliberal university's role as a service provider to extra-academic fields. This comes with increasing demands on philosophers to be of relevance to real-world policy and economic and political issues. The changing roles of institutions which Deleuze points towards is thus clearly visible, he notes, in a neoliberal present that puts pressure on philosophy to become a useful tool for achieving various entrepreneurial and practical ends. Patton picks up on the conceptualisation of 'field philosophy' as a means to respond to this situation. Noting the similarities between such post-disciplinary philosophy and Deleuze's conception of experimental philosophy, he notes that both can be seen as producing a 'rhizomatic Image of Thought', a concept which should be useful to us in further analysis of the relation between control culture and philosophy today.

Many thanks to Charlie Blake and Gregg Lambert for important and constructive comments on versions of this chapter.

REFERENCES

Beniger, James R. (1986), *The Control Revolution: Technological and Economic Origins of the Information Society*, Cambridge, MA and London: Harvard University Press.
Bratton, Benjamin H. (2015), *The Stack: On Software and Sovereignty*, Cambridge, MA and London: The MIT Press.
Deleuze, Gilles (1992a), 'Postscript on the Societies of Control', *October* 59, pp. 3–7.
Deleuze, Gilles (1992b), 'What is a Dispositif?' in *Michel Foucault Philosopher*, trans. Timothy J. Armstrong, New York and London: Harvester Wheatsheaf, pp. 159–66.
Deleuze, Gilles (1995), *Negotiations*, trans. Martin Joughin, New York: Columbia University Press.
Deleuze, Gilles (1998), 'Having an Idea in Cinema (On the Cinema of Straub-Huillet)', trans. Eleanor Kaufman, in *Deleuze and Guattari: New Mappings in Politics, Philosophy, and Culture*, ed. Eleanor Kaufman and Kevin Jon Heller, Minneapolis: University of Minnesota Press.
Deleuze, Gilles (2013), *Cinema II: The Time-Image*, trans. Hugh Tomlinson and Robert Galeta, London: Bloomsbury.
Flaxman, Gregory (2012), *Gilles Deleuze and the Fabulation of Philosophy*, Minneapolis and London: University of Minnesota Press.

Foucault, Michel (2008), *The Birth of Biopolitics: Lectures at the Collège de France, 1978–79*, ed. Michel Senellart, trans. Graham Burchell, Basingstoke: Palgrave Macmillan.
Franklin, Seb (2015), *Control: Digitality as a Cultural Logic*, Cambridge, MA and London: The MIT Press.
Galloway, Alexander (2004), *Protocol: How Control Exists after Decentralization*, Cambridge, MA and London: The MIT Press.
Galloway Alexander and Eugene Thacker (2007), *The Exploit: A Theory of Networks*, Minneapolis: University of Minnesota Press.
Harcourt, Bernard E. (2015), *Exposed: Desire and Disobedience in the Digital Age*, Cambridge, MA and London: Harvard University Press.
Hardt, Michael (1995), 'The Withering of Civil Society', *Social Text* 45, pp. 27–44.
Hardt, Michael and Antonio Negri (2000), *Empire*, Cambridge, MA: Harvard University Press.
Jameson, Fredric (1991), *Postmodernism, or, the Cultural Logic of Late Capitalism*, Durham, NC: Duke University Press.
Kelly, Mark G. E. (2015), 'Discipline is Control: Foucault contra Deleuze', *New Formations: A Journal of Culture/Theory/Politics* 84–5, pp. 148–62.
Massumi, Brian (1998), 'Requiem for Our Prospective Dead (Toward a Participatory Critique of Capitalist Power', in *Deleuze and Guattari: New Mappings in Politics, Philosophy, and Culture*, ed. Eleanor Kaufman and Kevin Jon Heller, Minneapolis: University of Minnesota Press.
O'Sullivan, Simon (2016), 'Deleuze against Control: Fictioning to Myth–Science', *Theory, Culture & Society* 33 (7–8), pp. 205–20.
Parisi, Luciana (2013), *Contagious Architecture: Computation, Aesthetics, and Space*, London and Cambridge, MA: The MIT Press.
Poster, Mark (2006), *Information Please: Culture and Politics in the Age of Digital Machines*, Durham, NC and London: Duke University Press.
Rouvroy, Antoinette (2013), 'The End(s) or Critique: Data-Behaviourism vs. Due-Process', in *Privacy, Due Process and the Computational Turn. Philosophers of Law Meet Philosophers of Technology*, ed. Mireille Hildebrandt and Katja De Vries, New York: Routledge, pp. 143–68.
Shaviro, Steven (2010), *Post-Cinematic Affect*, Winchester and Washington, DC: O-Books.
Terranova, Tiziana (2004), *Network Culture: Politics for the Information Age*, London and Ann Arbor: Pluto Press.
Thacker, Eugene (2004), 'Foreword: Protocol is as Protocol Does', in *Protocol: How Control Exists after Decentralization*, ed. Alexander R. Galloway, Cambridge, MA and London: The MIT Press.

CHAPTER I

Notes from an Investigation of 'Control Society'

Gregg Lambert

My title, of course, is an allusion to Althusser's famous meditation on the 'Ideological State Apparatus' (ISA), which will inform the following investigation of Deleuze's (and Guattari's) theory of the mechanism of control. As I have argued elsewhere, this allusion is not extraneous, since there is an internal and technical relationship between the two mechanisms (or *dispositifs*, employing Foucault's concept); therefore, Deleuze's programme to identify the sociopolitical mechanisms of control that are in the process of replacing the technical machines of disciplinary society can basically be understood as an updating of Althusser's earlier programme of ideological interpellation to forecast an emerging assemblage of power relations.[1] Nevertheless, in the following investigation I will argue that this teleology cannot be applied in a wholesale manner to analyse the political and social transformations of contemporary neoliberal society, which is how Deleuze's early sketch has so often been employed, since it contains an element of science fiction that spoils any direct application to the concrete phenomenon.

In order to grasp this generic element, it seems fitting to begin our investigation with the following scenario: '*Picture a man, one Mr. Leonard Mead, unemployed writer, who goes out for a stroll after dinner* – '*at 8 o'clock on a misty evening in November*' – *in 2053 and is arrested for 'just walking.*' In '7000 B.C.: Apparatus of Capture' (which appears in *A Thousand Plateaus* six years before the 'Postscript on Control Societies') Deleuze and Guattari employ this plot from Ray Bradbury's short story 'The Pedestrian' (1951; see Bradbury 1953) to first describe what they call a 'new machinic form of enslavement' that was replacing the earlier technical forms of subjection (i.e., disciplinary techniques). The story portrays an individual who is out for a walk in the moonlit night, posed against the background of a Kafkaesque village of darkened homes, the only signs of life being the ghostly light of the television flickering in the windows of each enclosure, as if linking them together in a larger apparatus composed of both human and technical parts. In defining the logic of the technical machine drawn from the Bradbury story, Deleuze and Guattari write:

> one is enslaved by the TV as a human machine insofar as television viewers are no longer consumers or users, nor even subjects who supposedly 'make' it, but intrinsic component pieces, 'input' and 'output,' feedback or recurrences that are no longer connected to the machine in such a way as to produce or use it. In machinic enslavement, there is nothing but transformations and exchanges of information, some of which are mechanical, others human. (Deleuze and Guattari 1987: 458)[2]

Before returning to read this passage from *A Thousand Plateaus*, I will simply list what I believe are the elements that must have attracted Deleuze and Guattari to employ Bradbury's futuristic vision as a primary example of their thesis concerning the relationship they draw between 'a technical form of subjection' and a 'machinic form of enslavement', that is between a disciplinary dispositif and a mechanism of control.[3]

1. A man takes a walk outside (perhaps recalling the figures of Lenz, Kerouac or Bartleby), representing an un-encoded movement or flow – of perception, thought, affect, desire.
2. This movement constitutes a 'line of flight' across a non-localisable space and time outside the series of enclosures of the darkened homes with their occupants, connected by means of a ghostly light that appears through the windows, as if constituting the walls of a singular enclosure. (The tomb-like houses form a series not unlike the one that they also find in Kafka's *The Castle*, a vast collective assemblage made up as a patchwork, and yet the presence of the whole being immanent at every point, constituting the homogenous form of interiority of an apparatus or machine.)
3. Finally, this un-encoded movement, as well as the subjective intensities it expresses, is suddenly and abruptly halted by an 'apparatus of capture' which determines 'Leonard Mead out for his walk in the desert' as abnormal and 'regressive tendency'. In other words, the multiple affects, thoughts and desires which are expressed by 'just walking' are subjected to a clinical and juridical form of judgement (e.g., the door of the police car opens directly to the interior of the psychiatric clinic where Leonard Mead is taken).

Turning to the passage, Deleuze and Guattari employ the transformation of the technical device of the television from the Bradbury story to describe society itself as a human machine that contains both human and technical parts, which now functions as an apparatus composed of micro-assemblages of subjection and control. The above example merely represents a case where enslavement and subjection are taken to their extreme poles that constantly reinforce and replenish each other – e.g., the regime of labour-time is transformed so that one never stops working, the nature of surplus value becomes machinic, appearing to function automatically and no longer requiring either an external motor action or user, and, finally, the framework [of capitalisation] expands to include all of society, including the interior and privatised space of the home (Deleuze and Guattari 1987: 458). Does this mean, however, that Deleuze and Guattari are suggesting that mass media in general become a new 'model of realisation' that, in some ways, replace the state-apparatus, or supplant the role played by former disciplinary dispositifs themselves (prisons, clinics, schools, etc.)? No, since as they also remind us, one is always enslaved by human machines, not by the technical machines themselves (correcting the common misinterpretations of both ideology and cultural critique), since 'information technology is also a property of the States that set themselves up as humans-machines systems' (Deleuze and Guattari 1987: 458). Moreover, as also illustrated in the Bradbury story, we discover that disciplinary enclosures and their technical dispositifs (e.g., the police car, the psychiatric clinic) continue to exist alongside the new machinic form of enslavement, as if comprising a form of exteriority and a prehistoric past of the new mechanism of control. Therefore, it is precisely this spatiotemporal distinction between disciplinary order first analysed by Foucault's and Deleuze's image of control that I would like to further investigate in the following sections.

I

Six years later, Deleuze explicitly proposes a programme to identify the new mechanisms of control in terms of the following problem: how to locate and identify all the elements of a multiplicity in an open or relative unlimited and smooth space. This is contrasted to the social problem of a disciplinary order, much like the one described by Althusser, which is how to locate a relative number of elements of a finite multiplicity within a closed space (the factory, the school, the prison, the hospital). If this dualism between open vs. closed spatial composition resembles a similar dynamic employed in Deleuze's cinema books – i.e., between the closed set proposed by the movement image and the open set linked to an 'outside' through the time image – perhaps this is because he was working on both projects around the same time as the lecture course on Foucault in 1985. For example, in the seminars Deleuze also explores the problem of control in the new art forms that employ serialisation to explore a new conception of spatiality and form, such as in the musical serialisation of Pierre Boulez (occupying without counting) or the cinemas of Jean-Luc Godard, Federico Fellini and Alain Resnais. It is at this point that he begins to theorise the difference between discipline and control according to the same problem of localisation in spatiotemporal forms, just as in the theory of ensembles. The question that I will return to address below is that this dualism can nowhere be found to operate in the analysis of Foucault himself according to the same temporal and spatial schema.

To summarise the formal convention that Deleuze will introduce into Foucault's analysis of disciplinary order, causing the effect of a mutation to occur between the diagrams of discipline and control, which first appears as a spatiotemporal difference of formed enclosure (striated) vs. unformed and open (smooth) spatiotemporal processes and relations. For example, in the 1985 seminar on Foucault, Deleuze defines the problem of localisation in the disciplinary diagram, just as in a theory of ensembles, as a finite multiplicity that determines the relative localisation of elements through analogically coordinated segments. For example, masses, classes and races can be quantified as homogenous elements of a finite multiplicity that can then be segmented and localised according to a diagram of geopolitical enclosure: villages or ghettoes in the city, zones or shanty towns in a district, regions or even entire continents in the striated arrangement of globalised segments according to development of international markets, etc. Each finite multiplicity operated according to the analogy provided by the disciplinary diagram that was employed to localise the elements, or individuals, that belonged to that assemblage. However, what Deleuze identifies as the problem that will emerge in the spatiotemporal diagram of control society – a diagram, however, that was only the 'just coming into view' – is the existence of an 'outside' that is composed of 'Reimanian patches' of unstriated or unstratified forces. These forces, however, are determined neither by enclosure nor analogy, thus creating the possibility of new un-encoded elements and a greater degree of movement between spatiotemporal relations that appear outside their former enclosures. As Deleuze and Guattari write,

> each [space] is characterized by the form of the expression that defines the square of the distance between two infinitely proximate points so that two neighboring observers in a Riemann space can locate the points in their immediate vicinity but cannot locate their spaces in relation to each other without a new convention [i.e., a new diagram]. (Deleuze and Guattari 1987: 485)

And yet, if we now observe the same phenomenon as described in the 'Postscript', it is precisely the emergence of a new convention of control that will suddenly become the source of the greatest threat. This is because Deleuze will also see the invention of newer technical machines (the internet, data banks, electronic collars), as well as new dispositifs that emerge to re-code these elements and establish localisation once again, even though this localisation no longer occurs through the apparatus of disciplinary enclosure. To illustrate this apparent danger, we could simply point to the example that Deleuze ascribes to Guattari, that of the prisoner who is no longer enclosed in a disciplinary space but allowed to remain in open society under the condition that his or her location is constantly monitored and thus regulated. Stripped of its practical application as a cheaper and more cost-efficient form of confinement (especially for non-violent offenders or petty and habitual criminals, or for juvenile delinquents), what would be required is simply the addition of a 'qualitative leap' whereby this technology would become employed universally to all subjects, especially through newer technological improvements such as GPS tracking and biometric monitoring, as in the case of Guattari's premonition of a city with districts controlled by digital pass-codes or biometric tags. Moreover, it is by means of a similar leap that several years later in the opening of the 'Postscript' Deleuze further revises and updates Bradbury's post-war dystopian vision with Burroughs' conception of 'soft machines', even though Burroughs' more paranoid vision was far more insidious in that it was constituted at the level of neuronal and chemical signals in the brain, and the so-called 'dividual' would not be able to discern which thought was organically autonomous and which was the signal communicated by a race of Senders, or in this the impudent breed of our new masters, the advertising men.

From the above examples, I think we have discerned the principle of the 'qualitative leap' that is performed not only of Deleuze and Guattari's interpretation of television as a new technical machine of control, but later Deleuze's interpretation (or as I have said, quite purposively *mutation*) of Foucault's entire analysis of the concrete dispositifs of discipline. Moreover, it is for this reason that the later description of Foucault's theory of disciplinary order acquires the distinctive feeling (a mood, or *melos*) of science fiction in Deleuze's description of control society, since it is precisely by means of a model borrowed from this genre and applied to Foucault's description of nineteenth-century phenomena that the diagram of discipline suddenly undergoes a strange mutation into the emergent diagram control, that is providing it with a supplemental and strategic dimension 'coming from the future' (i.e., the outside).[4] Here, the reference to science fiction is not accidental in determining the nature of this 'qualitative leap'. At this point, moreover, let me turn on the television again, since as in all the above examples we need to account for the principle that will allow Deleuze and Guattari to connect the technical forms of subjection and their concrete dispositifs, at one end, with a more generalised and machinic form of enslavement, at the other. Not surprisingly, this principle is drawn from a common theme that is often employed by the genre, which is why I have proposed the early story by Bradbury, in a certain manner, as the fictional double of Deleuze's brief 'Postscript on Control Societies'. However, this can also be confirmed by the footnote that appears immediately below the passage that I have quoted above, where we discover the following statement:

> One of the basic themes of science fiction is to show how machinic enslavement combines with processes of subjection, but exceeds or differs from them, performing a qualitative leap. Take Ray Bradbury: television not as an instrument located at the center of the house, but as forming the walls of the house. (Deleuze and Guattari 1987: 570, n. 57)

Finally, this qualitative leap is more clearly stated by Neil Gaiman as the 'what if' phrase, which is one of three generic methods employed in the genre of science fiction for creating possible worlds:

> There are three phrases that make possible the world of writing about the world of not-yet (you can call it science fiction or speculative fiction; you can call it anything you wish) and they are simple phrases:
> *What if . . . ?*
> *If only . . . ?*
> *If this goes on . . .*
> 'What if . . . ?' gives us change, a departure from our lives. *(What if aliens landed tomorrow and gave us everything we wanted, but at a price?)*
> 'If only . . .' lets us explore the glories and dangers of tomorrow. *(If only dogs could talk. If only I were invisible.)*
> 'If this goes on . . .' is the most predictive of the three, although it doesn't try to predict an actual future with all its messy confusion. Instead, 'If this goes on . . .' fiction takes an element of life today, something clear and obvious and normally something troubling, and asks what would happen if that thing, that one thing, became bigger, became all-pervasive, changed the way we thought and behaved. *(If this goes on, all communication everywhere will be through text messages or computers, and direct speech between two people, without a machine, will be outlawed.)* (Gaiman xi–xii)

In applying the third phrase, which is relevant to our discussion employed by Deleuze as well, we find that one can create a possible world simply by exaggerating or totalising the relation between a technical form of subjection and a machinic form of enslavement, that is employing the generic 'what if this goes on' method. For example, one can take a technical machine of media society and cause it suddenly to become more troubling by making it bigger, all-pervasive, a machine that changes our very thought and habits. Employing this same method to their interpretation of the television in Bradbury, therefore, Deleuze and Guattari are able to propose from their exaggeration of the technical machine of mass media that 'social subjection now proportions itself to the model of realization, just as machinic enslavement expands to meet the dimensions of an axiomatic that is effectuated in the model' (Deleuze and Guattari 1987: 459).

And yet, one question I will return to below is whether the two diagrams can exist in the same present, or for the same society, except in a mutant form that resembles science fiction? The question, as Deleuze says above, is precisely how to reunite two diagrams, especially when the diagrams themselves are always already in a process of mutation? In this sense, it is a bit like the future described in the story by Bradbury, where police no longer exist and a lonely police car roams the night, because all the subjects have internalised the confinement of the former apparatus – that is to say, they have subjectively internalised the form of enclosure that belonged to the previous diagram, which has now become what Deleuze and Guattari call a 'machinic form of enslavement'. We find, moreover, that a new form of exteriority now replaces the former enclosure or confinement of any concrete dispositif where the formerly subjected used to exist inside a nucleus, somewhat like the creature described in Kafka's 'The Burrow' (as Blanchot also defined this new form, confinement now refers to an outside, not to the nucleus of an interiority). The machinic form of enslavement is defined, once again, as a model in a Platonic sense, as effectuating the realisation of the virtual model in the machinic form. Here, the principal difference with Foucault's construction of the diagram is that for Foucault the diagram cannot be understood in terms of between 'the purity of the ideal and the disorderly impurity of the real'. In other words, as Mitchell Dean and Kaspar Villadsen have also recently observed: 'The history of diagrams . . . is not one that demonstrates their remarkable endurance and success; rather, it is a history of plans never realized. Foucault gives emphasis to the fundamentally unattainable nature of diagrams and their imperatives, comparing them to "a programming left in abeyance"' (Dean and Villadsen 2016: 110).

Contrary to this understanding of the failure of the diagram to realise a concrete dispositif of control, however, we find instead that the new forms of subjection described simply occur outside their former disciplinary enclosures (e.g., the prison replaced by a GPS tracking device, the proletariat ghetto by digitalised access on an individual level, the school by constant training in personal electives). The ideal model of control is thus constituted by the full realisation of the model itself since it now operates in a different dimension than the earlier concrete or technical dispositifs.[5] Consequently, we have discovered that primary distinction which defines the new convention (or diagram) of control society, which is that subjection no longer belongs to a specific dispositif to perform, but instead constitutes an outside, 'which is farther away than any external world and even any form of exteriority', and which, henceforth, also becomes 'infinitely closer and deeper than any form of interiority as well' (Deleuze 1988: 86).

2

Since we have identified Deleuze's diagram of control society as bearing all the characteristics of what Foucault would call an 'inflationary theory of the State Form', let us now turn to the seminar in *The Birth of Biopolitics* where Foucault first discusses this phenomena that belongs to the politics of the Left. In the lecture of 7 March, Foucault characterises two persistent themes or 'elements' which appear at the basis of what he defines as a 'critical morality' of anti-estatism or state phobia that could almost be taken as a direct commentary on Deleuze and Guattari's account of the inner teleology of the state form from the perspective of the Universal History of Capitalism, which was also presented earlier in the famous chapter 'Savages, Barbarians, Civilized Men' in *Anti-Oedipus*, which appeared in 1972. To vividly demonstrate this potential criticism of their theory of the state form as evidencing all the signs of an inflationary and paranoid style, in the following I will simply place Foucault's description of these themes alongside the description of the state form that we discovered earlier in *A Thousand Plateaus*:

a. (Foucault) 'First, there is the idea that the state possesses in itself and through its own dynamism a sort of power of expansion, an intrinsic tendency to expand, an endogenous imperialism constantly pushing to spread its surface and increase in extent, depth, and subtlety to the point that it will come to take over entirely that which is at the same time its other, its outside, its target, its object, namely, civil society.' (Foucault 2008: 187)
b. (Deleuze and Guattari) 'Social subjection proportions itself to the model of realization [i.e., the state form], just as machinic enslavement expands itself to meet the dimensions of the axiomatic that is effected in the model [i.e., the capitalist axiomatic]. We have the privilege of undergoing the two operations simultaneously, in relation to the same things and the same events. Rather than stages, subjection and enslavement constitute two coexistent poles. [. . .] For since the Paleolithic and Neolithic times, the State has been deterriteritorializing to the extent that it makes the earth an object of its higher unity [its imperial form of cosmopolis], a forced aggregate of coexistence [a mechanic form of enslavement of all the parts that serve this higher unity, whatever it is called], instead of a free play of territories among themselves and with the lineages.' (Deleuze and Guattari 1987: 454–9)

a. (Foucault) 'The second element which it seems to me is constantly found in these general themes of state phobia is that there is a kinship, a sort of generic continuity or evolutionary implication between different forms of the state, with the administrative state, the welfare state, the bureaucratic state, the fascist state, the totalitarian state, in no matter which of the various analyses, the successive branches of and same great tree of state control in its continuous and unified expansion.' (Foucault 2008: 187)
b. (Deleuze and Guattari) 'We may return to the different forms of the State, from the standpoint of Universal History [e.g., 1. imperial archaic states; 2. diverse early modern states such as administrative patriarchies, monarchies, autonomous cities, and feudal states; 3. modern nation states]. We find the revival of 1 in the Greek, Roman, and feudal worlds: there is always an Empire on the horizon, which for the subjective States plays a role of signifier and encompassing element [e.g., Christianity, Capitalism]. And the correlation between 2 and 3 is no less pronounced, for industrial revolutions are not wanting, and the difference between topical conjunctions and the great conjugations of decoded flows is so thin that one is left with the impression that capitalism was continually being born, disappearing and reviving at every crossroads of history. And the correlation between 3 and 1 is also a necessary one: the modern States of the third age do indeed restore the most absolute of empires, a new 'megamachine,' whatever the novelty or timelines of its now immanent form: they do this by realizing the axiomatic that functions as much by machinic enslavement as by social subjection. Capitalism has reawakened the *Urstaat*, and given it new strength.' (Deleuze and Guattari 1987: 459–60)

Point for point, Foucault's analysis of these themes could not be more relevant for illustrating my argument. But what is wrong about this theory of the state and how is it finally inflationary, implying that it is a phantasm and has no scientific value for either real historical analysis or effective political critique of actual states and their technical machines? In the following, I will attempt to boil down to their most direct problems:

1. First, what Foucault calls the problem of the inter-exchangability of analyses according to a model of kinship or heredity: anytime you begin with a genetic kinship between different forms of the state, for example, from the standpoint of a universal history, then these become eternal forms that can be reactivated at any point of the great chain of being, thus sacrificing any possible specificity in the analysis of the circumstances of the specific genesis or coming into being of actual states by proposing instead a hereditary model of evolution. For example, this hereditary model is clearly present in Deleuze and Guattari's division of the history of the state form into three types that can be reactualised in various hybrid combinations from the perspective of

universal history, but especially in their assertion that the most primitive state form, the archaic imperial or oriental despotic form, derived from early Marx, constitutes the absolute horizon of each historical transformation. In other words, there is the presence of an organic model of heredity and evolution, which is more than a little responsible for the organicism implicit in the concept of 'biopower' that has been derived mostly from Deleuze's writings. However, their analysis cannot and does not even attempt to account for the differences that occur within each generic species, which cannot be grouped under the same hereditary scheme, and this is particularly true in the case of the second major form under the heading of 'extremely diverse states' (monarchies, feudal systems, evolved empires, autonomous cities, etc.), and the loss of specificity or the dilution of differences between actual state forms of the same genre or species can certainly be applied to the third form, the modern nation states. Therefore, one result of employing a genetic or hereditary model of kinship – as in the case of any biological model that is applied to real historical phenomena – is that the understanding of specific causality is reduced to a mythical reproduction of eternal forms. For example, in addition to Deleuze and Guattari, here we might also recall the argument of Hardt and Negri who employ the same scheme of universal history of the state form (which they take from Marx as well as Deleuze and Guattari) to evoke the reactualisation of the 'autonomous polis' in their description of a new form of Empire constituted by the Multitude.

2. Second, the problem of 'the worst of the worst', according to the biopolitical model of enslavement: this directly results from the interchangeability of analyses and makes possible the reactualisation of the most extreme and despotic state form in any critique of the actual state and its technical forms of power. Everything ends up being immediately referred to the return of the most primitive and imperial of state forms as a paradigmatic representation of the actual state power. Foucault addresses his criticism of this inflationary tendency most directly: 'For example, an analysis of social security and the administrative apparatus on which it rests ends up, via some slippages and thanks to some play on words, referring to the analysis of concentration camps' (Foucault 2008: 189). In other words, because of the intrinsic dynamism of the state form, which has internalised its entire hereditary past in each instance of state power and violence, every actual instance of legal violence or the juridical expression of state power immediately evokes the realisation of the worst of the worst. As Foucault writes, 'it hardly matters what one's grasp of the reality really is or what profile of actuality is really present'. Mere suspicion is enough evidence for 'denunciation, to find something like the fantastical profile of the state and there is no longer any need to analyze actuality' (Foucault 2008: 188). Here, to exemplify this, we might cite the following passage about Paul Virilio's

Speed and Politics: that it is precisely beyond fascism and total war that the war machine finds its complete object, in the menacing peace of nuclear deterrence. It is there that the reversal of Clausewitz's formula takes on a concrete meaning, at the same time as State politics tends to wither and the war machine takes over a maximum of civil functions ('place the whole of civil society under the regime of military security', 'disqualify the whole of the planet's habitat by stripping the peoples of their quality of inhabitant', 'erase the distinction between wartime and peacetime'; see the role of the media in this respect). Or as Deleuze and Guattari write, 'certain European police forces could be taken as an example, when they claim the right to "shoot on sight": they cease to be a cogwheel in the State apparatus and become pieces in a war machine' (Deleuze and Guattari 1987: 570).

3. Finally, the third problem concerns what I will call the mythic return of the *Urstaat*, that is to say, the full realisation of the model of the great paranoid state form. However, in reality this problem is only the outcome of the first two, in that one no longer needs to concern oneself with the impurity of the real actualisations of the state form, since every appearance of the state form is immediately denounced for being intrinsically fascist, totalitarian, etc. This leads to Foucault's most severe criticism of this kind of analysis that employs an intrinsic or genetic model of the state form, one that always has – as in the case of Deleuze and Guattari – the archaic imperial empire as its absolute horizon, or, as in the case of Agamben, the concentration camp as its intrinsic model of realisation of a new convention (paradigm) of the biopolitical state form of neoliberalism. For example, in *Homo Sacer* the paradigm of the concentration camp is immanent to every state form and even functions as its model of realisation. Here, one can easily associate the principle paradigm of Agamben, and particularly how it is employed paradigmatically to analyse the new juridical forms of state control that have emerged because of the Patriot Act, but also Deleuze and Guattari's evocation of fascism, 'the seeds of fascism', and ultimately the return of the fascist state, that lurks in every overt expression of police violence. Here again, Foucault's criticism is relevant, the appeal to an intrinsic and immanent paradigm of fascism in each case only serves to mythologise the actual mechanisms of power, especially because there is no attempt to base this kind of analysis on the actual legal codes or jurisprudence, in order to see how this violence is made possible and really comes about in the event, but instead immediately resorts to a kind of inductive reasoning where the event serves only as an example of the most archaic and primitive of models as what it immediately demonstrates (i.e., that the state is becoming fascist, that its new technical machines are actually machinic forms of enslavement, or that the ultimate destination of the growing and interconnected neoliberal states is to imagine all life in a concentration camp on a global scale).

To conclude my brief investigation, I think I have developed enough comparison from Foucault's criticisms and Deleuze and Guattari's earlier depictions of the state form from *Anti-Oedipus* as well as the passages we have been reading from *A Thousand Plateaus*, which also contain all the characteristics of what Foucault is calling an 'inflationary theory of the state' (Foucault 2008: 187). Implicitly, what I am also suggesting is that this same inflationary tendency can be found today in many of the critiques of the neoliberal state as well, informing the character of the idea of neoliberalism today as a planetary and neo-imperial phenomenon. Of course, I am not saying that this is not part of its force that is coupled to unifying effects of global markets and the reactive effect this has on subjacent nation states, but, then, the question becomes one of either specificity and history rather than the appeal to a wholesale paradigm as exhibited in many contemporary representations of biopower as a universal form of control, a paradigm that has been influenced by Deleuze's earlier diagram of control. I realise that this conclusion might appear provocative but I would like to offer it as one of the possible mutations of the current diagram, along with the suggestion that we begin to develop different conventions for establishing our contemporary relationship between power and knowledge – and, especially, generic conventions other than those that were already employed in science fiction in the post-war period of 1950s onwards – to forecast the future of our society. Perhaps I am being a little too Spinozian in this regard, but I don't believe that philosophy has ever been that reliable of a machine for prognostication, nor for the interpretation of 'signs and wonders'. As a 'Deleuzian', moreover, I also realise that this might seem counterintuitive at first glance – was not Deleuze a Spinozist, after all? – and I must admit that there are many aspects of what I have called Deleuze's 'mutation' of Foucault's original theory of dispositifs that should be pursued today, just not all! As Kafka's dog once said, I am simply making a report of my investigation. I am only making a report, since in my view, the diagram of control has become too dominant and even mythic in proportions in its image of the new machinic form of enslavement.

Not all of this is Deleuze's responsibility, to be sure. So finally, I would recall that the 1990 'Postscript', and the collection of *Pourparlers* (1991) in which it appeared with other miscellaneous 'negotiations', was in fact written during a period when the philosopher was at his weakest and most reactive moment, having just retired from his position in the university, engaged in constant attack and 'counter-attack' with the new philosophers, the infamous 'potato war' with philosopher Alain Badiou, as well as with what Deleuze identifies as an 'impudent breed of new masters' that he associates with the marketing principles of the new media in the 'Postscript on Control Societies'. As Deleuze himself confesses in the foreword to the French edition, *Pourparlers* must be understood as strategic and tense negotiations for peace in a time of war (Deleuze 1991: 7). Consequently, if I have employed Bradbury's short story 'The Pedestrian', it was partly as an allegory of what I was imagining as an incident that occurred on autumn evening in November 1990 in the deserted streets of Paris when the recently retired philosopher goes out for a walk, looking with disdain at the phantom lights against the apartment windows on his street, imagining perhaps that inside the occupants were engrossed in the latest instalment of Alain Badiou's popular programme on 'French Philosophy'. Suddenly, a policeman hails him:

'Hey You! What do you think you are doing?'
'I am out for a stroll like Lenz or Bartleby', Deleuze replies.
'Oh really? That's funny! And what is your occupation?'
'Philosopher', replies Deleuze.
'Ah! So I see!' Exclaims the *flic*, 'You are unemployed.'

NOTES

1. An early version of this chapter was presented at the first meeting of the Society for the Study of Biopolitical Futures (Syracuse University, April 2013). The talk is archived at http://biopoliticalfutures.net/
2. Deleuze and Guattari refer to this new technical form of enslavement as a 'mega-machine', employing the term of Lewis Mumford, who had first described the machinic relationship between labour, knowledge and power as a system made up of interchangeable parts, organic and inorganic, human and animal, technical and institutional, that are organised and controlled. Quoting directly from Mumford's *Myth of the Machine*: 'Conceptually the instruments of mechanization five thousand years ago were already detached from other human functions and purposes than the constant increase of order, power, predictability, and, above all, control. With this proto-scientific ideology went a corresponding regimentation and degradation of once-autonomous human activities: "mass culture" and "mass control" made their first appearance' (Mumford 1967: 12).
3. For an alternative description of the machinic form of enslavement based on a reading of the same passage, see Lazzarato 2014: 43–52.
4. In the seminar of 1986, Deleuze observes: 'First, I would say, the diagram arrives from the outside, although we do not know exactly what Foucault understands by "the outside." Secondly, the diagram always emerges from another diagram. And why? Because every diagram is a mutation! Every diagram is the mutation of the preceding one, which was itself already a mutation. The diagram is fundamentally mutant and even expresses, within a given society, the mutations that are possible. Thus, the question is one of reuniting the two [diagrams].' Gilles Deleuze/Foucault – Le Pouvoir cours 13–25/02/1986 – 5 Transcription: Annabelle Dufourcq (avec l'aide du College of Liberal Arts, Purdue University) [my translation].
5. See also Mark G. E. Kelly's criticisms of the examples found in the 1990 'Postscript' in 'Discipline is Control: Foucault Contra Deleuze' (NEWF: 84/85.01.2015).

BIBLIOGRAPHY

Althusser, Louis (2001), *Lenin and Philosophy and Other Essays*, trans. Ben Brewster, New York: Monthly Review Press.
Bradbury, Ray (1953), *The Golden Apples in the Sun*, Garden City, New York: Doubleday & Co.
Bradbury, Ray (2012), *Fahrenheit 451*, New York: Simon and Schuster.
Dean, Mitchell and Kaspar Villadsen (2016), *State Phobia and Civil Society: Michel Foucault's Political Legacy*, Stanford: Stanford University Press.
Deleuze, Gilles (1988), *Foucault*, Minneapolis: University of Minnesota Press.
Deleuze, Gilles (1991), *Pourparlers*, Paris: Les Editions Minuit.
Deleuze, Gilles (1995), 'Postscript on Control Societies', in *Negotiations*, trans. Martin Joughin, New York: Columbia University Press, pp. 177–82.
Deleuze, Gilles and Felix Guattari (1987), *A Thousand Plateaus*, trans. Brian Massumi, Minneapolis: University of Minnesota Press.
Foucault, Michel (2008), *The Birth of Biopolitics: Lectures at the Collège de France 1978–79*, New York: Palgrave Macmillan.
Gaiman, Neil (2012), 'Introduction', in Ray Bradbury *Fahrenheit 451*.
Kelly, Mark G. E. (2015), 'Discipline is Control: Foucault Contra Deleuze', in *New Formations* (84/85, no. 1).
Lazzarato, Maurizio (2014), *Signs and Machines: Capitalism and the Production of Subjectivity*, trans. J. D. Jordan, Cambridge, MA: The MIT Press.
Mumford, Lewis (1967), *Myth of the Machine: The Technics of Human Development*, New York: Harcourt.

CHAPTER 2

Post-Mortem on Race and Control

Neel Ahuja

Control names a dynamic mode of power which seeks to proliferate difference in order to modulate and contain its disruptive force. Thus, one starting point for a critique of control is to think with and through its dependency on difference, including difference marked as racial. From this premise, it is possible to pursue how racial assemblages constitute the ideological grounds for accounts of control, and explore why control might become an increasingly salient metaphor for racial power as the political centrality of race intensifies with the global rise of ethnonationalism and outright fascism. Although thinking of race as a matter of technical control of bodies involves working through posthumanist and new-materialist methods for social analysis, it also involves retrospectively interpreting the role of racial difference in the constitution of control theory's paranoid figuration of technology and the state. In the works of William Burroughs and Gilles Deleuze, control exhibits a desire for the destruction of subjectivity through constant modulations of difference and the integration of individuals into networked aspirations of capitalist accumulation. This rhetoric on the technological penetration of the body by the state, I will argue, reflects a generalisation of existing forms of race war into the Cold War state form, allowing for control theory to appear deracinated and globalised. Nonetheless, the critique of control demonstrates the importance of the concept for grappling with deterritorialised models of empire, in which race is affectively modulated across media environments, biotechnologies and war apparatuses. From this vantage point, the engagement of race and control charts a different path for critical race theory than do the largely polemical critiques by some Deleuzeans of the structuralism and representationalism of racial formation theory. The intersection of race and control poses questions of whether and how contemporary forms of empire are able to take hold of race's plastic potential for differentiation.

* * *

The horror of control emerges not in the active attempt of a commanding operator to overcome resistance, but in the dream of a total realisation of the operator's control. At that point control itself vanishes. In William Burroughs' 1978 essay 'The Limits of Control', the capability of the state to exercise control over a population is presented as inherently limited by the agency of subjects who potentially resist the control order. However, the imagined realisation of control also marks control's vanishing point, as the transformation of a responding subject into an object of domination also marks its release from a dynamic of control into one of mere use:

> Control also needs opposition or acquiescence; otherwise it ceases to be control . . . I control a slave, a dog, a worker; but if I establish complete control somehow, as by implanting electrodes in the brain, then my subject is little more than a tape recorder, a camera, a robot. You don't control a tape recorder – you use it . . . All control systems try to make control as tight as possible, but at the same time, if they succeeded completely, there would be nothing left to control. Suppose for example a control system installed electrodes in the brains of all prospective workers at birth. Control is now complete. Even the thought of rebellion is neurologically impossible. No police force is necessary. No psychological control is necessary, other than pushing buttons. (Burroughs 1978: 38)

Control thus names a dynamic mode of power that is not dependent on a specific structure of production and labour. If the slave, the dog or generic 'worker' are the more-than-human labouring figures of this potential difference that defines control, it is the coloniser who provides the figure for the disruption of control's totalisation and, simultaneously, its total dissolution. Positing that the precolonial Mayan calendar schematised the total control of the population even as its use atrophied without existential enemies, total control meant that the Mayans could not 'repel invaders': 'such a hermetic control system could be completely disoriented and shattered by even one person who tampered with the control calender [sic] on which the control system depended more and more heavily as the actual means of force withered away' (Burroughs 1978: 39). If colonialism may disrupt this process of turning animal life into machine life, reinforcing a narrative of the vanishing Indian coincident with US settler–imperial nationalisms (Byrd 2011), it also massifies as a political desire for control. Turning to the ascendance of empires and the problem of their inability to cope with change, Burroughs thus concludes that control's ultimate dependence is not on labour nor technology but on time itself. Once a control system totalises, it is only a matter of time before contradictions rend it apart. Moving from the enforced control of the slave or the dog to the totalised control of the indigene, empire models control on ever-massified scales only to inevitably dissolve in the face of aleatory complexity.

Yale cyberneticist José Manuel Rodriguez Delgado's infamous experimental use of brain electrodes to pacify a bull was the ostensible occasion for Burroughs' essay. Yet the Cold War expansion of the US security state – from the CIA's experiments in torture to produce 'learned helplessness' to the expansion of FBI surveillance – formed its public context. With the report of the Church Committee and the public revelation of the COINTELPRO programme in 1971, decades of state spying on black Communist and black Muslim activists was the justification for the creation of the mass surveillance apparatus that forms the backdrop of Burroughs' paranoid literary oeuvre. Given the long rise of US policing techniques in the contexts of Indian war, slave patrols and renditions, and Asian counterinsurgency from the Philippines occupation through those of Vietnam, Afghanistan and Iraq (Singh 2017), the entanglement of militarised anti-Communism, anti-blackness and Islamophobia in the history of US technological surveillance and mind control programmes are severed from accounts of control's novelty (Guenther 2013). If these disavowals of colonisation and anti-black racism form the discursive context of control theory, Burroughs and the Beat writers are more likely to displace the central axes of US race war in order to figure control through a mediation between primitivism and futurism which allows for control's relation to the state to be generalised across the social field. Timothy Yu claims that rather than focusing on the black/white axis of racial power during the civil rights era along the lines of prominent essayists like Norman Mailer, Burroughs fashioned a techno-orientalism that made the global city a site of both fantasy and danger in his literary oeuvre. In the process, the orient becomes the site for fashioning a speculative vision of advanced capitalist control (Yu 2008). Although the spectre of the orient is not explicit in 'The Limits of Control', Burroughs' rendering of control as the postcolonial future of capitalist security is complemented by a primitivism in which the figure of the Mayan native provides a millenarian vision of social totality and its dissolution. Despite this displacement of race as an organising dimension of imperial surveillance and militarisation, the figures of the slave and the native in the essay suggest that control might be configured as a technology for managing dissent against a racial order, even as the control regime seeks to modulate and dissipate the identities that allow that order to function.

* * *

In Gilles Deleuze's reflections on the topic, race plays no explicit role in the arsenal of control. However, as with Burroughs, the theory of control is implicitly racialised; its critiques of digital communication and plastic subjectivity rely on specific understandings of how race spatialises the globe under capitalism. For Deleuze, control marks a transition from a disciplinary society reliant on schools, prisons and other institutions towards an informational society permeated by market logics that smooth speech, imagination and conduct into capitalist prerogatives. Deleuze thinks control from the vanishing point identified by Burroughs: there is simply no free subjectivity from which to resist the regime of control, only the integration of the brain into a kind of mass nervous system. For Deleuze, the brain is not the site of a deep internal subject but rather a folding of the environment into an event:

> The brain's precisely this boundary of a continuous two-way movement between an Inside and an Outside, this membrane between them. New cerebral pathways, new ways of thinking, aren't explicable in terms of microsurgery; it's for science, rather, to try and discover what might have happened in the brain for one to start thinking this way or that. I think that subjectivation, events, and brains are more or less the same thing. (Negri and Deleuze 1995: 176)

Control constantly communicates, constantly modulates response: 'Controls are a modulation, like a self-transmuting molding continually changing from one moment to the next, like a sieve whose mesh varies from one point to another' (Deleuze 1995: 179). Control dissipates the power of difference by proliferating and modulating it, displacing and postponing identity.

Distinct in emphasis from the affirmation of becoming evident in Deleuze's co-authored works with Guattari, control suggests the seamless evacuation of political resistance brought about by the technical integration of the brain into capitalist systems of circulation. While control entails specific associations with cybernetics, debt and media, the concept of control is not reducible to a single historical referent. Control's normative association with the rise of modern computing and digital media is complicated by Deleuze's references to early twentieth-century histories evident, for example, in his reference to Kafka's writings as illuminating the juridical logic of control. The most detailed book-length study of control to date locates origins of the cultural logic of digitality in the nineteenth century, with the rise of computerised forms of processing and the early theoretical underpinnings of cybernetics (Franklin 2015).

Regardless of how one conceptualises the history of control, Deleuze does geopolitically bracket control and locate it within certain logics of post-industrial capitalism. The implicitly racialised grounding for the theory of control is the international division of labour. Deleuze writes:

> Capitalism is no longer directed towards production, which is often transferred to remote parts of the Third World . . . What it seeks to sell

is services, and what it seeks to buy, activities . . . Control is short-term and rapidly shifting, but at the same time continuous and unbounded . . . A man is no longer a man confined but a man in debt. One thing – it's true – hasn't changed: capitalism still keeps three-quarters of humanity in extreme poverty, too poor to have debts and too numerous to be confined: control will have to deal not only with vanishing frontiers, but with mushrooming shantytowns and ghettos. (Deleuze 1995: 181)

There is an ambivalence in this diagnosis, which at first seems to radically separate the Third World from control (as the site of both production and captivity) but then smuggles the intensification of Third World violence into control's logic: it 'will have to deal' with massified confinements of shanty towns and ghettoes. Deleuze's comment that the Third World 'hasn't changed' suggests that control involves superseding earlier forms of power based on sovereignty and discipline, even if its integration of subjects as 'dividuals' within a cybernetic system may be guided by the modes in which it manages those with which it disposes on the other side of the international divide.

Such a schema fits uneasily into a contemporary geopolitical scene in which US empire has transitioned in form through its economic dependencies on Asian capital, and where the evisceration of the social state unites logics of control and disposability. The right-wing assault on redistributive and welfarist policies across continents energises fascistic policing and surveillance schemes that network precisely because their ethnonationalist forms delimit them spatially – the regimes in the US, Israel, Turkey, Russia, India and the Philippines can complement one another in racially targeted social wars precisely because such wars depend on the *form* of the state use of violence rather than its content (the specific social groups that are securitised or expunged). If the political-economic dynamics which generate this form of state violence lie in debt-driven US military and security spending fuelled by Gulf oil extraction and East Asian production, then China, India and the Southeast Asian 'Tiger' economies function less as simple sites of disposable manufacturing labour than as spatial locations in which differential legal regimes allow for war accumulation. The multiplication of exceptions in the intra- and interstate form of Asian neoliberal production allows for post-industrial capital to develop a gradated juridical form that is both extensively profitable and institutionally opaque (Ong 2006). From this vantage point, it is difficult to locate control's geographic logic or racial form in binary distinctions separating first from third worlds, manufacturing from service labour, white from dark continents, despite the fact that systemically empire intensifies policing of racial difference. The networking of Islamophobic ethnonationalisms overlaps with processes that are not in advance fully epidermalised, such as religious conversion, the development of group identities through warfare, the digital mediatisation of executions, protests and police/military violence, and the slow violence of economic blockade and ecological warfare. The schema of an international division of labour captures an important part of these processes, but not the dimensions of scale and ecology that render them deep in the planetary matter.

Deleuze's adaptation of Foucault's historical schema for sovereignty, discipline and security (the analogue to control) provides another point of difficulty, as the scholars of race and colonialism have for decades contested the assertion that incarceration, torture and other forms of direct state violence have dissipated with the rise of modern logics of capital and statecraft. However, Deleuze does not make a simple claim that sovereign power is on the decline, but he does emphasise that confinement is not a primary site for the exercise of control: 'we're moving toward control societies that no longer operate by confining people but through continuous control and instant communication'. The 'breaking down' of the prison and other institutions lumped together with them by Foucault and Deleuze (schools and hospitals, for example) coincides with a withering of the possibility of ideology and civic discourse as sites of resistance. If resistance is possible after control, claims Deleuze, 'it would be nothing to do with minorities speaking out. Maybe speech and communication have been corrupted ... The key thing may be to create vacuoles of noncommunication, circuit breakers, so we can elude control' (Negri and Deleuze 1995: 174). For Deleuze, this does not mean that prisons simply disappear, but that they are remade by a different apparatus of power. Jared Sexton concurs with this vision of the foreclosure of resistant minoritised speech even as he suggests that sovereign violence (incarceration, gratuitous police violence) represent the basic form of power, with discipline and control layered on top. Critiquing the construction and cultivation of a black electorate in the US during the Obama presidency and the development of the terrorism prison system, Sexton frames the control logic as epiphenomenal to the primary and long-standing violence of policing and prisons, permanent exceptions to the liberal order: 'organized, systemic racial violence against blacks, gratuitous violence that traverses the conceptual distinction between state and civil society is ... the opening gesture of western modernity as such' (Sexton 2007: 198).

* * *

Despite their different characterisations of sovereignty, the fact that Sexton's afro-pessimist dismissal of black resistance echoes Deleuze's rendering of minority voicelessness points to the novel ways in which theories of control might appeal to particular strands of critical race theory. To date, the largely polemical criticisms against racial formation theory (Omi and Winant 1986) by theorists engaged with Deleuze and Guattari has often pitted ontology against epistemology, affect against ideology, becoming against dialectics, making Deleuzean writing on race incompatible with the trends towards racial exceptionalism and diagnoses of historically durable racial structure evident in some afro-pessimist and decolonial theories. Because these extant polemics highlight Deleuze's philosophical affirmation of becoming, their emphasis on the creative potential of race sits in tension with control's paranoid evisceration of resistance. In the introduction to the volume *Deleuze and Race*, Arun Saldanha argues for an immanent philosophy of race, one defined against representationalist and structuralist social critique in its insistence that 'like all power relations, racism operates first of all through the materialities of desire and landscape far "below" any mental or linguistic detectability' (2013: 34; see further Rai 2012). So, unlike the majority of studies in the field, which centre on historical narratives about racial discourse, images and statecraft, Deleuzean approaches to race have thus far been more intimately concerned with the micropolitics of embodiment, technology and affect, connecting with feminist and queer theories that undermine the holism of the body. The agenda of such a critical programme which understands race as a material assemblage is not to act as a supplement to structuralist analysis of race but to reformulate an understanding of racial ontology in ways that require a radical rethinking of the scales, bodies and affective forms that constitute the matter of race. For Saldanha, race exhibits a certain viscosity, and in its proliferation rather than its suppression lies the possibility for a new antiracism (Saldanha 2006).

The polemics against the structuralist bent of racial formation theory can, however, be productive if it helps to elucidate how the deep histories of racial violence energise the embodied plasticity of racial form, its biopoliticisation and productive capacity. This often means a deep engagement of race, Deleuze and feminist and queer technoscience scholarship. Jasbir Puar suggests a new critical dialogue between more structuralist forms of race critique (such as intersectional analysis) that develop schemas for race's interrelation with other forms of social domination and an assemblage theory that crosses the discursive with affective and temporal dimensions of relation (Puar 2012). Putting Catherine Malabou's writings on the brain in conversation with Deleuze, Jairus Grove explains that one of the unfinished projects for theorising control is to think with the destructive potential of plasticity as a more radical refusal of humanism than is available in Burroughs' paranoid framing of control (Grove 2015: 250-1). Furthermore, attempts to open critical race theory to media, war and biotechnical apparatuses might help us understand how racial assemblage does not only operate as an ideological struggle over stereotyped images or content, but through mutations of form. In such analyses, form can govern racial difference and intensify racial crisis while remaining rather disinterested in content or even generating its viral transformation. (Consider, for example, the scandals over Russian state promotion of racial conflict in US social media, where media bots proliferated contradictory content on race in order to intensify the speed and intensity of race's public articulation.) One possible outcome of the current collision of Deleuzean thought and critical race theory, however, is that such productive openings might be jettisoned in favour of a totalising view of control. As in Sexton's reading, which dispenses with Burroughs' paranoia in order to posit lack of speech as the mundane racial product of modernity, there is a potential for invigorating rhetorical tendencies towards racial exceptionalism and nihilistic, transhistorical readings of racism's psychosocial inevitability. Given the intensity with which race is itself the object of proliferating scales of analysis and meta-analysis in contemporary digital culture – often bent on convincing us of the impossibility of moving racial structure – the narrative of control itself can be taken up as an element in race war, not just a theorisation of it.

Up to now, the relative lack of engagement by critical race theorists with control as a concept may be a result of the short treatment of the control concept by Deleuze, but it is also likely influenced by several other factors, including the generally hostile approach towards the field by followers of Deleuze and Guattari who have made race only one object of criticism in a broader assault on structuralist social theory. Nonetheless, recent contexts in which the virtuality of race appears to accelerate its violence and specular intensity are likely to invigorate interest in theories of control (Puar 2017). In the very disruption of existing racial orderings girded by the system of nation states, post-Cold War conflicts and migration flows crossing the Persian Gulf, Southwest Asia, the Maghreb and North Africa are ripe contexts for thinking how media and war ecologies modulate race's emergent potential. Here we witness the cacophony of state militaries and non-state war machines vivisecting Syrian, Yemeni and Palestinian landscapes; the informational architectures of social network analysis that digitise the planet and produce the figure of the terrorist as a data aggregate; the dronised becoming-insect of both the Islamist insurgent and the security state; the massive dispossession and commoditisation of migrant outflows to Europe; the dispersal of ad hoc regimes of imprisonment and torture that experiment with the plasticity of the body–brain relation; the improvised border surveillance and sorting out of the racially disposable who cannot be redeemed through asylum. The racial assemblage of control in this context appears to work through the double movement of transiting the state as arbiter of racial domination and the reconstitution of media, war and biotechnical apparatuses around the modulation of new sites of racial crisis that are unleashed as a result. If the geographically dispersed violence instantiated in the current Islamophobic wars appears predictable based on a long-entrenched schema of phenotypic hierarchy – a lethally militarised intermingling of anti-blackness and orientalism sedimented in the deep time of slavery and colonialism – the mutations of racial form also invigorate the most spectacular dissipations of structure, dissipations which fragment and reconfigure the racial in a manner that suggests that time generally and speed in particular constitute significant concerns for how race is subject to modulation and affective management (Rai 2012). In the planetary conflagrations emanating between the 9/11 attacks and the current rise of fascist politics worldwide, we witness the proliferation of Islamophobias, preemptive killings, carceral violence, mass surveillance, ethnoracialisation of religious forms, and imminent death of the mythic postcolonial social democracy and integrationism of the West. Across these disparate phenomena, racial form cannot be anticipated solely in the contexts of citizenship or exclusion but must be assembled from planetary ecologies of sensation that define a posthuman relation to media, technical and interspecies environments. Theories of control can play a part in developing such an understanding, as long as the relation of control and race can be rethought from the inside out.

REFERENCES

Burroughs, William (1978), 'The Limits of Control', *Semiotexte* 3:2, pp. 38–42.
Byrd, Jody A. (2011), *The Transit of Empire*, Minneapolis: University of Minnesota Press.
Deleuze, Gilles (1995 [1980]), 'Postscript on Control Societies', in *Negotiations 1972–1990*, trans. Martin Joughin, New York: Columbia University Press, pp. 177–82.
Franklin, Seb (2015), *Control: Digitality as Cultural Logic*, Cambridge, MA: The MIT Press.
Grove, Jairus (2015), 'Something Darkly This Way Comes: The Horror of Plasticity in an Age of Control', in *Plastic Materialities: Politics, Legality, and Metamorphosis in the Work of Catharine Malabou*, ed. Brenna Bhandar and Jonathan Goldberg Hiller, Durham, NC: Duke University Press, pp. 233–64.
Guenther, Lisa (2013), *Solitary Confinement: Social Death and Its Afterlives*, Minneapolis: University of Minnesota Press.
Negri, Antonio and Gilles Deleuze (1995), 'Control and Becoming', in *Negotiations 1972–1990*, trans. Martin Joughin, New York: Columbia University Press, pp. 169–76.
Omi, Michael and Howard Winant (1986), *Racial Formation in the United States*, New York: Routledge.
Ong, Aihwa (2006), *Neoliberalism as Exception*, Berkeley: University of California Press.
Puar, Jasbir (2012), '"I'd Rather Be a Cyborg Than a Goddess:" Becoming-Intersectional in Assemblage Theory', *philoSOPHIA* 2:1, pp. 49–66.
Puar, Jasbir (2017), *The Right to Maim*, Durham, NC: Duke University Press.
Rai, Amit S. (2012), 'Race Racing: Four Theses on Race and Intensity', *WSQ* 40:1–2, pp. 64–75.
Saldanha, Arun (2006), 'Reontologising Race: The Machinic Geography of Phenotype', *Environment and Planning D: Society and Space* 24:1, pp. 9–24.
Saldanha, Arun (2013), 'Introduction: Bastard and Mixed-Blood are the True Names of Race', in *Deleuze and Race*, ed. Jason Michael Adams and Arun Saldanha, Edinburgh: Edinburgh University Press, pp. 6–34.
Sexton, Jared (2007), 'Racial Profiling and the Societies of Control', in *Warfare in the American*

Homeland: Policing and Prison in a Penal Democracy, ed. Joy James, Durham, NC: Duke University Press, pp. 197–218.

Singh, Nikhil Pal (2017), *Race and America's Long War*, Berkeley: University of California Press.

Yu, Timothy (2008), 'Oriental Cities, Postmodern Futures: "Naked Lunch," "Bladerunner," and "Neuromancer"', *MELUS* 33:4, pp. 45–71.

CHAPTER 3

Periodising (with) Control

Seb Franklin

What kinds of critical possibilities become legible if one reads Gilles Deleuze's conceptualisation of control societies both as a work of periodisation theory and as a theory of periodisation? In other words, how might one read the concept of control in methodological terms? Central to my attempt to respond to these questions is Fredric Jameson's observation that periodising hypotheses 'tend to obliterate difference and to project an idea of the historical period as massive homogeneity (bounded on either side by inexplicable chronological metamorphoses and punctuation marks' (1991: 3–4). Jameson's solution to this problem centres on the concept of the 'cultural dominant' that replaces the concept of style within aesthetic analysis and that thus allows for 'the presence and coexistence of a range of different, yet subordinate, features' (1991: 4). The specific features which Deleuze attributes to control societies suggest the possibility that this analytical rubric can be extended to the analysis of 'dominant' features that occur not only in spheres conventionally described in aesthetic (or stylistic) terms – such as architecture, literature and visual art – but also in arrangements that operate across and demonstrate the close imbrication of discursive and material registers: governmentality, technology and economics. A close reading of Deleuze's writings on control reveals an understanding of these co-constitutive registers that both invites and thwarts 'clean' periodisation. Because of this, the concept and the historical logic of control necessitate modes of analysis that can account for complex assemblages of epistemic abstractions *and* the concrete situations that undergird and (for worse and for better) exceed them.

It is certainly the case that a specific periodising gesture grounds the essays 'Having an Idea in Cinema' (1998; first delivered as a lecture at La Fémis in 1987) and 'Postscript on Control Societies' (1995b), as well the conversation with Antonio Negri published as 'Control and Becoming' (1995a; first published in 1990).[1] Across these texts Deleuze names and sketches the contours of a sociopolitical and economic shift away from the regimes of sovereignty and discipline theorised by Michel Foucault. In the earliest of what one might call the control texts, ostensibly a commentary on the cinema of Jean-Marie Straub and Danièle Huillet, Deleuze itemises the predominant mechanism of disciplinary societies – 'the accumulation of structures of confinement' (prisons, hospitals, workshops and schools) – in order to demarcate a period in which emerge 'societies of control that are defined very differently' (1998: 17). In this initial account, the newer type of society is distinguished by a specific and intentional mode of social management: the age of control comes about when 'those who look after our interests do not need or will no longer need structures of confinement', with the result that the exemplary forms of social regulation begin to 'spread out' (1998: 17–18).

This dissolution of now-defunct institutional spaces marks the first characteristic of control societies and, Deleuze suggests, establishes their difference from arrangements centred on 'classical' sovereignty or disciplinary power. The exemplary diagram and material expression of this regime is the highway system, in which 'people can drive infinitely and "freely" without being at all confined yet while still being perfectly controlled' (1998: 18). In 'Control and Becoming', Deleuze once again speaks of the passage through sovereignty and discipline, the breakdown of the latter's sites of confinement, and the concomitant emergence of distributed mechanisms of control. And he adds a second valence to this historical passage through a discussion of technology that is only hinted at in the earlier piece's allusions to information and communication. In developing this facet of control societies, Deleuze again appears to define that system in terms of a historical break: he suggests that sovereign societies correspond to 'simple mechanical machines', disciplinary societies to 'thermodynamic machines', and control societies to 'cybernetic machines and computers' (1995a: 175).

These two intertwined narratives – of distributed governmentality and the techniques and technologies of computation – represent the two main vectors through which the concept of control has shaped subsequent critical writing. Michael Hardt and Antonio Negri's concept of empire (2000) emphasises the former, and Alexander R. Galloway's *Protocol: How Control Exists After Decentralization* (2004) privileges the latter, although in truth each addresses both technology and power in some ratio. More broadly, it is possible to identify commonalities between the lineaments of control societies and a still-growing body of periodising concepts, both celebratory and critical, that do not mention Deleuze's concept but that define a similar set of historical movements (and a similar relationship between technology and social structure) in more universal terms: the information age; digital culture; the network society; post-industrial society; the age of big data; and so on, and so on, and so on.

So many ways to imagine a 'new' economy of services and informatic exchanges. But what do these periodising phrases occlude? Does 'postindustrial society' really describe the full, evenly distributed inclusion and valorisation of all social activity? Or does it describe a specific imaginary that rests on and obfuscates a complex of material conditions, conceptual operations, and imaginaries that are organised around abstract principles for the efficient extraction of surplus value? Do the structural and regulatory functions of racialised, gendered, sexualised, disabled and debilitated populations take on new forms in the movement from discipline to control, or does the abjection and violent management of such populations represent a continuity that undergirds the shifting conditions overhead?

Across the control texts it is possible to identify a more complex system of periodisation, one that is less concerned with linear (albeit staggered and layered) progression than with the multiplication of different, often competing systems of historical knowledge that make claims about the absolute novelty and specificity of control societies impossible to sustain. This movement, which starts to appear with a some passing remarks in 'Control and Becoming' and comes more fully into view across the six pages of the 'Postscript', suggests that Deleuze is concerned not only with extending Foucault's periodising project but also with complicating the kind of historical thinking that produces the various totalising concepts listed above. Could it be that the final sketch of control, the 'Postscript on Control Societies', encrypts the kind of multi-threaded historical method that is necessary for engaging with the epistemic demands of the period it ostensibly defines? Might this, rather than the specific characteristics that Deleuze attributes to control, represent the real import of his intervention? In this chapter, I examine the three strands touched upon in this introductory discussion – power, technology and economy – in order to foreground these historical-methodological possibilities. Having established these components of control and the complex historical questions they invite, I'll briefly consider the kind of cultural work that might be understood as constituting and/or expressing the cultural logic of the present conjuncture.

POWER

As cleanly as the discipline-control sequence appears to function, across the control texts Deleuze makes it clear that the relationship between the two terms cannot be reduced to one of direct succession or linear extension. In 'Having an Idea in Cinema', for example, Deleuze points out 'there are all kinds of things left over from disciplinary societies, and this for years on end' (1998: 17). In the conversation with Negri he further complicates the relationship between the two periodising concepts by stating that Foucault was 'one of the first to say that we're moving away from disciplinary societies, we've already left them behind' (1995a: 174). And in the 'Postscript' he writes that 'Control is the name proposed by Burroughs for this new monster, and Foucault sees it fast approaching' (1995b: 178). There is nothing like a consensus across these three temporal relations. Each, however, makes it clear that the relationship between the terms cannot be understood in terms of a clear break. This opens up a series of questions that have methodological as well as historical implications. What is the precise nature of the temporal relationship between discipline and control? What role does sovereign power play in the two 'later' periods? What drives the globally uneven movement between discipline and control, and how can the latter function as a periodising device if it cannot be detached from the former? One possible answer is that the logic of control does not emerge through the 'invention' of new relations, but rather rests on, mobilises and reorients techniques and technologies whose origins and prior uses predate it. Such techniques and technologies must thus be understood as recursive; they both originate in and 'belong' to a specific regime and perform essential functions within subsequent regimes. Because of this, any historically attentive analyses of control cannot remain in the twentieth and twenty-first centuries, but must locate objects and practices that first become legible in earlier moments. One way of doing this is by considering the specific phenomena to which Deleuze refers when he suggests that Foucault already identified the roots of control in disciplinary societies.

In the 'Postscript' Deleuze identifies two systems of management unearthed by Foucault: the first produces the individual subject through techniques of discipline, and the second biopolitically formats a given society as a mass through the use of statistical methods. Where disciplinary power sees 'no incompatibility at all' between masses and individuals – so that signatures can stand in for the latter while lists or registers account for the former – technologies of control reformulates masses as 'samples, data, markets, or banks' and thus recast individuals as 'dividuals' (1995b: 180). The similarity between this process and Foucault's theorisation of biopolitics and biopower is marked: what are samples and data if not technologies for the production of the 'forecasts, statistical estimates, and overall measures' that Foucault positions as emblematic of biopower (Foucault 2003: 246)? What are markets and banks if not extensions of the 'subtle, rational mechanisms' of biopolitics that for Foucault include 'insurance, individual and collective savings, safety measures, and so on' (Foucault 2003: 246)? What is the dividual if not the person mapped in terms of universalised, discrete predicates (race, class, gender, sexuality, ability, age)? What, in other words, is the exact nature of the relationship between control, biopower and biopolitics?

The proximity between the cybernetic inflections of Deleuze's control societies and Foucault's conceptualisation of biopolitical mechanisms as those which seek 'homeostasis' (Foucault 2003: 249) is registered in the odd way in which Hardt and Negri formulate the relationship between the two regimes in *Empire*. In discussing the political-economic character of millennial global capitalism they write that 'Foucault's work allows us to recognise a historical, epochal passage in social forms from *disciplinary society* to *societies of control*' (2000: 22–3). Only in the footnote to this claim do they reveal that this epochal passage is 'not articulated explicitly by Foucault but remains implicit in his work', an observation that is, in Hardt and Negri's telling, only guided (rather than made possible) by 'the excellent commentaries of Gilles Deleuze' (2000: 419, n1). Within Foucault's oeuvre, *The Birth of Biopolitics* (delivered as lectures at the Collège de France in 1978 and 1979; English translation 2008) might be the place in which something like a genealogy of what Deleuze names control is most explicitly articulated, although it is notable that this text focuses on political-economic (rather than governmental) imaginaries. *'Society Must be Defended'* (lectures 1975–6; English translation 2003) and Volume I of *The History of Sexuality* (1976; English translation 1978), both of which focus on techniques of governmentality, disclose connections between discipline, biopower and control that make theories of linear succession unworkable.

So, the identification between biopower and control appears so overt that Hardt and Negri more or less conflate the two and are able to attribute the full identification of the latter to latent content in Foucault's writings (on which Deleuze's control texts are mere 'commentaries', albeit 'excellent' ones). They then make the claim that '[i]n the passage from disciplinary society to the society of control, a new paradigm of power is realised which is defined by the technologies that recognise society as the realm of biopower' (Hardt and Negri 2000: 24). Following this logic, control societies come about when the ratio of biopower to discipline shifts in favour of the latter. What, then, is revealed about the historical specificity of control societies when one locates the emergence of the techniques of biopower in the eighteenth century? For this is the claim that grounds Foucault's introduction to the concept in *'Society Must be Defended'*, where he states that 'the two sets of mechanisms – one disciplinary and one regulatory [biopolitical]' are 'not mutually exclusive, and can be articulated with each other' (2003: 250). This is restated in Volume I of *The History of Sexuality*, where Foucault writes that power over life evolves in 'two basic forms' from the seventeenth century onwards (1978: 139). These two forms again correspond to the regimes of discipline and biopower. While the second of these appears 'somewhat later' than the first, it is clear that Foucault does not theorise the two as discrete, successive developments. Nor are they theorised as 'antithetical' (Foucault 1978: 139). Rather, they form 'two poles of development linked together by a whole intermediary cluster of relations'

(1978: 139). This diagram – two poles linked by intermediary clusters – suggests that control emerges not from a waning of disciplinary power, but rather through a shift in the articulations of discipline and biopower that cannot be fully understood through the image of a simple transition or change in ratio. Equally, although the former might appear to be organised around inclusion and exclusion and the latter around integration, thinking of the two as articulated logics emphasises a more complex relationship: biopower operates through and produces thresholds that render legible certain populations while occluding (or rendering as non-populations) certain others, while different applications of disciplinary techniques regulate the education, productivity and health of 'normal' individuals and manage (often by incapacitating or otherwise destroying) the bodies that fall below the line separating the normal from the abnormal (or that which should be made to live from that which can be left to die). And, as Alexander G. Weheliye has observed, this process of sorting also structures critical theorisations of biopower: in considering racism as a function of biopolitics, Weheliye notes, Foucault distinguishes

> European state racism and biopolitics from those primeval forms of racism that linger in . . . the philosophical, geographical, and political quicksands of an unspecified elsewhere; at least this is what we are asked to infer as a consequence of Foucault's taciturnity about the reach and afterlife of those other modalities of racialisation. (2014: 57–8)

The historically-specific articulations of discipline and biopower which Deleuze associates with control must thus be understood in terms of *sorting* and *disposal* as well as *scale* and *conceptual emphasis*. Furthermore, these shifts can be connected to the function of technologies that not only facilitate specific practices of capture, representation and management but also generate and modify the conceptual bases around which specific social formations are imagined and normalised. The articulations of hinged and lockable thresholds (such as those of plantations, prisons and factories) with the logic gates of electronic devices might consequently be understood in terms of specific movements between enclosures that are larger than and that confine, include and exclude certain bodies, and microscopic enclosures that operate on data, are premised on logics of selection, and position non-selected beings as non-existent or structurally invisible rather than aberrant but existent.[2] These non-selected beings are then either left in states of accelerated debilitation and slow death (Puar 2017) or subject to disciplinary techniques (incarceration and its concomitant forms of slave labour) and punishment (extrajudicial murder by police forces and armies, and so on). This is the process that Grace Kyungwon Hong has identified, albeit in relation to a different but undoubtedly related periodising concept (neoliberalism), as one in which the 'previously unimaginable' integration of certain 'racialised, gendered, and sexualised subjects' into circuits of capital and citizenship 'do[es] not alleviate, but rather exacerbates the conditions that led to the devaluation of poor, racialised, and sexual- and gender-deviant populations, and the relegation of these populations to premature death' (2015: 11–12).

Consider, for example, the ways in which the necropolitical regimes identified by Achille Mbembe (2003) and the genealogical link between panopticon and slave ship that Simone Browne traces so brilliantly in *Dark Matters* (2015: 31–62) persist and are reframed or modulated through the shifts in articulation sketched here. As Browne demonstrates, the emergence of more granular and distributed modes of control neither eliminate and replace racialised forms of sovereign and disciplinary violence nor exist apart from the historical logics that motivated and rationalised these forms of violence. In the light of these interventions it becomes essential to frame the relationship between the individual and the dividual in terms of the difference between the social rendered bio-mechanically (as bodies) and the social rendered informatically (as data). But it is equally important to note that these rendering techniques tend to be densely imbricated, and that the difficulty of privileging one over the other in a given context tends to reveal a great deal about the dynamics of racialisation, gender, sex and (dis)ability that organise that context. Information can't be separated from (but tends to occlude) the mechanisms that process it. The rendering of information is always also the production of non-information. Techniques and technologies of informatic surveillance can't be separated from (but tend to occlude) earlier technologies of violent subjection, including those of the slave ship and the plantation. The management of life is always also the production of death.

TECHNOLOGY

Considered in isolation, 'machines don't explain anything' (Deleuze 1995a: 175); rather, they 'express the social forms capable of producing them and making use of them' (Deleuze 1995b: 180). At the same time, the 'language' of discipline can be specified as '*analogical*', while control operates through languages that are '*digital* (although not necessarily binary)' (1995b: 178). Analogue and digital, while associated with certain classes of machine, must thus be understood to exceed concrete technologies and to function as conceptual operators within discursive-material fields (which might include systems of production, management and regulation). With this in mind, how might one derive a non-deterministic theory of the relationship between technology, power and economy from the control texts? This question lurks in the background of the 'Postscript on Control Societies', and it constitutes one of the most telling ways in which that text can be read as an encrypted theory of historical method as well as a diagram of a specific period.

As I suggested at the end of the preceding section, technologies are assemblages of specific social relations and specific technological developments. Such relations and developments also come to undergird epistemological claims about fundamental categories such as thinking, the human and sociality. And, as the discussion of discipline and biopolitics above should make clear, the historical, concept-generating function of specific technologies that Deleuze sketches with his claim about 'collective apparatuses' impedes linear periodisation by implementing a recursive temporality: specific technologies give concrete form to collective social forces that precede them, and in so doing intensify and reorient these forces, coming to function as what Hans-Jörg Rheinberger (1997) calls 'epistemic things'. In other words, a specific technology might come to concretise and exemplify the abstractions undergirding a given political-economic regime, but it does so by securing or amplifying certain conceptual structures or operations that logically and historically precede it, as well as by reorienting concepts and facilitating new practices and relations that point (again, for better and worse) towards different sociopolitical arrangements. For example, as Bernhard Siegert (2012, 2015) shows, the door permits a body to pass through when it is open and prevents a body moving through it when it is closed, thus both expressing and securing the inside/outside distinction (and, by extension, the logic of disciplinary power). Conversely, the logic gate permits a signal to pass through only when it is closed, thus securing a conceptual system that permits conceptual mixtures of inside and outside, and human and nonhuman, that exemplify distinctive regimes of accumulation and management.

This recursive theorisation of specific technologies as products, expressions and determiners of social forces is one of the moments at which continuities between the control texts and Deleuze's earlier collaborations with Félix Guattari are most overt. Consider the similarities between the 'collective apparatuses' of which machines form one element and the 'social machine' that Deleuze and Guattari identify in their book on Kafka:

> a machine is never simply technical. Quite the contrary, it is technical only as a social machine, taking men and women into its gears, or, rather, having men and women as part of its gears along with things, structures, metals, materials. Even more, Kafka doesn't think only about the conditions of alienated, mechanised labour – he knows all about that in great, intimate detail – but his genius is that he considers men and women to be part of the machine not only in their work but even more so in their adjacent activities, in their leisure, in their loves, in their protestations, in their indignations, and so on. (1986: 81)

This claim makes it clear that 'collective apparatuses' centred on technology include concepts, systems of management and normative ways of living as well as procedures of extraction, definition and occlusion. The mechanical factory of 'gears', 'structures', 'metals', and 'materials' is one such apparatus, and it is imbricated with specific orientations of 'leisure', 'loves', 'protestations', and so on. What kinds of orientations are similarly formed around the apparatuses of electronic digital computation?

Jeremy Bentham's 1787 essay 'Panopticon, or, the Inspection House' begins with a grand announcement: *'Morals reformed – health preserved – industry invigorated – public burthens lighted – Economy seated, as it were, upon a rock – the gordian knot of the Poor Laws not cut, but untied – all by a simple idea in architecture!'* (1843; emphasis in original). Resisting the oft-repeated distinction between discipline and biopower, Bernhard Siegert locates in the universality of Bentham's proclamation an unexamined genealogy of digital-social technologies that, perhaps surprisingly, includes ostensibly disciplinary technologies such as the panopticon and the penny post as well as the nascent computing machines theorised and developed by Charles Babbage and Ada Lovelace. 'The Panopticon was applicable to every kind of bio-politics', Siegert writes of Bentham's opening pronouncement, because on it, like on the penny post and the analytical engine, 'contents and applications were programs that ran (or would run)' only because 'such machines were blind to them' (Siegert 1999: 126–7). This leads him to a theorisation of power that is compelling for thinking through the historical logic of technology that the control texts insist upon:

> That the machine or power became abstract, Deleuze has said, merely meant that it became programmable. But power itself became machine-like in the process. The rationality of power – functionality or universality – requires the prior standardisation of the data it processes – via postage stamps or punch cards, it makes no difference . . . Disciplinary machine, postal machine, adding machine: after their interconnection was established, bodies, discourses, and numbers were one and the same with regard to the technology of power: data, and as such, contingent. (Siegert 1999: 127)

The critical movement here is towards *abstraction*, not *enumeration*. In Siegert's account one finds a description of the disciplinary technology *par excellence* in which the latter appears not as a thermodynamic machine (in line with Deleuze's periodisation) but as a digital information processor which functions through abstraction, remains structurally indifferent to the specifics of the purpose to which it is turned, and thus formats its human subjects as unmarked inputs and/or outputs. This isn't to say that the concrete formations that are shaped by these technologies are all shaped in the same way – Browne's argument in *Dark Matters* (as well as earlier theorisations, most notably Saidiya V. Hartman's *Scenes of Subjection*) should make this clear. However, Siegert's position clarifies the need for analyses of technology and culture to take into account the conceptual operations and the concrete preconditions and outcomes that both undergird and extend out of particular machines, connecting them, in often surprising ways, to past devices and practices as well as to current and future formations.

Siegert does not speak of the value form in his theorisation of panopticon, penny post and computing machine as abstract machines of power, but the resonance between his account and that most important of Marxian concepts is pronounced. With this provocation in mind, the theory of technology that Deleuze sketches in the 'Postscript' suggests some compelling directions for the integration of media theory and history within studies of economics and governmentality. Siegert's work on cultural techniques (2015) could prove useful here, as might the writings of Friedrich Kittler, Cornelia Vismann, Sybille Krämer, Wolfgang Ernst, Markus Krajewski, and others. Equally, Galloway's work on François Laruelle (2014) is instructive for the ways in which it points towards a relationship between modern thought and digitality that takes shape long before and far away from the invention of the electronic digital computer. Counterpoised with these recent media-theoretical interventions, the mode of historical analysis diagrammed in the 'Postscript' invites one to consider the ways in which investigations into cultural techniques, the materiality of signifying systems, the conceptual character and epistemic effects of digitality, and the concept-generating function of specific technologies might illuminate the economic dynamics of the post-1970s period – a period in which Marxian analysis appears both essential and incessantly troubled by what appear to be spectacular transformations in regimes of labour, value extraction and accumulation.

ECONOMY

'Today', Deleuze states in a 1995 interview in *Le Nouvel Observateur*, 'I can say I feel completely Marxist. The article I have published on the "society of control," for example, is completely Marxist, yet I write about things that Marx did not know' (1995c). If the 'Postscript' is 'completely Marxist' then it is remarkable for the challenges it poses to classical Marxist categories of historical analysis. Perhaps this is most overt in the theorisation of spatiotemporal dispersion, the movement from the 'body' of the factory to businesses that are a 'soul' or 'gas' (Deleuze 1995b: 179), the account of the movement of art away from 'closed sites' and into 'the open circuits of banking', (1995b: 181), and the baleful description of 'speech and communication' becoming 'thoroughly permeated' by 'money' (1995a: 175). Each of these phenomena resonates with recent theorisations that rest on and extend Marx's concept of real subsumption (Marx 1994: 93–116). In Hardt and Negri's exemplary account, this concept describes nothing less than a total capture of social relations and their orientation towards capital accumulation. 'With the real subsumption of society under capital', they write:

> capital has become a world. Use value and all the other references to values and processes of valorisation that were conceived to be outside the capitalist mode of production have progressively vanished. Subjectivity is entirely immersed in exchange and language, but that does not mean it is now pacific. Technological development based on the generalisation of the communicative relationships of production is a motor of crisis, and productive general intellect is a nest of antagonisms. (2000: 386)

As writers from Timothy Brennan (2003) to the authors of the journal *Endnotes* (*Endnotes* 2010) have observed, this notion of real subsumption far exceeds that found in Marx's writing, where it describes the processes through which commodity production is restructured in order to maximise efficiency, for example by increasing the proportion of production that is automated by machinery (a process described as an increase in the organic composition of capital).[3] This process leads both to a decline in capital's capacity to absorb labour (which leads to the growth of surplus populations) and a decline in the absolute surplus labour that can be extracted from a given production process. The practices and theories glossed by the term 'neoliberalism' might all be understood as responses to this historical process. The phenomena that Guy Debord theorises in *The Society of the Spectacle* furnish other examples, as does the exponential growth of the so-called tertiary (service) sector. Critically, none of these regimes of extraction and management are evenly distributed; participation in each is contoured and fragmented by geography, processes of gendering and racialisation, related constructions of physical and cognitive capacity, and other procedures for defining certain forms of attention, rationality and affective capacities as valorisable. As such, the notion that the flexible or modulating economic conditions associated with the control era progressively integrate whatever might once have existed outside circuits of capitalist valorisation must be resisted.

As Rosa Luxemburg writes, capitalism 'depends in all respects on noncapitalist strata and social organisations existing side by side with it' (2003: 345). The essential role played by so-called 'non-productive' labour (childbirth and child-rearing, cooking, cleaning, emotional and physical care) in the production and reproduction of labour power is perhaps the most obvious example of this. Consequently, for subsumption to function as a useful concept within a given periodisation theory it is necessary to replace the notion of a single process through which capital in all senses encircles 'the world' with specific, materialist examinations of the shifting dynamics of inside and outside, representation and occlusion, and integration and suspension as they operate in concert with the structural transformations glossed by ideas of post-industrial or post-Fordist production. In the 'fully Marxist' pages of the 'Postscript' Deleuze at least faintly insists that one account for both sides of this dialectic: on the one hand, he tracks specific changes in labour relations and modes of accumulation detailed above (the shifts from the factory to the business, from goods to services, and so on); on the other hand, he makes it clear that the forms of dispersal and modulation that characterise these transformations are secured against the 'three quarters of humanity in extreme poverty, too poor to have debts and too numerous to be confined' (1995b: 181). Extending this relation beyond Deleuze's brief sketch, today one might observe that even if they cannot directly access their questionable benefits, racialised, sexualised, gendered, disabled and debilitated surplus populations are increasingly bound to mechanisms of accumulation, debt, sovereign violence and disciplinary organisation. Today such populations are positioned as proxy, object or raw material within certain modes of accumulation, from the 'commodified' life of inmates in prisons and detention centres (Tadiar 2012) to the forms of service, surrogacy and outsourced labour that are understood not to generate value directly but to facilitate the productivity and reproduction of other, more directly valorisable lives (Vora 2015). And, again, the distinctions upon which these sorting procedures are premised precede the period that might be glossed as that of control societies. Both Tadiar and Vora clearly demonstrate how these newer dynamics of accumulation-by-enclosure and accumulation-by-proxy closely limn longer-term colonial structures, while Ruth Wilson Gilmore (2007: 12) points out that

> during most of the modern history of prisons, those officially devoid of rights – indigenous and enslaved women and men, for example, or new immigrants, or married white women – rarely saw the inside of a cage, because their unfreedom was guaranteed by other means.

In the end, it is this dialectical, materialist impulse that grounds the movement between 'clean' periodisation and the coexistence of unmatched and even conflicting areas of inquiry within the 'Postscript'. Tracking the techniques and technologies of distributed, modulating sovereignty, mapping the affordances and epistemic effects of digital technologies, and itemising the implications of and preconditions for an imagined economy without commodities are all necessary endeavours. But the analysis of sociopolitical distribution must take into account the persistence of violent processes of differentiation, abjection and corralling supported by the legal and discursive framing of unemployed people, disabled people, migrants, prisoners and other detainees as oscillating between structurally invisible and hypervisible, qualifiedly human and fully nonhuman. The analysis of computational media must remain attentive to the historicity and materiality of devices, their users and the people that labour, often precariously and in deleterious conditions, to produce them; it must also address the ways in which all of these are abstracted, with a range of quite different implications, by the cultural and technical operations of the media in question. And, for now at least, the analysis of 'immaterial' economic formations must include the ongoing presence of older formations and the emergence of newer but less widely discussed methods for the violent extraction of value from human life and the ongoing abjection of lives from which no value can currently be extracted.

Since abstraction, capture and measurement are themselves social relations whose changing articulations are registered in the passage designated as that from discipline to control, the impossibility of periodisation is as important as – and registers the critical value of – the diagnostic utility that periodisation affords. The radical promise of periodisation (if there is one) thus lies in its capacity to provisionally impose a set of historical markers against which one might (1) observe and measure specifically new forms of interaction between abstractions and social formations, (2) register the ways in which these new forms of interaction are determined by longer-term social formations (such as the structural production of gendered, sexed and racialised abjection), and (3) identify how both the newer and the longer-term formations rest on a surplus that exceeds or is too faint to register within the dominant markers associated with a given period. This is the procedure that Lisa Lowe (2005: 412) insists on when, against the kinds of control-by-governmentality that promise to integrate difference in exchange for the further abjection of certain gendered and racialised groups, she calls for 'a *genealogical* study that would *both* situate "difference" within the modern mode of comparison *and* attempt to retrieve the fragments of mixture and convergence that are "lost" through modern comparative procedures'. The appropriate concept to tie together those fragments and modes of comparison might be *disposal*, since that term encompasses both *having people and things at one's disposal* (exploitation, value extraction) and *making things disposable* (abjection, exhaustion/using up).

REPRESENTATION

This uneven, multilayered genealogy, which encompasses both the novel features of the current conjuncture and the older structures of thought, action and violence that are retained and (at times) repurposed within it, requires a commensurate approach to the forms of cultural production that express and/or exemplify the logic and material operations of control. In other words, discussions of the cultural logic of control must begin from the premise that expressions of this logic precede and exceed the direct representation of computer technologies, post-industrial forms of work and leisure, and sci-fi projections of both into various imagined futures. The 'positive' (i.e., legible) marks of this historical logic are evident in theoretical analyses such as Foucault's location of the parallel emergence of disciplinary and biopolitical modes of regulation and Siegert's discussion of the ways that panopticon, postal service and adding machine each effect a comparable 'standardisation of the data' – i.e., the people – that power processes. The 'negative' marks are locatable in critical-theoretical interventions that insist on the centrality of race and racialisation to disciplinary and biopolitical techniques, Marxist theorisations of the mechanical relationship between subsumption and surplus populations, and Lowe's reminder that contemporary valorisations of difference are predicated on loss.

Where might one locate the cultural expressions of this logic? Deleuze provides a few concrete suggestions. 'Kafka', he writes, 'already standing at the point of transition between the two kinds of society, described in *The Trial* their most ominous juridical expressions: *apparent acquittal* (between two confinements) in disciplinary societies, and *endless postponement* in (constantly changing) control societies' (1995b: 179). To the literature of bureaucracy, one might add that of predictive intelligence and policing – Poe's *The Purloined Letter*, in which disciplinary policing through grids and direct applications of force is counterpoised with the detective Dupin's abstract permutational mechanism (which is directly associated with computing machines in Lacan's *Seminar* II), might be exemplary here. But, as I've been suggesting above, it is equally important to understand how the dynamics of control are undergirded by forms of violence that have longer genealogies – genealogies that are occluded by the notion of a general shift away from exploitation, enclosure, incarceration and exclusion and towards flexible, predictive and speculative forms of accumulation and management in the passage from discipline to control.

With such methodological questions in mind, I suggest that M. NourbeSe Philip's *ZONG!* (2008) represents an invaluable expression of both (1) the complex of more and less visible historical structures, and (2) the imbrication of logical, juridical and embodied violence upon which the ostensibly novel components of control are premised. In other words, *ZONG!* (and the baleful events upon which it is based) makes clear what is occluded by a sole focus on the 'free floating' and predicative dynamics of accumulation and management that are conventionally evoked to characterise societies of control.

Philip's cycle of poems is based on the text of *Gregson v. Gilbert* (1783), 'the formal name of the case more colloquially known as the *Zong* Case' in which between 130 and 150 enslaved Africans (the exact number being, for Philip, a 'slippery signifier' that attests to the violence of the event) were massacred, thrown overboard from the ship transporting them to Jamaica so that the ship's owners ('the Messrs Gregson') could claim against their loss from their insurers ('the Messrs Gibson') (Philips 2008: 189). In the 'Notanda' that follows the poems in *ZONG!* Philip states that,

> [M]y intent is to use the text of the legal decision as a word store; to lock myself into this particular and peculiar discursive landscape in the belief that the story of these African men, women, and children thrown overboard in an attempt to collect insurance monies, the story that can only be told by not telling, is locked in this text. (2008: 191)

This story – which is the story both of the living African men, women and children and the racialised violence foundational to financial speculation – represents a specific instance of the erasures that produce and are produced by the abstracting mechanisms of legal and financial language and by practices of accumulation by speculation. In locating in these languages 'the story that can only be told by not telling', Philip restores the foundational (but oft-occluded) connection between the historical precursors to putatively immaterial technologies of control (in this case, financial-legal instruments such as insurance policies) and the excessive violence, ontological dehumanisation and spatial confinement (the massacre, the legal definition of the slaves as property and the ship's hold) upon which capital accumulation in general – including accumulation via 'flexible', distributed, financialised, or so-called 'immaterial' means – is premised.

Consider the ways in which the relationships between abstract universality, speculation and racialised violence are figured in this excerpt from Philip's *ZONG! #20*:

> this necessity of loss
>
> this quantity of not
>
> perils underwriters
>
> insurers
>
> of
>
> the throw in circumstances
>
> the instance in attempt

PERIODISING (WITH) CONTROL 59

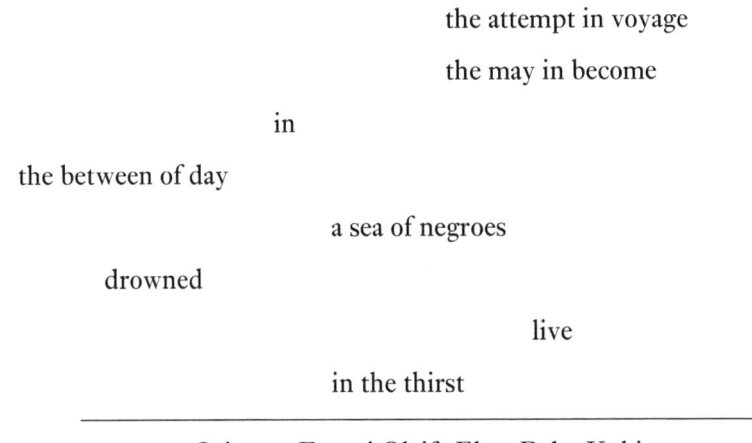

The first nine lines of the poem map the speculative temporality and the interactions among material and putatively immaterial (imaginary, logical, conceptual, legal) registers that connect eighteenth-century finance to the range of economic, legal and carceral structures that tend to be evoked to characterise societies of control. The imagined possibility of profit or loss is a structuring precondition for the existence of the insurance claim whose phrasing is oriented towards absolute control (including control of the future); the possibility of the future absence of a specific quantity structures makes necessary the preliminary quantification of cargo (in this instance people rendered as chattel) that strips African men, women and children 'of all specificity, including their names' while recording and preserving 'their financial value for insurance purposes' (Philips 2008: 194). Underwriters are insurers of the contingencies that are encoded in but always exceed the formal language of the policy: circumstances that play out under the 'cover' of a given insurance policy always imply the play of chance (a 'throw'); every attempt at X produces a concrete instance that jars with the abstract universality of legal discourse and financial logic; every voyage constitutes an 'attempt' whose outcome cannot be concretely guaranteed; every concrete process entails contingency ('the may in become').

Below the orderly pattern of these nine lines, beneath these orderly abstractions that promise to protect the future economic value extractable from a complex arrangement of ship, bodies, ocean and weather, Philip inscribes the concrete violence that makes possible but cannot be fully accommodated by these formations. The use of the text of *Gregson* v. *Gilbert* as a source that is subject to 'fragmentation and mutilation' (2008: 197–8) inverts the fact that the violent fragmentation and mutilation of bodies and social relations is the unmarked content of property law and the forms of discipline and control that extend from it. The technologies of control emerge – historically and logically

– out of these relations: between legal and financial abstractions; between abstraction and racialisation; between the terms of the insurance policy and the content of the ship's hold; between control, speculation, subjection and immediate, excessive violence.

Drawing (as Philip does) on Ian Baucom's *Specters of the Atlantic*, Brenna Bhandar (2014) argues that racialisation, modern property law and finance capital are linked by a logic of abstraction that (to return to a periodising terminology that Bhandar does not specifically mention) persists across disciplinary and control regimes. For Baucom, Bhandar observes, the *Zong* massacre is instructive for what it reveals about how 'new epistemological structures' of credit and debt 'required above all faith in the imaginary values promised by ocean-crossing bills-of-exchange, promissory notes and other financial instruments that made the slave trade possible' (2014: 214). And, as Bhandar demonstrates, these instruments are premised on a speculative temporality premised on Benthamite notions of property ownership as the 'expectation that one can utilise a thing' (as distinct from 'mere physical possession') that themselves emerge with the historical production of 'the abstract figure of the slave, the native, the savage' (2014: 210, 208). Consequently, Bhandar concludes, the

> contradictory mixture of attributes that are . . . metaphysical, embodied, and affective shape the very constitution of modern legal-political subjectivities. Notions of privilege and entitlement shape the contours of one's consciousness, based on the possession of particular qualities and characteristics that constituted the pre-requisites of one's ability to own property. Understanding the historical development of the interrelationship between the legal form of property and the racial remains crucial to accounting for contemporary iterations of a globalised capital firmly rooted in histories of slavery and colonialism. (2014: 218)

In other words, the legally attributed capacity to own and dispose of property – as well as the elaboration of legal and economic structures centred on this capacity, whether organised around confinement or modulating modes of distributed management – is secured against those marked as ontologically unable to own property and, consequently, subject either to being treated as property or having their land rendered as property owned by others. In so far as the legal and conceptual form of the property relations that make such definitions possible undergird the 'imaginary values' upon which financialisation is premised, the 'contemporary iterations of . . . globalised capital' that characterise contemporary cultures of control – distributed management; modulation; samples, data and markets; the 'open circuits of banking' (Deleuze 1995b: 181) – must be seen not as a successive regime to but rather *directly informed* by the violence of slavery and settler colonialism.

NOTES

1. It is possible to identify a larger archive of texts that, while not naming control as such, certainly examine the same historical tendencies; see the chapter '7000 B.C.: Apparatus of Capture' (Deleuze and Guattari 1987: 424–73) and the appendix to Deleuze 1999: 102–10.
2. This argument can be extended to other discursive formations that operate in the present. For example, one can follow Jordy Rosenberg and take the molecule (rather than the logic gate) as an exemplary epistemic object in order to examine a different valence of the contemporary moment (Rosenberg 2014).
3. For a rigorous account of real subsumption as it pertains to periodisation see *Endnotes* (2010).

BIBLIOGRAPHY

Bentham, Jeremy (1843), 'Panopticon, or, the Inspection-House', in *The Works of Jeremy Bentham, Vol. 4*, Edinburgh: William Tait.
Bhandar, Brenna (2014), 'Property, Law, and Race: Modes of Abstraction', *UC Irvine Law Review* 4:1, pp. 203–18.
Brennan, Timothy (2003), 'The Empire's New Clothes', *Critical Inquiry* 29:2.
Brown, Wendy (2003), 'Neo-Liberalism and the End of Liberal Democracy', *Theory and Event* 7:1.
Browne, Simone (2015), *Dark Matters: On the Surveillance of Blackness*, Durham, NC: Duke University Press.
Deleuze, Gilles (1995a), 'Control and Becoming', in *Negotiations*, trans. Martin Joughin, New York: Columbia University Press.
Deleuze, Gilles (1995b), 'Postscript on Control Societies', in *Negotiations*, trans. Martin Joughin, New York: Columbia University Press.
Deleuze, Gilles (1995c), 'Le "Je me souviens" de Gilles Deleuze', *Le Nouvel Observateur*, 16–22 November.
Deleuze, Gilles (1998), 'Having an Idea in Cinema', trans. Eleanor Kaufman, in *Deleuze and Guattari: New Mappings in Politics, Philosophy, and Culture*, ed. Eleanor Kaufman and Kevin Jon Heller, Minneapolis: University of Minnesota Press.
Deleuze, Gilles (1999), *Foucault*, trans. Seán Hand, London: Continuum.
Deleuze, Gilles and Félix Guattari (1986), *Kafka: Toward a Minor Literature*, trans. Brian Massumi, Minneapolis: University of Minnesota Press.
Deleuze, Gilles and Félix Guattari (1987), *A Thousand Plateaus*, trans. Brian Massumi, Minneapolis: University of Minnesota Press.
Endnotes (2010), 'The History of Subsumption', *Endnotes 2*.
Foucault, Michel (1978), *The History of Sexuality, Volume I*, trans. Robert Hurley, New York: Pantheon Books.
Foucault, Michel (2003), *'Society Must Be Defended': Lectures at the Collège de France 1975–1976*, trans. David Macey, London: Allen Lane.
Foucault, Michel (2008), *The Birth of Biopolitics: Lectures at the Collège de France 1978–1979*, trans. Graham Burchell, Basingstoke: Palgrave Macmillan.
Franklin, Seb (2015), *Control: Digitality as Cultural Logic*, Cambridge, MA: The MIT Press.
Galloway, Alexander R. (2004), *Protocol: How Control Exists After Decentralization*, Cambridge, MA: The MIT Press.

Galloway, Alexander R. (2014), *Laruelle: Against the Digital*, Minneapolis: University of Minnesota Press.
Gilmore, Ruth Wilson (2007), *Golden Gulag: Prisons, Surplus, Crisis, and Opposition in Globalizing California*, Berkeley: University of California Press.
Hardt, Michael and Antonio Negri (2000), *Empire*, Cambridge, MA: Harvard University Press.
Hong, Grace Kyungwon (2015), *Death Beyond Disavowal: The Impossible Politics of Difference*, Minneapolis, MN: University of Minnesota Press.
Jameson, Fredric (1991), *Postmodernism, or, the Cultural Logic of Late Capitalism*, Durham, NC: Duke University Press.
Lowe, Lisa (2005), 'Insufficient Difference', *Ethnicities* 5:3, pp. 409–14.
Luxemburg, Rosa (2003), *The Accumulation of Capital*, trans. Agnes Schwarzschild, London, New York: Routledge.
Marx, Karl (1994), *Economic Manuscript of 1861–63*, trans. Ben Fowkes, in *Karl Marx Frederick Engels Collected Works*, Vol. 34, London: Lawrence and Wishart.
Marx, Karl (1996), *Capital*, Vol. 1, trans. Richard Dixon, in *Karl Marx Frederick Engels Collected Works*, Vol. 35, London: Lawrence and Wishart.
Mbembe, Achille (2003), 'Necropolitics', trans. Libby Meintjes, *Public Culture* 15:1, pp. 11–40.
Pasquinelli, Matteo (2009), 'Google's PageRank Algorithm: A Diagram of Cognitive Capitalism and the Rentier of the Common Intellect', in *Deep Search*, ed. Konrad Becker and Felix Stalder, London: Transaction Publishers.
Philip, M. NourbeSe (2008), *ZONG!* Middletown, CT: Wesleyan University Press.
Puar, Jasbir K. (2017), *The Right to Maim: Debility, Capacity, Disability*, Durham, NC: Duke University Press.
Rheinberger, Hans-Jörg (1997), *Towards a History of Epistemic Things: Synthesizing Proteins in the Test Tube*, Stanford: Stanford University Press.
Rosenberg, Jordy (2014), 'The Molecularization of Sexuality', *Theory and Event* 17:2.
Siegert, Bernhard (1999), *Relays: Literature as an Epoch of the Postal System*, trans. Kevin Repp, Stanford: Stanford University Press.
Siegert, Bernhard (2012), 'Doors: On the Materiality of the Symbolic', trans. John Durham Peters, *Grey Room* 47, pp. 6–23.
Siegert, Bernhard (2015), *Cultural Techniques: Grids, Filters, Doors, and Other Articulations of the Real*, trans. Geoffrey Winthrop-Young, New York: Fordham University Press.
Tadiar, Neferti X. M. (2012), 'Life-Times in Fate Playing', *South Atlantic Quarterly* 111:4, pp. 783–802.
Vora, Kalindi (2015), *Life Support: Biocapital and the New History of Outsourced Labor*, Minneapolis: University of Minnesota Press.
Weheliye, Alexander G. (2014), *Habeas Viscus: Racializing Assemblages, Biopolitics, and Black Feminist Theories of the Human*, Durham, NC: Duke University Press.

CHAPTER 4

Subjects of Sovereign Control and the Art of Critique in the Early Modern Period

Carin Franzén

Early modern France is usually described as a society of sovereignty. Yet, its centralised administration as well as state-controlled art and literature during the seventeenth century point to a transition not only towards disciplinary societies to come – it also shares similarities with what Deleuze defines as our contemporary control societies (Deleuze 1995: 177–82). To be sure, in absolutist France the despotic power of Louis XIV – his right to dispose over his subjects' life and death – diminished during the end of the century and gave way to more disciplinary forms of power by 'an explosion of numerous and diverse techniques for achieving the subjugation of bodies and the control of populations' (Foucault 1998: 140). Nonetheless, around the turn of the seventeenth to eighteenth centuries there existed also a kind of social formation that Norbert Elias in a classic study from 1969 described as the *court society*, characterised by imposed self-restraint due to the development of an increasingly differentiated and interconnected web of power relations in the early modern state (Elias 2006: 4–5). In this chapter, I want to show that former societies of sovereignty have more in common with contemporary control societies than we usually think. The idea that the early modern court society already functions as a form of control society affirms in a sense Deleuze's suggestion that it 'may be that older means of control, borrowed from the old sovereign societies, will come back onto play' (Deleuze 1995: 182). Or, more precisely, I want to highlight the parallels between early modern sovereign societies and contemporary neoliberal societies regarding the ambiguity of control as both enslaving and liberating, and how the 'older means of control' functioned both ways – as mechanisms of subjugation and as potentials for a resistance – an ambiguity that has gained new actuality today.

The motivation for this juxtaposition is that the ubiquitous character of control mechanisms in court society – where there were also subtler ways of modulating subjectivity than sovereign subjugation or disciplining as such – can be associated with a flexibility that forms the contemporary subject submitted to the ideology and function of global capitalism. I also argue that the subjective strategies of obedience or resistance developed within the French regime of absolute monarchy point to problems for every elaboration of a critical practice in relation to power, in the early modern period as well as in our contemporary society of control.

SOVEREIGN RATIONALITIES

As Foucault points out (in his Collège de France course from 1978–9, *The Birth of Biopolitics* (2008)), referring to the concept of *raison d'état*, control during the early modern period takes 'the form of the rationality of the state understood as sovereign individuality'. In seventeenth-century France, this governmental rationality is 'the rationality of the sovereign himself', that is Louis XIV, who in order to exercise his power was enmeshed in a specific interdependence that Foucault describes as a transition from the rationality of the sovereign to 'the rationality of the governed' (Foucault 2008: 312). This form of transferred control can be linked to what Elias labels 'court rationality', which is a characterised by a competition for prestige and status by a development of 'a specific control of affects' among the people concerned by the king's favours (Elias 2006: 102). In a more general sense, this transition of control from the king to his subjects was also promoted by Descartes as his philosophical ideal. For example, in a famous letter to Swedish Queen Christina from 1647, Descartes writes that free will is the sovereign good because it makes the subject similar to God – the sovereign above (Descartes 1953: 168). And two years later, in his treaties *The Passions of the Soul*, he states that 'the greatest benefit of wisdom is that it teaches us to master the passions so thoroughly and handle them so skilfully that the evils they cause are perfectly bearable, and can even, all of them, be a source of joy' (Descartes 2015: 280). However, governmental rationality, wisdom and free will can direct subjects only in so far as they are based on *reason*, which is the faculty that according to Descartes defines the human being.

Reason is not only what is used in order to defend the powers that be – *raison d'état* – it also dictates cultural expressions during the classical period, as Nicolas Boileau (1636–1711) writes it in his famous poem on the doctrines of French Classicism, 'The Art of Poetry' from 1670: 'So cherish Reason: all your work should show' (Boileau 2007: 21). However, in the French seventeenth century there were also smoother forms of control that did not take reason as its reason, as it were. The ways libertines and freethinking moralists handled 'court rationality' gave rise to other forms of subjectivity than the ones reflected by classicist ideals, court competition for prestige or philosophical self-mastery by reason and will. Against a very short backdrop of early modern subjectivity that also functions as a genealogy of the modern subject, I will try to highlight these more liberating forms of subjectivity. In a first step, by assessing scepticism as a condition for the libertine resistance to sovereign rationality and control, and, in a second step, by focusing on some concrete examples taken from classical freethinking moralists and libertines who, in the wake of Montaigne and through the salon culture, developed minor genres such as maxims, letter writings and fables, and through them a style and an art of critique confronting or negotiating the above-mentioned dominating control mechanisms.

A SHORT GENEALOGY OF THE MODERN SUBJECT

The modern subject seems to be in crisis in our contemporary age, not only from a trans- and posthuman perspective but also in relation to neoliberalism and global capitalism provoking a 'fatigue of being oneself', to use Ehrenberg's diagnosis in the book *The Weariness of the Self* from 1998. This 'fatigue' follows from a modification of the ideal of an autonomous subject into a neoliberal subject with the ability to bend and with a docility that joins together 'in constituting a new structural norm that function[s] immediately to exclude' the one who is not flexible enough – to use Catherine Malabou's razor-sharp description of the formation of subjectivity in our contemporary society of control (Malabou 2008: 46). Before this critical turning point in the history of subjectivity that passes from sovereign rationality and discipline to infinite flexibility as a new form of enslavement, we can see how the modern subject emerges from a specific discursive practice.

Speaking as a first-person subject and making oneself the subject of examination mark a revision away from a conception of thought as deriving from God and his authorities on earth towards thought as an individual, lived experience through empirical observations and the linguistic and literary resources at one's disposal. Modern ideals of autonomy, self-realisation, and the ability to act by oneself can thus be derived from a new experience of the subject initiated among others by Montaigne's address to the reader in the preface to his *Essays*: 'I am the matter of my book' (Montaigne 1991: lxii).

Descartes also takes himself as a starting point for his philosophical search after certain knowledge and self-mastery. In his *Discourse on the Method* (1637) he writes that as soon as he 'reached an age that allowed me to escape from the control of my teachers' he decided to 'pursue only that knowledge which I might find in myself or in the great book of the world' (Descartes 2006:10).

However, although there are similarities between Montaigne's and Descartes' empirical observations and interest for the inner workings of the self, their methods and aims are strikingly different. The former develops a critical attitude that leads to an insight of the limitations of reason and self-mastery:

> I have not seen no more evident monstrosity and miracle in the world than myself. Time and custom condition us to anything strange: nevertheless, the more I haunt myself and know myself the more my deformity amazes me and the less I understand myself. (Montaigne 1991: 1164; translation modified)

As has been pointed out, in contrast to Montaigne's acceptance of the limitations of his own subject throughout his writing, 'Descartes emphasizes the importance of converting objects of wonder into that of knowledge' (Zalloua 2009: 17). Thus, if epistemological certainty as well as rational control over passions are essential goals for Descartes, Montaigne's scepticism informs the shape and manner of his essays. Further, if doubt is a driving force for both of them, the one uses it in order to conduct his reason and find truth while the other takes 'reason itself to court' as Claude Lévi-Strauss put it in his rereading of Montaigne (Lévi-Strauss 1995: 212). While Descartes never doubts that human beings have a divine, sovereign reason that distinguish them from animals, Montaigne's process against reason dismisses the idea of human sovereignty straightaway – most clearly in the famous and longest of his essays, 'Apology for Raymond Sebond', where Montaigne also deploys his ideas on scepticism. Among other things he states that the human being 'has no true privilege or pre-eminence' in nature and if the 'freedom to think' is exclusively human, the person who thinks this 'has little cause to boast about it, since it is the chief source of the woes which beset him: sin, sickness, irresolution, confusion and despair' (Montaigne 1991: 514).

According to Lévi-Strauss it is the discussion of the New World in this essay that gives Montaigne the opportunity to undermine the idea of a sovereign reason by comparing ethnographic data as 'a mess of customs and beliefs that are either common to or opposite in the Old and New Worlds' (Lévi-Strauss 1995: 213). However, Montaigne's scepticism regarding a rational basis of these resemblances and differences does not lead him to an absolute cultural relativism but to a more general disbelief in a stable or essential truth about human nature. The search for certainty in human matters is vain according to Montaigne's argument that life is a movement from birth to death, which becomes a paradoxical ground for a being that constantly changes – and 'reason, that there looks for a real substance, finds itself deceived' (Montaigne 1991: 680; translation modified). However, if Montaigne's scepticism can be described as a deceived rationalism it does not stay there. Instead, it leads to a practice that has a more empirical than rational foundation, or in Lévi-Strauss' words:

> A consistent skepticism would only lead to suicide or to the most extreme asceticism, if it were not for its butting against an empirical fact: without having to justify them in another way, human beings find sensory satisfactions in living life as if it had a meaning, this even though intellectual honesty assures us that this is not so. (Lévi-Strauss 1995: 216)

To live *as* if life has a meaning is also to develop an art of existence. At any rate, in the wake of Montaigne, French libertines and moralists during the following century seek not to control the passions by self-mastery through reason as in the case of Descartes and his followers but to transform them into a practice that 'carries certain aesthetic values and meets certain stylistic criteria' as Foucault puts it in the introduction to *The Use of Pleasure* (Foucault 1985: 10–11). Also, in his lecture at Collège de France 1981–2, *The Hermeneutics of the Subject*, Foucault (2005) suggests that there is a connection between the ethics and the aesthetics of the self in the Greek and Latin authors he was studying during this year and the sixteenth century, especially Montaigne. It will be my contention that these ancient and early modern forms of subjective practices also could give later forms of returning to the self an ethical and political meaning, and more precisely counteracting the 'fatigue of being oneself' in our contemporary control society. The more so if it is, as Foucault suggests in this lecture, 'that there is no first or final point of resistance to political power other that in the relationship one has to oneself' (Foucault 2005: 252). So, let us look a little closer to how Montaigne's legacy was brought into practice by his first readers – the libertines of the French seventeenth century.

AN ART OF EXISTENCE

The very concepts libertine (*libertin*) and libertinism (*libertinage*) were not used as self-designations during the early modern period but rather as labels in order to stigmatise a certain lifestyle and liberty of thought that deviated from religious doctrines and official politics. It was not until the end of the nineteenth century that the terms were used in order to categorise 'minor authors from the seventeenth century that did not get a place in the history of philosophy and represented a counter-movement opposing classicism' (Cavaillé 2017: 25). Actually, this 'counter-movement' is constituted by a set of phenomena that transgress boundaries between philosophy, literature and lifestyle. It is for example significant that Charles de Saint-Évremond (1613–1703) – whom the nineteenth century classified as a libertine – describes himself as a philosopher writing on various subjects and in different minor genres such as short stories, chronicles, essays and most often letters addressed to friends. In one of his more famous essays, 'The Man who Wants to Know Everything does not Know Himself' ('L'Homme qui veut connaître toutes choses ne se connaît pas lui-même'), probably written in 1647–8, he starts warning the imaginary addressee, 'the man who wants to know everything', that he risks losing his sociability in this specific search: 'You are not as sociable as you were. Study [has] something sombre over it, spoiling your natural charm, taking away your intellectual ease and free expression of wit that are required in conversation by honest people' (Saint-Évremond 2004: 651).

Inspired by Montaigne's scepticism and by philosopher Pierre Gassendi (1592–1655), who had introduced him to the atomistic theories of Epicurus, Saint-Évremond defends a lifestyle based on an art that the French court society called *honnêteté*. It is a complex notion difficult to translate and in many senses it is the essence of 'court rationality'. On the one hand it designates a utilitarian use of social and verbal qualities in order to suceed at court and gain nobilitary status. The most famous treatise of this kind of social *arrivisme* that *honnêteté* could imply was probably Nicolas Faret's *The Honest Man or the Art to Please in Court* from 1630 that was reprinted no less than eleven times during the century. On the other hand there were more subtle uses of the term deriving from Montaigne, whose *Essays* were regarded as 'the breviary of *honnêtes gens*' (Stanton 1980: 21). For Montaigne, *honnêteté* is clearly linked to life as art, and in this sense it can also be connected to 'a discourse of resistance to tyrannical domination' (Vance 2009: 80). With Foucault, this resistance can be understood as a certain 'return to the self' that at the same time functions as critical attention paid to 'the order of the world and with its general and internal organization' (Foucault 2005: 260). Thus, the use of this crucial notion in seventeenth-century court society can work both ways, as the sovereign regime's controlling instrument that courtiers quickly learned to use on themselves, and as a return to the self in the form of a critique and a resistance to this enslaving force. For both uses of the ideal of *honnêteté* a relation to style is required. Hence, style is an ambigous notion as well.

Style in the early modern society can be seen as part of the courtly codes deriving from the Middle Ages and developed during the following centuries in different treatises, as in Baldesar Castiglione's *Il Cortegiano*, first published 1528 and followed up in Faret's book, where didactically it is turned into signs at the service of the powers that be – signs that were especially important for the upcoming bourgeoisies as well as for a nobility that was losing its power in absolutist France. Thus, the discourse of *honnêteté*, as Michael Moriarty points out, 'postulates a subject participating in a nobiliary scheme of values under the aegis of a monarchichal order' (Moriarty 1988: 93). However, in the margins of French court society there was also a possibility to develop an internal strategy of resistance precisely through style. Even though the court had a formative influence on convivial culture, social life was slowly decentralised into the so-called *salons* of private homes (*hôtels particuliers*) where style was turned into a more playful practice and an art of existence making room for a more critical than hypocritical attitude.[1]

A MATTER OF STYLE

Salon culture and libertine thought after Montaigne was concerned with the description and analysis of the moral character of humanity. Writers in this tradition were also sometimes called moralists, but it is important to keep in mind that a moralist is not necessarily a moraliser. Their writings are descriptive rather than prescriptive as Moriarty states in relation to La Rochefoucauld's *Maxims* (Moriarty 1988: 12). Moreover, they all share with Montaigne a sceptical view of the human.

To be sure, Montaigne readers in the seventeenth century are a rather heterogeneous group with different opinions. For example, Blaise Pascal (1623–62), one of the major classical moralists, wanted to convince a certain class of libertine philosophers, usually described as *libertins érudites*, that 'they must rationally accept the limitations of human knowledge and the necessity of Christian faith' (Boitano 2002: 29). However, regardless of confessionalism the libertines that I am concerned with here accepted the limitations of human knowledge by a 'riskier practice that seeks to yield artistry from constraint', to quote Judith Butler's comment on Foucault's idea of a possible critical agency counteracting hegemonic control through stylisation (Butler 2004: 321). Furthermore, libertine scepticism can be seen as 'a certain risk-taking that happens at the limit of the epistemological field', as Butler also says when she describes the specific practice that follows from Foucault's notion of critique in terms of his 'virtue' (Butler 2004: 319). I would like to suggest that this *virtue* – in terms of a specific returning to the self that implies a critical attention payed to the order of the world – is a salient feature also in libertine circles that appropriated 'court rationality' by developing it as a critical practice.

Further, if there is no possible resistance to our contemporary control society other than *internal* as Catherine Malabou contends in the preface to the second edition of *Que faire de Notre Cerveau?* (Malabou 2011: 24), the same goes for the early modern court society – at least if we are to follow Elias' definition of court society as an instrument of social control that intensified the subordination of nobility. Nevertheless, I see the development of *honnêteté* not just as result of this subordination but also as a virtue in Butler's sense, which furthermore could be linked to Malabou's concept of 'plasticity' that she uses as a critical alternative to the flexibility of the neoliberal subject. In other words, I suggest that this connection of style to plasticity or artistry rather than to sovereign rationality and controlling powers can be a way of assessing and actualising the virtue of early modern libertine subjects.

Belonging to a mundane cultural elite the libertines developed a discursive practice and specific techniques of the self by using their passions as a matter of style, focusing on manners and the art of conversation. It is worth underlining that the term conversation had a more complex significance than today. According to Antoine Furetière's *Dictionnaire universel* (1690) it implied the art of 'living, talking in a familiar way with someone' (Parmentier 2000: 10). And they probably agreed with Montaigne who praised the art of conversation as 'the most fruitful and most natural exercise of our minds [. . .] I find the practice of it the most delightful activity in our lives' (Montaigne 1991: 1045). Further, as Marc Schachter has clarified, Montaigne's view of this art reveals a form of a critical practice that Foucault identifies as 'the art of not being so governed' (Schachter 2009: 124). Hence, Foucault's concept of governmentality (first developed in his 1977–8 Collège de France course, *Security, Territory, Population* (2007)) does not only designate the power over subjects but includes corollary forms of resistance that can be put to use in order to assess the political dimensions of cultural expression of the libertines.

Foucault underlines throughout his thinking – but more clearly in his work from 1980 onwards – that resistance is not an opposition to power but a strategy making subjection into a care of the self or a technology of the self by stylisation. However, as I have already pointed out, style is a form of control and self-constraint that could be lived as both a submission to and as a critical response to the powers that be. This ambiguity of the subject that is 'compelled to form itself within practices that are more or less in place' (Butler 2004: 321) can also be sensed in the early modern period's praise of conversation. Thus, this art could be used in a competitive manner by paying close attention to speech and searching for hidden intentions in order to gain advantages and advance one's position at court or in the mundane salon culture. Yet, more importantly in my perspective is that the libertine lifestyle and art of conversation bring into play the basic structure of control that during the classical age was still linked to Christian confession.

Libertine thinking and writing in the wake of Montaigne reveal if not an impossibility at the core of the Christian imperative to confess then a potential resistance to what Foucault sees as a key in the history of Western subjectivity, namely the revelation of one's inner secrets by putting oneself into discourse (in his 1979–80 Collège de France course, *On the Government of the Living* (2014)). If the consequence of the Christian imperative is an 'indefinite spiritual doubt' (Foucault 2014: 304) that can be sensed in the period's governmental as well as philosophical rationality, the libertines use doubt or scepticism in a way that departs from the practice of confession, especially regarding the search for truth.

As Elias also underlines, when religious self-observation contemplates the inner self in order to 'discipline its hidden impulses', self-observation in court society aims at 'self-discipline in social life' (Elias 2006: 114). I will develop the relation of these two major types of early modern forms of control of the subject (confession and the courtly art of human observation) to 'the art of not being so governed' below, but I want to emphasise already here that when Descartes transformed doubt into a rational method or, as Foucault points out, transformed spiritual doubt into a philosophical affirmation (Foucault 2014: 304), the libertines remained sceptical and put doubt to use in a rather different technology of the self.

To be sure, libertine conversations which can be seen in letters and genres such as maxims or essays are also forms of adaptation to the classicist rules of *plaire* and *bienséance* (to please and to follow decorum) that were essential in court society, but they are also based on an earlier humanist idea that there are forces that transgress will and reason. In that sense, they keep to Montaigne's famous maxim of scepticism, 'What do I know?' (*Que sçay-je?*), and his conviction that human beings are inconsistent in themselves, as he puts it in the essay 'On the Inconstancy of our Actions': 'We float about among diverse counsels: our willing of anything is never free, final or constant' (Montaigne 1991: 375). As Foucault has shown, in Christianity the response to this fickle and mobile subjectivity has been confession, and a belief that a stable truth (God's truth) within the subject could counteract its inconstancy. Further, as a self-technique confession gave rise to an 'introspective turn of literary culture' during the seventeenth century that was reinforced by a rediscovery of the works of Stoic and Epicurean philosophers (Lyons 2016: 75). Introspection was also adopted by the libertines, but following Montaigne's more essayistic approach to the human subject's inconstancy they twisted the search for truth in a way that in the final analysis resists sovereign control, be it in the name of the subject's free will as in Descartes or in the service of governmental rationality.

The introspective turn for example can be clearly sensed in François de La Rochefoucauld (1613–80), who identifies his project – the writing of the *Maxims* that he published between 1664 and 1678 – as an 'anatomy of all the folds in the heart' (La Rochefoucauld 1976: 270). However, the most striking features in La Rochefoucauld's analysis of the human 'heart' are the acceptance of forces that escape control, most clearly sensed in his descriptions of the passion of love that early modernity called *amour propre* (translating the church father Augustine's term *amor sui* designating what he considered to be a sinful love). In the maxims which analyse this passion rationality is disclosed and connected to forces that conduct the subject rather than the other way around, as in: 'Self love is more cunning than the most cunning man in the world' (La Rochefoucauld 1976: 44). However, La Rochefoucauld's sceptical view of the power of free will and sovereign reason, unmasking the subject's self-interest and narcissism (if we are to translate *amour propre* to more modern notions), is conditioned by a certain art of observation that also includes the observer and serves as a controlling as well as self-controlling instrument in court society. Human observation and verbal art go hand in hand and, as Elias states: 'The forms of literature and knowledge characteristic of court society match its specific needs and demands [. . .] that grow directly or indirectly out of the incessant conversation of society' (Elias 2006: 115). To be sure, this literature plays an essential role in the transition of control from the king to his subjects during the period. What Elias does not notice in his sociological analysis is that literature even during the classicist period can also function as a form of resistance. Especially early modern libertine and moralist writers developed an art of critique based on scepticism regarding human sovereignty that counteracted classicist docility towards royal demands.

I will try to assess this resistance by turning to Saint-Évremond and to Ninon de Lenclos (1620–1705), the latter one of the few freethinking women during this period. Ninon de Lenclos is usually described as a libertine transgressing the traditional early modern feminine subject position (and gender role) without being banished from society. Even if her relation to the libertine movement and activity as *salonnière* is often underlined in literary history she is presented mainly as a courtesan and a starting point for this reputation was probably the diarist Saint-Simon (1675–1755) who dedicated a passage to her in his *Memoirs* from 1705. Among other things he describes her as: 'a new example of the triumph of vice carried on cleverly and repaired by some virtue' (Saint-Simon 1983: 636). The description is revealing of her art of making matters of love into a matter of style.

Ninon de Lenclos' reputation is to a large part based on what others have said about her, but there exists a correspondence between her and Saint-Évremond (based on eleven letters by Saint-Évremond and thirteen by Ninon de Lenclos) bearing witness of a lasting and affective friendship. The letters were written over a long period, from 1669 until 1699, and the majority of them are responses to lost letters. Further, letters were an important aspect of the period's mundane lifestyle and a social media in the salon culture, which this line from Ninon de Lenclos indicates: 'There are twenty of your letters in my hands: they are read here with admiration' (quoted from Lallemand 2000: 117). Ninon de Lenclos' attitude towards passions – in this correspondence but also in other writers' descriptions of her – is interesting because it underlines art rather than rationality as a form of controlling the passions, which can be exemplified by another correspondence where Ninon de Lenclos writes to the young marquis de Sévigné.[2] Here she describes love as 'a blind instinct, which one must know how to appreciate' (Lenclos 1999: 17). Thus, instead of submitting to reason there is an emphasis on practice – 'know how' – and 'appreciate' appears as a key word that relates to a cultural practice actualising the social and linguistic conventions of love displayed in the salons. In matters of love the libertines shared only to a certain point the ideal of *honnêteté* that according to Stanton demanded 'total control over internal feelings' (Stanton 1980: 136). Instead of trying to gain power over passions in this sovereign way they developed an art that rested on an acceptance of them through appreciation. Moreover, another word for appreciation is critique in the sense of the lived experience that both reflects and transgresses the self-discipline developed in court society.

It could be argued that the libertines turned the philosophical as well as courtly rationalisation of passions into 'thinking-feelings' to use a term from contemporary affect theory (Massumi 2015: 94), shaped by a sensual experience that always and first passes in-between subjects or subjects and objects. It is significant that the equivalence of the Cartesian *cogito ergo sum* in the writings of Saint-Évremond is conjugated into a more embodied and transindividual experience, as in this line: 'I feel myself in what I'm saying' (Saint-Évremond 2004: 704). Or more explicitly in a letter to an unknown addressee: 'I think, therefore I am, that drives Monsieur Descartes' philosophy, is a rather cold and languid conclusion. I love, therefore I am, is an absolutely lively consequence' (Saint-Évremond 1967: 296).

Thus, libertine subjects recognise themselves in a discursive and aesthetic practice that eludes philosophical self-mastery as well as 'court rationality' with its docility to follow the king's orders. To be sure, the libertines were also bound to the court society but their position within it was precarious and many of them were also excluded from it – Saint-Évremond lived his last forty years in exile and La Rochefoucauld belonged to a nobility that, after the civil war called the *Fronde*, not only lost its independence but also the possibility of a social advancement.[3] Further, during the year 1656 Ninon de Lenclos was imprisoned at a convent because of her libertinism – the target was probably both her support of freethinking thoughts and her lifestyle.

What I want to suggest is that the libertines turned the intensification of control in court society into an art of critique that if it seems frivolous nevertheless and furthermore reveals a way of treating passions, affects and emotions as relational and social before they become subjective and rationalised. To further highlight the relevance of this specific early modern subjectivity for the actual crisis of the modern subject in our contemporary control society, I will give another example of how a libertine writer in the wake of Montaigne could turn cultural representations informed by a sovereign politics of control into a subtle critique of the same. Or, more precisely, I will further assess how cultural expressions during the classical age functioned both ways – as control and resistance – by turning to La Fontaine.

ANIMAL REASON

Jean de La Fontaine (1621–95) belongs to the first generation of Montaigne readers during the seventeenth century, or more correctly to a cultural milieu where the influence of his *Essays* is apparent. The poet's sceptical attitude towards the idea of human sovereignty goes hand in hand with his main concern – the animals – in the *Fables*. This connection can be sensed throughout La Fontaine's writing, but most clearly in his playful assessment of one of the period's debated philosophical questions – namely Descartes' theory of animal mechanism.

The fable where the question is treated, 'Discourse to Madame de la Sablière' (1678), is a mix of philosophical reflexions and *galant* conversation fixed in verse. As in his other fables La Fontaine uses a well-known material, giving it a new critical and moral sense. Further, the question of the animal can be understood as an exploration of the boundaries of human identity actualised by the epistemic shift that marked the classical age according to Foucault, which was also a confrontation between two forms of reason. On the one hand, a continuation of the sceptical thought that in wake of Montaigne 'was vividly conscious of the forms that limited it and the forces that contradicted it' (Foucault 2006: 34). On the other, the establishment of a sovereign reason that for Descartes is the fundament of and a condition for a knowledge implying a control over life – or as he puts it in his *Discourse on the Method* – that can 'make ourselves as it were the masters and possessors of nature' (Descartes 2006: 51).

La Fontaine's discourse to Madame de la Sablière bears witness to a more general debate between libertines and Cartesians in her salon.[4] La Fontaine shared her hospitality for over ten years and the name he gives her in the fables is Iris, a personification of the rainbow associated with communication and hospitality. The poet's description of what is needed for the art of conversation at the beginning of his fable is also a praise of the specific humanist culture in her salon:

> Along with serious learning and imagination
> That sees what eyes cannot – all these,
> From grand concerns to less-than-trivialities,
> Are needed, I maintain, in good conversation.
> (La Fontaine 1991: 383)

Conversation is not just talk, it is a practice that is constantly turned towards the exterior, towards communication and pleasure, but it also needs to be sensitive to the affects and effects of power relations displayed in the court society and its margins. The art of conversation as it was practised in Madame de la Sablière's salon (to judge from the lines quoted from La Fontaine) can be said to displace sovereign control as well as the philosophical *ratio* by embracing intersubjective diversity in this sense.

At any rate, in the poem La Fontaine opposes Descartes' philosophy – 'That has been talked about as new, / Ingenious, daring, keen' (La Fontaine 1991: 383) – to Epicureanism. La Fontaine could have been introduced to this ancient philosophical tradition through Madame de la Sablière's tutor, François Bernier, who had written a summary of Gassendi's work, and if he had not read Descartes he certainly knew of Nicolas Malebranche who had developed the official Cartesian doctrine in his book *The Search after Truth* (1674). Thus, in La Fontaine's discourse to Madame de la Sablière, Descartes is called the 'rival of Epicurus', against whom he develops his argument by using his art as a fabulist. In order to refute the idea that animals are machines without souls the poet lists counter-examples of the diversity of the species that echo Montaigne's 'Apology for Raymond Sebond', including ethnological findings from the New World.

As Judith Still demonstrates in a thorough commentary on Derrida's seminars on the man–animal borderline, the discourse to Madame de la Sablière is closer to natural history than La Fontaine's fables in general with their more anthropomorphic and allegorical representation of animals as men (Still 2015: 191). Here, La Fontaine seems to draw on the early modern encounter with the New World, informed by the colonial idea of its people as 'savage' as well as on contemporary natural history.[5] With a reference to animals living in a region 'near the north pole', the poet states against Descartes: 'That beavers are mere bodies void of intellect / Is an idea that I forever will reject' (La Fontaine 1991: 386). Further, when Descartes wants to uphold the demarcation between the species by stating that animals 'have no mental powers whatsoever' even though he admits that there are some similarities (Descartes 2006: 48), the importance for La Fontaine is to demonstrate that all living beings belong to the same nature. There are differences between all living beings, but it is not an ontological difference as in Descartes. Instead, living beings are thought of on a scale that can be rephrased with Joanna Zylinka's word as a 'shared materiality of the universe' (Zylinska 2014: 25). At the end of the fable, La Fontaine argues that there is a:

> soul found equally in all
> Blank idiots and children, the foolish and the wise,
> And every other being that we think to call
> By the term animal, of any shape or size.
> (La Fontaine 1991: 385)

Thus, it could be argued that La Fontaine, by the way he inscribes Epicureanism and scepticism in his fables, articulates a more liberating use of the control mechanisms in early modern court society. At any rate, the idea of self-mastery foreshadowing the modern subject is here parallelled by another form of plastic subjectivity based on 'shared materiality', which includes shared passions and interests in the name of 'pleasing' rather than control by reason and will.

If it may be 'that older means of control, borrowed from the old sovereign societies, will come back into play', to recall this line from Deleuze again, there is a possibility that it is not just the enslaving forces that return in modified forms, such as the docility and flexibility of subjects in a system of global capitalism reflecting early modern 'court rationality'. The need for 'new forms of resistance against control societies' (Deleuze 1995: 182) also actualises the verbal arts as well as the codes for courtesy that freethinking moralists and libertines developed in the salon culture, which I would like to link to the way in which Malabou interprets Foucault's notion of critique – 'in one word, to be plastic' (Malabou 2011: 15).

In minor genres such as fables, epistolary writing, maxims, and in conversation in general, *honnêteté* is conjugated in a way that eludes the enslaving forces of courtly self-discipline as well as the anthropocentric and instrumental rational subject that Descartes establishes. It can even be argued that the libertines' more materialist than rationalist idea of the subject also functions as a critique against any sovereign claim of power over others. In the final analysis, this is what La Fontaine's fable critiquing Descartes' theory of animal mechanism is about. Although La Fontaine's 'Discourse to Madame de La Sablière' can be accused of dividing living beings into categories, 'which might have different relations to reason, perfectibility and language', as has been pointed out (Still 2015: 192) these subdivisions are precisely divisions or *folds* in the universe, and not demarcations making possible the distinction between human beings and the rest, and hence a certain power over them. La Fontaine is usually described as a classicist but the definition of the living being in his writing draws more on Montaigne and perhaps even on the baroque philosophy that Deleuze detected in Lebiniz – that is based on a nomadic subject in the process of becoming.[6] At any rate, the importance for La Fontaine as for the libertines in general is the development of an art of living together with others by using inescapable control mechanisms with plasticity – that is with an art of critique. At least for a moment.

RATIONAL SUBMISSION

In the wake of Montaigne's materialistic view of the human being and essayistic approach towards his own subjectivity, libertines turned 'court rationality' into an art of critique. And they did this at a moment when the questions of 'how to govern oneself, how to be governed, by whom should we accept to be governed, how to be the best possible governor' (Foucault 2007: 127) were of central importance. According to Foucault these are questions linked to the convergence of two historical movements, namely the state centralisation on the one hand, and on the other hand the Reformation and following Counter-Reformation. However, early modern governmentality not only reflects a period of transition that creates ambiguous cultural expressions like *honnêteté* and courtly stylisation, it also makes palpable an ambiguity that is operative in processes of subjectification in general, namely that our 'ability to resist control, or our submission to it, has to be assessed at the level of our every move' (Deleuze 1995: 176). This ambiguity inherent in the question of governmentality and subjectification also explains why there is a conflict within every regime or system of power – be it early modern sovereign societies or contemporary control societies – 'between the ways they free and enslave us' (Deleuze 1995: 178).

Both La Fontaine's and Madame de la Sablière's life stories exemplify rather clearly the ambiguous process of subjectification, or more precisely the conflict between the ways control does both 'free and enslave us'. In his last fable from 1692 and after ten years as a member in the French Academy La Fontaine writes: 'To gain self-knowledge is the primal task assigned / By nature's majesty to all of humankind' (La Fontaine 1991: 537). These lines seem to affirm what Foucault describes as the dominance of a specific organisation of subjectivity, namely the adaptation of the Ancient Greek aphorism *gnothi seauton* by early Christian culture into a basic form of obedience in spiritual direction and confession, as I mentioned earlier. According to Foucault it is the verbalisation of this ancient form of self-technology that marks Western subjectivity from early Christianity onwards: 'putting oneself in discourse is in actual fact one of the major driving forces in the organization of subjectivity and truth relationships in the Christian West' (Foucault 2014: 311). Even though 'court rationality' serves the struggle for prestige and status among the courtiers this agency is pegged on a transference of control from the king to the subject that the Counter-Reformation reinforces. As Katherine Ibbett puts it with a reference to cultural historian Peter Burke, after the Revocation of the Edict of Nantes (1685), which made Protestant worship illegal in France, there was a 'high point of representational fervour in the "fabrication" of Louis XIV' (Ibbett 2014: 19). Thus, La Fontaine's last fable can be seen as part of this fabrication, in the form of an obedient response to his government and following an introspective turn in front of 'nature's majesty'. At any case, the movement from an earlier freethinking sceptical attitude based on stylisation and a critique of sovereignty to the last fable, which has been called La Fontaine's spiritual testament, gives the idea of a rationalisation and adaptation to a society of sovereignty and its controlling mechanism – that with Foucault's words is an 'inflection of the subject towards its own truth' (Foucault 2014:

311). In other words, at the end of his life La Fontaine accepted the king's sovereignty, and subjected himself to its less liberating and more enslaving forces.

The same movement – that is conversion to Catholicism and spiritual retreat – occurs during last year of Madame de la Sablière's life. The acceptance of giving up salon life and freethinking in favour of Catholicism can hence be understood as 'rational'. As Elias argues:

> What is considered 'rational' depends at any time on the structure of society. What we reify as 'reason' comes into being whenever adaptation to a particular society and survival within it demand a specific foresight or calculation and therefore a constraint of short-term individual affects. (Elias 2006: 120)

However, parallel to 'rational' submission to the enslaving forces in court society – and with a potentiality to counteract the whole rational system installed by the classical age that was reinforced by the disciplinary societies during the centuries to come – there were other cultural forms and expressions resting on internal strategies of resistance. So, let me wrap up by pointing out what I see as the central trait in these strategies by returning to La Fontaine and his fables, before his conversion.

CODA: THE ART OF NOT BEING SO GOVERNED

La Fontaine's preface to his fables reads: 'The apologue consists of two parts, one of which might be called its body, the other its soul. Its body is the fable; its soul the moral' (La Fontaine 1991: 9). If the moral of a fable is its soul the poet nevertheless sets it in motion, and does so in a different way than the philosopher. When Descartes in his *Meditations on First Philosophy* (Meditation 2) says that his mind 'loves to wander' and that he gives it 'the freest rein', he does this to get better control over it – 'so that when afterwards we seize the proper occasion for pulling up, it may the more easily be regulated and controlled' (Descartes 1911: 11). La Fontaine for his part uses another form of control that is more aesthetic than cognitive, which simply put is the one that comes from art itself. In the preface, the poet also refers to what he calls *la grande règle* during the classical age: 'In France, the only consideration is whether a thing is pleasing: that is the primary rule, not to say the only one' (La Fontaine 1991: 9). In the salon culture that developed outside the court this 'pleasing' art was used 'not only in order to bring one's conduct into compliance with a given rule, but to attempt to transform oneself into the ethical subject of one's behaviour' with Foucault's description of 'the arts of existence' in *The Use of Pleasure* (1985: 10). Libertinism in this perspective is neither a self-sufficient activity nor a rational instrument of control, but a cultural practice based on conversation and social relations that needs – as La Fontaine put it in his discourse to Madame de la Sablière – everything 'from grand concerns to less-than-trivialities' to be maintained. Further, libertinism is a *virtue* that promotes a critical use of 'court rationality' by transforming it into strategies that modifies or counteracts its dominance. And it may be that this moment in the Western history of the subject can come back and function as a reminder of the potentials of artistry as a strategy of resistance for a subject in crisis formed by neoliberal rationality and its engulfing control.

NOTES

1. According to Elias the shift of gravity from court society to 'good society' occurred during the eighteenth century (Elias 2006: 87). However, there already existed an extensive cultural practice of intellectual and artistic gatherings often conducted by noblewomen in their private homes that from the mid-seventeenth century also hosted people who were exiled from court by different reasons.
2. The correspondence *Lettres au marquis de Sévigné* has been attributed to various writers and editors in the eighteenth century, for example to the novelist Crébillon fils who published it in 1750. See Vergé-Franceschi (2014: 410). But even though the letters might be constructed by another writer, they articulate a libertine discourse.
3. It is an established fact that the defeat of this insurrection (1648–53) that aimed to protect the ancient aristocratic liberties from royal sovereignty only enforced it with the consequence that 'the power of the French nobility became largely symbolic' (Stanton 1980: 69).
4. Madame de la Sablière (1640–93) cultivated La Fontaine's career in her salon between 1669 and 1680 and was renowned for her scientific and philosophical interests. Her salon was one of the more distinguished in Paris at time. See Conley (2002: 77–8).
5. The general figure of the 'savage' dominated early modern literature. As Lévi-Strauss points out regarding Montaigne, despite his critique of sovereign reason and ontological hierarchy, he 'does not stray from the sixteenth- and seventeenth-century answers the explorers' and missionaries' contemporaries [. . .] provided to the questions raised by the discovery of America' (Lévi-Strauss 1995: 218).
6. See Deleuze's book on the fold as a characteristic trait of baroque art and thinking, *Le Pli. Leibniz et le Baroque* (1988).

REFERENCES

Boileau, Nicolas (2007), *Selected Poems*, trans. Burton Raffel, New Haven: Yale University.
Boitano, John F. (2002), *The Polemics of Libertine Conversion in Pascal's* Pensées, Tübingen: Gunter Narr Verlag.
Butler, Judith (1997), *The Psychic Life of Power: Theories in Subjection*, Stanford: Stanford University Press.
Butler, Judith (2004), 'What is Critique? An Essay on Foucault's Virtue', in *The Judith Butler Reader*, ed. Sara Salih, Malden, MA: Blackwell.

Cavaillé, Jean-Pierre (2017), 'Qu'est-ce qu'un "philosophe libertin" au XVIIe siècle?', in *Philosophie et libre pensée / Philosophy and Free Thought*, ed. Lorenzo Bianchi et al., Paris: Champion.
Conley, John J. (2002), *The Suspicion of Virtue: Women Philosophers in Neoclassical France*, Ithaca: Cornell University Press.
Deleuze, Gilles (1995), *Negotiations 1972–1990*, trans. Martin Joughin, New York: Columbia University Press.
Deleuze, Gilles (1988), *Le Pli. Leibniz et le Baroque*, Paris: Minuit.
Descartes, René (1911), *The Philosophical Works of Descartes*, trans. Elizabeth S. Haldane, Cambridge: Cambridge University Press, http://selfpace.uconn.edu/class/percep/DescartesMeditations.pdf
Descartes, René (1953), *Œuvres et lettres de Descartes*, ed. André Bridoux, Paris: Gallimard.
Descartes, René (2006), *A Discourse on the Method of Correctly Conducting One's Reason and Seeking Truth in the Science*, trans. Ian Maclean, Oxford: Oxford University Press.
Descartes, René (2015), *The Passions of the Soul and Other Late Philosophical Writings*, trans. Michael Moriarty, Oxford: Oxford University Press.
Ehrenberg, Alain (2010 [1998]), *The Weariness of the Self: Diagnosing the History of Depression in the Contemporary Age*, trans. Enrico Caouette et al., Montreal: McGill-Queen's University Press.
Elias, Norbert (2006), *The Court Society*, trans. Edmund Jephcott, Dublin: University College Dublin Press.
Foucault, Michel (1985), *The Use of Pleasure. History of Sexuality*, vol. 2, trans. Robert Hurley, New York: Pantheon.
Foucault, Michel (1998), *The Will to Knowledge: The History of Sexuality*, vol. 1, trans. Robert Hurley, London: Penguin Books.
Foucault, Michel (2005), *The Hermeneutics of the Subject: Lectures at the Collège de France, 1981–1982*, ed. Frédéric Gros, trans. Graham Burchell, Basingstoke: Palgrave Macmillan.
Foucault, Michel (2006), *History of Madness*, trans. Jonathan Murphy and Jean Khalfa, New York: Routledge.
Foucault, Michel (2007), *Security, Territory, Population: Lectures at the Collège de France 1977–1978*, ed. Michel Senellart, trans. Graham Burchell, Basingstoke: Palgrave Macmillan.
Foucault, Michel (2008), *The Birth of Biopolitics: Lectures at the Collège de France 1978–1979*, ed. Michel Senellart, trans. Graham Burchell, Basingstoke: Palgrave Macmillan.
Foucault, Michel (2014), *On the Government of the Living: Lectures at the Collège de France 1979–1980*, ed. Michel Senellart, trans. Graham Burchell, Basingstoke: Palgrave Macmillan.
Ibbett, Katherine (2014), 'Being Moved: Louis XIV's Triumphant Tenderness and the Protestant Object', *Exemplaria* 26:1, pp. 16–38.
La Fontaine, Jean de (1991), *Œuvres complètes*, vol. 1, ed. Jean-Pierre Collinet, Paris: Gallimard.
La Fontaine, Jean de (2011), *The Complete Fables of La Fontaine: A New Translation in Verse*, trans. Craig Hill, New York: Arcade Publishing.
Lallemand, Marie-Gabrielle (2000), 'Saint-Évremond et Ninon de Lenclos: Correspondance', in *Saint-Évremond entre Baroque et Lumière*, ed. Suzanne Guellouz, Caen: Presses universitaire de Caen.
La Rochefoucauld, François de (1871), *Reflections; or, Sentences and Moral Maxims*, trans. John William Willis Bund and James Hain Friswell, https://www.gutenberg.org/files/9105/9105-h/9105-h.htm
La Rochefoucauld, François de (1976), *Maximes et Réflexions diverses*, ed. Jean Lafond, Paris: Gallimard.

Lenclos, Ninon de (1903), *Life, Letters and Epicurean Philosophy of Ninon de L'Enclos*, trans. Charles Henry Robinson and William Hassell Overton, Chicago: Lion Publishing Co., http://aelliott.com/reading/ninon/index.htm

Lenclos, Ninon de (1999), *Lettres au marquis de Sévigné ou l'Art de se faire aimer*, Paris: L'Arche.

Lévi-Strauss, Claude (1995), *The Story of Lynx*, trans. Catherine Tihanyi, Chicago: The University of Chicago Press.

Lyons, John D. (2016), 'Tragedy and Fear', in *French Literature*, ed. John D. Lyons, Cambridge: Cambridge University Press.

Malabou, Catherine (2008), *What Should We Do with Our Brain*, trans. Sebastian Rand, New York: Fordham University Press.

Malabou, Catherine (2011), *Que faire de Notre Cerveau?*, Paris: Bayard.

Massumi, Brian (2015), *Politics of Affect*, Cambridge: Polity Press.

Montaigne, Michel de (1991), *The Complete Essays*, trans. M. A. Screech, London: Penguin.

Moriarty, Michael (1988), *Taste and Ideology in Seventeenth-Century France*, Cambridge: Cambridge University Press.

Parmentier, Bérengère (2000), *Le siècle des moraliste: de Montaigne à La Bruyère*, Paris: Seuil.

Saint-Évremond, Charles de (1967), *Lettres*, vol. 1, ed. René Ternois, Paris: Marce Didier.

Saint-Évremond, Charles de (2004), 'L'Homme qui veut connaître toutes choses ne se connaît pas lui-meme', in *Libertins du XVIIe siècle*, vol. 2, ed. Jacques Prévot, Paris: Gallimard.

Saint-Simon, Louis de Rouvroy (1983), *Mémoires 1701–1707*, vol. 2, ed. Yves Coirault, Paris: Gallimard.

Schachter, Marc (2009), '"Qu'est-ce que la critique?", La Boétie, Montaigne, Foucault', in *Montaigne After Theory, Theory After Montaigne*, ed. Zahi Zalloua, Washington, DC: University of Washington Press.

Stanton, Domna C. (1980), *The Aristocrat as Art: A Study of the* Honnête Homme *and the* Dandy *in the Seventeenth-Century and the Nineteenth-Century French Literature*, New York: Columbia University Press.

Still, Judith (2015), *Derrida and Other Animals: The Boundaries of the Human*, Edinburgh: Edinburgh University Press.

Vance, Jacob (2009), 'Duty, Conciliation, and Ontology in the *Essais*', in *Montaigne After Theory, Theory After Montaigne*, ed. Zahi Zalloua, Washington, DC: University of Washington Press.

Vergé-Franceschi, Michel (2014), *Ninon de Lenclos: Libertine du grand siècle*, Paris: Payot & Rivage.

Zalloua, Zahi (2009), 'Introduction: What is Theory?', in *Montaigne After Theory, Theory After Montaigne*, ed. Zahi Zalloua, Washington, DC: University of Washington Press.

Zylinska, Joanna (2014), *Minimal Ethics for the Antropcene*, Ann Arbor: Open Humanities Press.

CHAPTER 5

Posthumanism, Social Complexity and the Political: A Genealogy for Foucault's *The Birth of Biopolitics*

Cary Wolfe

What does rethinking the concept of the political from a posthumanist point of view entail? More specifically, I want to ask here, what resources are made available to us for this task in Michel Foucault's lectures at the Collège de France published in translation under the title, *The Birth of Biopolitics*? My approach to these questions may be usefully contrasted with Wendy Brown's account of the waning of the political sphere in her recent book, *Undoing the Demos*, where she laments the weakening of the political as such under the pressure of neoliberalism. More specifically, she identifies the incursion of the neoliberal logic of the market into what was heretofore the autonomous, or at least largely autonomous, realm of the political, where popular sovereignty should be allowed to express itself and be articulated by a set of values not subject to neoliberalism's logic of the market. Taking off from a critical reading of *The Birth of Biopolitics*, she argues that 'neoliberal reason, ubiquitous today in statecraft and the workplace, in jurisprudence, education, culture, and a vast range of quotidian activity, is converting the distinctly *political* character, meaning and operation of democracy's constituent elements into *economic* ones' (Brown 2015: 17). For neoliberal reason, as she characterises it,

> both persons and states are construed on the model of the contemporary firm, both persons and states are expected to comport themselves in ways that maximize their capital value in the present and enhance their future value, and both persons and states do so through practices of entrepreneurialism, self-investment, and/or attracting investors. Any regime pursuing another course faces fiscal crises, downgraded credit, currency and or bond ratings, and lost legitimacy at the least, bankruptcy and dissolution at the extreme. (Brown 2015: 22)

As she notes, critics of neoliberalism typically focus on four main negative effects of this shift: intensified inequality between polarised haves and have nots, with a stagnant (or worse) middle class caught in between; the commercialisation of activities that ought not be subject to the logic or discourse of commercialisation (education, wilderness, green space and carbon emissions, but also organ trafficking); increasingly inappropriate intimacy between finance capital, corporations and the state; and, finally, an increasingly unstable economic landscape brought on by the volatility of the financial markets themselves (epitomised by the 2008–9 'bubble' and meltdown), which only dramatises the disconnection between how that instability affects Wall Street and how it impacts the millions of human beings caught up in Wall Street's financial instrumentalisation of the economy (again epitomised by the phenomenon of Credit Default Swaps and other financial instruments during the 2008 bubble) (Brown 2015: 28–30).

A cornerstone of Brown's reading is that she sees part of Foucault's distinctive contribution as drawing our attention to not just the *economic* effects of neoliberalism, but also to the fact that it is a new 'normative order of reason', a 'governing rationality' that extends 'a specific formulation of economic values, practices, and metrics to every dimension of human life' (Brown 2015: 31). She then adds two sub-points which, when taken in tandem, open onto a larger set of problems with her analysis that I will engage in more detail below. First, she adds, 'economization may not always involve monetization', that 'to speak of the relentless economization of all features of life by neoliberalism is thus not to claim that neoliberalism literally *marketizes* all spheres', but rather that 'neoliberal rationality disseminates the *model of the market* to all domains and activities – even where money is not at issue – and configures human beings exhaustively as market actors, always, only, and everywhere as *homo oeconomicus*' (Brown 2015: 31). She gives plenty of examples of this dominant logic in action, the most compelling and appalling of which, perhaps, is the *Citizens United* US Supreme Court ruling to which she devotes an entire chapter. And anyone who works in a university in North America (but not just there) will recognise the portrait she paints later in the book of a higher education system in which the 'relentless configuration of liberal arts research by academic market norms' has transformed students into 'investors' and 'consumers' focused on the cash value of a degree, in a setting where it is more and more common 'to judge every academic endeavor by its uptake in nonacademic venues (commerce, state agencies, NGOs)' and the like (Brown 2015: 196).

But while *Citizens United* is every bit as appalling as Brown makes it out to be, I think we are well within our rights to ask if it is actually the case that individuals under neoliberalism are 'always, only, and everywhere "*homo oeconomicus*"'; and are the effects of market discourses, models and so on as omnipresent – in political force and not just discursively, as it were – as

Brown makes them out to be? Or to put it another way, is using an economic explanatory framework (which need not be limited, either historically or theoretically, to either capitalism or its more recent financialised versions, after all) as uniformly deleterious and politically corrosive as she categorically argues? And is that logic as ubiquitous as she suggests? As for the latter, it seems easy, after all, to point to all sorts of social activities that do not obey the logic of the market or demand that individuals always and only behave as *homo oeconomicus*. Think, for example, of the resurgent place of religion in US popular culture since the 1970s. Now one might well argue that such a resurgence is, in fact, a compensatory one for the processes of neoliberalisation that Brown identifies, but that is not an argument she is making, dialectically or otherwise. Similarly, one might observe that religion in the US is indeed Big Business, but that is not a claim that Brown is making either; and in any case, the fact that religion *is* Big Business obviously predates the rise of neoliberalism (or even modern capitalism, for that matter).

If 'the relentless economization of all features of life' is divorced from marketisation and monetisation specifically, as Brown suggests, then the claim that 'we are always, only, and everywhere "*homo oeconomicus*"' (Brown 2015: 33) seems far too sweeping and theoretically imprecise to be of much use. After all, many disciplines have for many years used what Brown would call an 'economic' methodology, but without endorsing neoliberal imperatives. For example, well-known scientist and futurologist Joël de Rosnay sums up the entire drift of modern ecological thought when he argues that 'the transition from economics to ecoenergetics' is crucial for thinking complex problems of ecology, where 'the basic tool of ecoenergetics is *energy analysis* . . . In order to find and put to work new sources of energy or to choose the most advantageous ways of saving energy', he continues, 'we must first be prepared to set up complete and detailed energy balance sheets' (de Rosnay 1979: 114–15). Does this 'economization of all features of life', as Brown puts it, make de Rosnay a neoliberal? Hardly. In fact, he argues for a form of what he calls 'ecosocialism' (de Rosnay 1979: 223). Other important figures in this lineage such as Gregory Bateson clearly exemplify how the conceptual power of 'economic' models need not be wedded to ideals of competition and warring 'capitals' at all (though it is certainly true, as Donna Haraway has pointed out in *Simians, Cyborgs, and Women* and elsewhere, that it *can* take this form). Bateson argues, for example, that 'every species has a primary Malthusian capacity', and that 'in a balanced ecological system whose underpinnings are of this nature, it is very clear that any monkeying with the system is likely to disrupt the equilibrium' (Bateson 1972: 430–1).

Does this make Bateson a neoliberal? Why not – *especially* if, as Brown argues, the 'economization of all features of life', and not just monetisation, is the fundamental issue here? In fact, Bateson, as is well known, is far from being a fan of the neoliberal fetishisation of competition, for as he argues in his classic essay, 'Form, Substance, and Difference',

> if an organism or aggregate of organisms sets to work with a focus on its own survival and thinks that that is the way to select its adaptive moves, its 'progress' ends up with a destroyed environment. If the organism ends up destroying its environment, it has in fact destroyed itself. (Bateson 1972: 452)

My point here, in other words, is that you can use an economic theoretical model to explain various forms of complexity – be they biological, historical or social – without being an apologist for, or an operative of, neoliberalism, whose deleterious effects Brown quite rightly criticises. The economic model of population genetics, for example, can lead us to Bateson or it can lead us to Richard Dawkins, but that does not in itself mean that it is evidence of – much less the result of – neoliberalisation. There are two different issues here: one has to do with the historical development of particular disciplines (in this case, economics) within the increasingly specialised and differentiated space of modernity understood, in Niklas Luhmann's terms, as a phenomenon of 'functional differentiation' (and – a subsidiary point – the extent to which those particular disciplinary developments, their theories and methodologies, may be shown on a deeper level to be isomorphic); and the other has to do with the extent to which *any* particular disciplinary paradigm or any particular social subsystem possesses the capacity to steer and overcode any or *all* of the others (as Brown claims, more stridently still – 'we are everywhere *homo oeconomicus* and only *homo oeconomicus*') (Luhmann 1995: 123–9).

As I have discussed elsewhere, both of these questions were taken up, after a fashion, in Deleuze's late speculations on 'control society' (Wolfe 2017) and the qualitatively different kind of social logic we find there from earlier social formations; and both point to a fundamental limitation in Brown's analysis: namely, an inadequate theory of social complexity – a problem that must be tackled *first* before we can presume to understand what the 'political' is and how it functions in relation to the other social instances. This is not just a theoretical and methodological problem; it is also, as I will discuss in a moment, a practical one. This is precisely the cluster of problems that forms the focus of Foucault's lectures at the Collège de France (and not just *The Birth of Biopolitics*, of course). As Foucault emphasises time and again, the larger quarry here – and it is one that political philosophy per se is only partially equipped to handle – is the historically transmogrifying character of social complexity itself as we move from disciplinary societies to the forms of governmentality associated with neoliberalism: a qualitative shift that has to change how we think the political and its forms of effectivity.

For Brown, the major limitation of *The Birth of Biopolitics* stems in no small part from Foucault's 'notorious late-1970s antagonism to Marxism'. As she puts it,

> The wholesale refusal of Marxist categories, logics, and historiography allows Foucault to bring forth undertheorized aspects of the emergence of political economy and permits a novel staging of the relationships between liberalism, the state, the economy, and the modern subject. However, this refusal also has its costs, especially in taking the measure of the unique dominations entailed in neoliberalism. Thus, Foucault's seemingly light judgments against neoliberalism pertain not only to his admirable commitment to excavating the novelties that only a genealogical curiosity can discover . . . Rather, Foucault averted his glance from capital itself as a historical and social force. (Brown 2015: 74–5)

I would argue, however, that Foucault is interested in the neoliberalism of the Chicago School, the ordoliberalism of the German variety, and the like, primarily because he recognises that these are attempts to think a new kind of social complexity to which traditional Marxist explanatory models had long since been inadequate – a problem that is rigorously taken up, of course, *within* the Marxist tradition itself, and nowhere more so than by Foucault's early mentor and teacher, Louis Althusser, in his attempt to theorise the problems of 'overdetermination', 'structure in dominance' and 'structural causality', which required an anti-humanism that

> replaced the old postulates (empiricism/idealism of the subject, empiricism/idealism of the essence) . . . by a theory of the different specific *levels* of *human practice* (economic practice, political practice, ideological practice, scientific practice) in their characteristic articulations, based on the specific articulations of the unity of human society. In a word, Marx substituted . . . a concrete conception of the specific differences that enables us to situate each particular practice in the specific differences of the social structure . . . On this condition it is possible to define humanism's status, and reject its *theoretical* pretensions while recognizing its practical function as an ideology. (Althusser 1969: 229)[1]

Foucault's entire project in the lectures *begins* by taking for granted not just this critique of humanist Marxism necessitated by Althusser's own work, but also the need to think more carefully the problem of social complexity that resulted in Althusser's theorisation of 'structural causality' as '*the existence of the structure in its effects*', where 'structure, which is merely a specific combination of its particular elements, is nothing outside its effects' (Althusser and Balibar 1970: 188–9; emphasis added).

While the lines of relation to Foucault's own work on social complexity are perhaps clear enough here, it is worth stressing, with Hans-Georg Moeller, their relation to Niklas Luhmann's ramping up of the problem in his social systems theory. For Luhmann, Moeller notes,

> With Marx it became possible to conceive of society as an autopoietic, self-constructing mechanism that operated of its own accord rather than under the unchangeable laws of some trans-social realm. This theoretical step is wholeheartedly embraced by social systems theory. Only a couple of further steps were needed, and one of these was to deny the primacy of the economic structure for the self-construction of society. (Moeller 2006: 178)

In a sense, that shift had already been announced in Althusser's famous insistence on 'determination in the last instance' by the economic, only to admit that 'the last instance never comes' (Althusser 1969: 113); and it is certainly completed by Foucault's reorientation and recalibration of the questions of the economic and of determinism. And once we acknowledge *that*, we can see the direct line of descent from Althusser's insistence that the 'fundamental problem' was 'to think the determination of the elements of a whole by the structure of the whole' (Althusser and Balibar 1970: 187) to Luhmann's contention that,

> in the definition of society as a whole in economic terms, what is lacking is a sufficient appreciation of the inherent dynamics of the economy and its effects on other functional areas and the ecological conditions of social evolution. What is lacking above all is a sufficient appreciation for parallel phenomena in different functional areas. Missing is a basis for comparing systems and for distilling abstract characteristics of modernity, which can be found in more or less all function systems. (qtd Moeller 2006: 179)

Indeed, as Althusser notes about this 'fundamental problem',

> it is clear that by other paths contemporary theory in psycho-analysis, linguistics, other disciplines such as biology, and perhaps even physics, has had to confront it, without suspecting that Marx had 'produced' it in the true sense, long ago . . . [A]lthough Marx *'produced this problem' he did not pose it as a problem*, but set out to solve it practically in the absence of its concept. (Althusser and Balibar 1970: 187; emphasis added)

From this vantage point, then, I think we can identify a clear through-line from Althusser's structural Marxism, to Foucault's work in the lectures, to

Niklas Luhmann's analysis of social systems – a shared anti-humanist orientation whose footings Althusser excavates in *For Marx* and *Reading Capital*, and that gets further radicalised, for example, in Luhmann's own anti-humanist claim that communications, not people, are the fundamental elements of social systems – a claim shared, as I have discussed elsewhere (Wolfe 2017), by Deleuze's characterisation of control society and, before that, by the work of William S. Burroughs and its wild reimagining of the relationship between the communicational, the psychic and the social that so influenced Deleuze's own formulations.[2]

To return to Foucault, then: this complex manifold is, everywhere and always, the repeated point of emphasis in his framing of his interest in liberalism and neoliberalism in the lectures collected in *The Birth of Biopolitics*. As he puts it in the course summary, for example,

> Liberal thought does not start from the existence of the state, finding in government the means for achieving that end that the state would be for itself; it starts instead from society, which exists in a complex relation of exteriority and interiority vis-à-vis the state . . . Instead of turning the distinction between the state and civil society into an historical universal enabling us to examine every concrete system, we may try to see in it a form of schematization peculiar to a particular technology of government. (Foucault 2008: 318)

And the problem of this new 'particular technology of government' is referred, in turn, to the problem of *complexity* – a new and evolving kind of social complexity ('society') that the state form does not know how to think, for reasons Foucault elaborates in some detail in the lectures. Or more precisely, it knows how to think it, but with an inadequate power of what Foucault in the lectures will call 'formalization'. 'Political economy is able to present itself as a critique of governmental reason', Foucault writes, when it tells the sovereign,

> not even you can know the totality of the economic process. There is no sovereign in economics. There is no economic sovereign. This is a very important point in the history of economic thought, certainly, but above all in the history of governmental reason. (Foucault 2008: 283)

In other words, the fundamental issue here is not about economics – or 'the market' or 'enterprise' or 'competition' – per se, but rather about the challenges that new forms of social complexity pose for governing, which first make themselves most dramatically manifest in the economic domain, beginning with political economy. And that, in turn, calls for a redefinition of what the 'political' is outside and beyond the discursive arsenal that had been available to the 'state.' As Foucault writes later in the lectures,

> How can this rationality of the sovereign who claims to say 'I' be exercised with regard to problems like those of the market or, more generally, economic processes in which rationality *not only completely dispenses with a unitary form but absolutely excludes both the unitary form and the bird's-eye view*? Hence, there is a new problem, the transition to a new form of rationality to which the regulation of government is pegged. (Foucault 2008: 312; emphasis added)

This is precisely the problem of the complexity differential between system and environment in relation to system self-reference that is central to Luhmann's social systems theory. And, as for Luhmann, 'rationality' for Foucault does not mean the 'reason' (communicative or otherwise) that is often invoked in defence of liberalism (as Carl Schmitt rightly protested).[3] For as Foucault writes in the very first lecture,

> I do not mean that at this moment politics or the art of government finally becomes rational. I do not mean that at this moment a sort of epistemological threshold is reached on the basis of which the art of government could become scientific. I mean that the moment I am presently trying to indicate is marked by the articulation of a particular type of discourse and a set of practices, a discourse that, on the one hand, constitutes these practices as a set bound together by an intelligible connection and, on the other hand, legislates and can legislate on these practices in terms of true and false. (Foucault 2008: 18)

And these are precisely the reasons that Foucault concludes at the end of the eleventh lecture that:

> Economic science never claimed that it had to be the line of conduct, the complete programming of what could be called governmental rationality. Political economy is indeed a science, a type of knowledge (*savoir*), a mode of knowledge (*connaissance*) which those who govern must take into account. But economic science cannot be the science of government and economics cannot be the internal principle, law, rule of conduct, or rationality of government. Economics is a science lateral to the art of governing. One must govern with economics, one must govern alongside economists, one must govern by listening to the economists, but economics must not be and there is no question that it can be the governmental rationality itself. (Foucault 2008: 286)

Brown writes about this passage that 'this seems importantly wrong today. The claim relates in part to his belief that economics is separated off from civil society, again, an implicit quarrel with Marx' (Brown 2015: 77). But what this reading of Foucault misses, I think, are the two main questions that drive the passages just quoted. The first is whether it is possible, in a context of increasingly opaque social complexity as we move from disciplinarity to governmentality, for one particular social system or discourse to be more proficient or coherent than others in capturing this complexity (and, again, this is not a matter of being more 'rational' but of being more *effective*). This is precisely the point of Foucault's discussion of the neoliberal break with *laissez-faire* economics early on in the lectures, and in particular of Husserl's influence on the German ordoliberals. For them, Foucault writes,

> When you deduce the principle of laissez-faire from the market economy, basically you are still in the grip of what could be called a 'naïve naturalism' . . . something produced spontaneously which the state must respect precisely inasmuch as it is a natural datum. But the ordoliberals say – and here it is easy to spot the influence of Husserl – this is naïve naturalism. For what in fact is competition? It is absolutely not a given of nature . . . Competition is a principle of formalization. Competition has an internal logic; it has its own structure. Its effects are only produced if this logic is respected . . . Just as for Husserl a formal structure is only given to intuition under certain conditions, in the same way competition as an essential economic logic will only appear and produce its effects under certain conditions which have to be carefully and artificially constructed. (Foucault 2008: 120)

Here, I think – and again the invocation of Husserl makes it clear – we find just how far apart Foucault and Brown are in thinking the question of society, and how Foucault's entire project is to think a *non-representationalist* logic of the social which in turn calls for a reconceptualisation of what the 'political' is and how it may be rethought beyond the inadequate lexicon of the 'state.' As for the second point – the ability of any particular social system or domain to steer and overdetermine the other social instances – Foucault's insistence that 'economic science cannot be the science of government' would appear rather commonsensical; or as Luhmann might say, 'the economy can't govern; only government can govern'. That it does so by drawing on models from economics does not in the least change that fact. The government can create various incentives and disincentives, or it can (as in the case of Quantitative Easing 2 and 3 after the 2008 economic bubble in the US) print money and manipulate interest rates. But it can in no way guarantee directly what the economic effects of these actions will be, as was quite candidly acknowledged by the Federal

Reserve during QE2 and QE3. Moreover, the use of economic concepts and administrative models within various domains of civil society is a far cry indeed from serving as evidence of the ability of the economic system to steer and dictate the autopoiesis of these other social systems.[4]

Let me be clear about this: it's not that I disagree with Brown's diagnosis of the various social ills created by neoliberalism run amok. I agree with her, and I imagine many other academic intellectuals in the humanities and interpretive social sciences would as well. But that, I think, is the easy part. The hard part is instead precisely the project that Foucault takes up with regard to reconceptualising the 'political' in relation to social complexity. To put it another way, what we find in Brown's argument is the conflation of two points: the claim, which I (and, I imagine, many others) agree with, that neoliberalism has taken forms and had effects that the Foucault of the lectures could not have foreseen;[5] and the claim that Foucault's analysis is insufficient because it is insufficiently Marxist. In fact, as we have already seen, Foucault *does have* a profound relationship to the Marxist tradition, but it's not the humanist Marxism that orients Brown's reading – the very humanist Marxism that Althusser rejected. To put it another way, underneath Brown's claim that Foucault is not Marxist enough is, in fact, the deeper complaint that Foucault is not *humanist* enough.

This is made especially clear in her defence of *homo politicus* against *homo oeconomicus*. Brown writes that 'what is missing' from Foucault's account, which she calls 'flat and highly behavioral',

> is the creature we may call *homo politicus*, the creature animated by and for the realization of popular sovereignty as well as its own individual sovereignty, the creature who made the French and American Revolutions and whom the American constitution bears forth, but also the creature we know as the sovereign individual who governs himself. (Brown 2015: 86)

'This subject, *homo politicus*', she continues, 'forms the substance and legitimacy of whatever democracy might mean beyond securing the individual provisioning of individual ends; this 'beyond' includes political equality and freedom, representation, popular sovereignty, and deliberation and judgment about the public good and the common' (Brown 2015: 87).

There are at least three distinct problems, however, with Brown's concept of *homo politicus*. The first is that we have to ask, as Althusser and Foucault had already done, whether individual subjects (even if we were to take the semantics of Brown's *homo politicus* at face value) have the ability to align, in a way that meaningfully steers the political system, their own actions and positionality with the larger environment of social complexity in which they find themselves, and through which political effectivity operates. This is not just a theoretical quibble; it's also a practical problem regarding the relationship between individual emotions, aspirations and the mechanisms of actual political change. As Althusser and even Marx before him had warned, can we really assume a linear and determinative relationship between the macroeconomic logic that would eventuate in neoliberalism and the micro-political expression of that logic in the self-conceptions and actions of individuals? The issue can be put quite bluntly: is the neoliberal subject's self-conception of its place in the world of financialised neoliberalism, and of its ability to align its 'asset-building' activities with its actual place in that world, as straightforward and representationally transparent as Brown thinks it is? In my view, one of the great lessons of the 2008 bubble and economic crisis is that the answer is clearly 'No.' The difference between what subprime mortgagees in South Florida or Phoenix *thought* they were doing – 'entrepreneurially', we might say (buying and 'flipping' houses 'on spec', buying more house than they could afford, and so on) – and what they were *actually* doing (as sites of throughput for the commodification and financialisation of risk) is precisely what is on display in subprime mortgage crisis. This misrecognition – which need not be seen as a failure of intelligence or cognition on the part of the social subjects in question, of course, but rather as an index of new and increasingly opaque forms of social and economic complexity – is precisely the question that Foucault is concerned with in his exploration of new social logics of subjectification and the forms of politicisation that might emerge from them. And it is precisely the question that his teacher Althusser was intensely interested in in his contention that ideology is a 'relation between relations, a second-order relation' (Althusser 1969: 233) which in turn means – and this is a very Foucauldian point, after all – that

> this action can never have been purely *instrumental*, the men who would use an ideology purely as a means of action, as a tool, find that they have been caught by it, implicated by it, just when they are using it and believe themselves to be absolute masters of it. (Althusser 1969: 234)

To put it this way is to move immediately to the second problem with Brown's concept of *homo politicus*, and that is the assumption, endemic to various forms of humanism on both the left and the right, that individual persons are the constitutive units of social and political analysis. We have already touched on this problem above, but here I would simply defer to a whole army of political philosophers – from Derrida to Luhmann to Althusser to Esposito and of course to Foucault himself – who have presented quite compelling critiques of this assumption. Of these, perhaps Luhmann's is the most trenchant, clinical and technical, with its insistence on the constitutive difference between autopoietically closed psychic systems and social systems, which first have to be disarticulated *before* we can explain more precisely how they can (and cannot) be structurally coupled and interact. As is well known from his debates with Habermas, Luhmann is not at a loss for the acerbic turn of phrase when it comes to this point, and he dismantles with maximum rigour the desire to index the mechanisms of social and political effectivity to the emotions and ideas of concrete individuals (Brown's 'aspirations'). As he writes in a characteristically withering, but also quite funny, passage:

> In whatever way the traditional concepts, especially 'reason,' are continued, obviously not everything that individualizes humans (if anything) belongs to society. Society does not weigh exactly as much as all human beings together, and its weight also does not change with every birth and death ... Society is therefore not a living thing. The neurophysiological processes of the brain that are inaccessible even for consciousness will not be seriously regarded as social processes; and the same is true for all that goes on in the form of perceptions and sequences of thoughts within the actual area of awareness of a single consciousness. (qtd Moeller 2006: 231)

To the humanist, this will seem counterintuitive, even outlandish, but in fact the point is quite straightforward and common-sensical, for as Luhmann points out, in all seriousness,

> Such a confusion, however, makes it impossible to precisely indicate the operation that performs the autopoiesis in the respective cases of organic, neurophysiological, psychic, and social systems. Typically, the concession is still made that the whole human being is not part of the social system, but only insofar as the human being interacts with or actualizes sense-identical (parallel) experiences with others ... This does not help the case, but worsens it, because then one can less than ever before indicate which operation processes this 'insofar' distinction – obviously neither cellular chemistry nor the brain nor consciousness nor social communication, but if need be, an observer who distinguishes accordingly. (qtd Moeller 2006: 230, n.2)[6]

While Luhmann offers what we might call an empirical objection to many of the assumptions underneath Brown's *homo politicus*, Esposito provides an acute observation about what he calls the 'ideologeme' of the 'person' that is in a more philosophical tenor, as it were, and it bears rather differently, but just as gravely, upon Brown's humanist subject of politics. As he observes, the concept of the 'person clarifies not only the role of a certain juridical figure, but also something that pertains to the general functioning of law, that is to say, the power to include by means of exclusion'. He continues,

> If the category of the person coincided with that of human being, there would have been no need for it. Ever since its original juridical performance, personhood is valuable exactly to the extent to which it is not applicable to all, and finds its meaning precisely in the principled difference between those to whom it is, from time to time, attributed and those to whom it is not or from whom, at a certain point, it is subtracted. (Esposito 2011: 209)

Both arguments – Luhmann's and Esposito's – offer a more pointed development of Foucault's framing of his own position at the very beginning of *The Birth of Biopolitics:* a remarkably original set of methodological and theoretical innovations that in no small part made possible the work carried out by Luhmann, Esposito and many others. 'I would like to point out straightaway', Foucault writes,

> that choosing to talk about or to start from governmental practice is obviously and explicitly a way of not taking as a primary, original, and already given object, notions such as the sovereign, sovereignty, the people, subjects, the state, and civil society, that is to say, all those universals employed by sociological analysis, historical analysis, and political philosophy in order to account for real governmental practice. For my part, I would like to do exactly the opposite and, starting from this practice as it is given, but at the same time as it reflects on itself and is rationalized, show how certain things – state and society, sovereign and subjects, etcetera – were actually able to be formed, and the status of which should obviously be questioned. (Foucault 2008: 3)

Now one might rightfully ask at this point, 'So what? Isn't this just an academic quibble?' I think not, and for reasons that point towards the *third* problem with Brown's concept of *homo politicus*. And that is the extent to which the discourse of Marxian humanist 'critique' is really outside of and opposed to that which Brown criticises. The problem, in other words, is not only the one that we have just noted: that it uses a theoretical framework inadequate to the contemporary reality it describes. It is also that such a semantics may well reinforce rather than challenge the order of things that it criticises, taking for granted its fundamental concepts. As Luhmann writes, 'It had always been clear to me that a thoroughly constructed conceptual theory of society would be much more radical and much more discomforting in its effects than narrowly focused criticisms – criticisms of capitalism, for instance – could ever imagine' (qtd Moeller 2006: 116). Indeed, Moeller argues, such criticisms 'do not criticize the fundamental self-descriptions of the leading semantics (today notions like "democracy," "liberty," and "human rights" are central elements of these semantics), but rather fully embrace them. Anti-globalization activists share their values and vocabulary with those they criticize', it's just that those doing the protesting 'claim that the leading powers and institutions use those values and vocabularies hypocritically whereas they themselves are the true protectors of these semantics' (Moeller 2006: 116).

But the *pragmatic* issue here is not just a shared commitment to a conceptual framework and a semantics; it is also a shared belief in what Luhmann calls 'steering', and this is just as true of Marxian humanist critiques as it is of liberal free market ideologists. As Moeller puts it, 'both the G8 summit and the demonstrations against it in the streets constitute the political system and share the belief that humans can and should politically steer society. They only disagree on the means and ends of political steering' (Moeller 2012: 30–1). And here is where Luhmann in fact *radicalises* Foucault's theoretical and methodological position announced at the beginning of *The Birth of Biopolitics*. Where Foucault's emphasis falls on the ability of 'certain concrete practices' to successfully constitute (as least largely) the realties they materialise, some of his most interesting insights in fact concern what Kenneth Burke would call the 'unintended by-products' of those practices (regarding, for example, how madness and sexuality are constituted as social phenomena, to take two of his most well-known objects of study) (Burke 1984: 282). This is the side of Foucault amplified by Luhmann's insistence that all such practices – because of the constitutive 'blind-spot' of their own self-reference – unavoidably produce unintended by-products that they themselves are, by definition, unable to see or to predict, much less steer and control in any consistent way.[7] In a very real sense, 'society' is thus an affair of various social systems – including the political system – trying to reduce and manage an overwhelmingly complex environment, not in the mode of optimisation or maximisation, but in the mode of an often haphazard adaptive survival.

The question then becomes how society copes with this harsh reality, in which all social systems operate in an environment far more complex than any single system can be, and Luhmann's answer is: it creates utopias, such as the 'free market' and 'social welfare'. As Luhmann puts it, 'political utopia is the form by which the uncontrollability of society is copied into the political system' (qtd Moeller 2012: 28). It's not that governmental policies and actions associated with the laudable goals of social welfare are impossible; such policies can be undertaken, and are, all the time, as the historical record well shows. It's rather that such policies are always undertaken with an inescapable and unavoidable blindness regarding the ability to anticipate and steer their unintended by-products and the complexities they create in their larger environment. There is, in other words, a constitutive asymmetry between the policy's semantics and its actual effects *vis-à-vis* the problem of social complexity. Sometimes there is more or less frank admission of this fact – as with the

Federal Reserve's candour about influencing the economic system in the US during QE2 and QE3 – but more often there is not. And this is understandable, given the fact that professional politicians depend for their livelihood upon sustaining the fantasy of being able to unilaterally use the political system to steer the other social systems – hence the familiar spectacle, on the left and the right, of campaign promises loudly made and then routinely broken once office is assumed.

Luhmann's observation about 'political utopias' and the function they serve *vis-à-vis* the actual uncontrollability of society is interesting to contemplate as the backdrop to the final reservation I would like to register about Brown's *homo politicus*, and that is the question of *populism* that it obviously begs – especially as that made itself manifest, on both the Left and the Right, during the 2016 US presidential electoral cycle. To put it very schematically, populism from both the Left and the Right seems to mistake the actual *inability* of the 'government establishment', 'professional politicians' and the like to use the political system in the services of steering for an *unwillingness* to steer society towards the various 'utopias' that the populists deem worthy (whether that is, say, the redistribution of wealth via taxation for the purposes of social welfare on the one hand, or 'getting tough on immigration' and 'protecting American jobs' on the other).

But the fundamental question dramatised by populism in its recent incarnations for Brown's *homo politicus*, is, in short, who is this 'we' of 'popular sovereignty'? This is precisely the question begged by Brown's formulation early on that:

> I want to release democracy from containment by any particular form while insisting on its value in connoting political self-rule by the people, whoever the people are. In this, democracy stands opposed not only to tyranny and dictatorship, fascism, or totalitarianism, aristocracy, plutocracy, or corporatocracy, but also to a contemporary phenomenon in which rule transmutes into governance and management. (Brown 2015: 21)

But the paradox, well noted by Derrida and others, is that it stands opposed to these unless of course it decides, democratically, that it doesn't.[8] In other words, it is always possible that popular sovereignty will decide that popular sovereignty should not decide, that the only way to protect democracy is to suspend democracy: a point that, as Foucault discusses in some detail, was not lost on the ordoliberals because of their experience of Nazism (Foucault 2008: 105–14).[9] Who decides 'democratically' who gets to be a 'person' or part of the collective body of the *demos*? And to put it bluntly and pragmatically in the contemporary US context, how can there be a 'people' and 'popular sovereignty' as a ground for the political when half the voting population thinks the other half is insane? Now Brown's rejoinder might be that the dominance of neoliberalism is precisely what has created this situation – not least, of course, through the consolidation of corporate ownership of the mass media – but here it need hardly be noted that the phenomenon of populism in the US (and its ideologically wild-card status) predates neoliberalism and reaches back well into the nineteenth century, most canonically to the Jacksonian democracy of the 1830s.

The problem is thus indeed, as William Rasch trenchantly observes, 'who decides?' As he writes,

> Who decides on what is and what is not peace, what is and is not violence, what is and is not sin? And we know the answer: the sovereign . . . Does negating the presupposition of violence negate the sovereign, or is not the negation itself a sovereign act? (Rasch 2004: 16)

Moreover, he argues (and here we return to Luhmann's discussion of the 'blind spot' of observation in the light of social complexity, but in a more Derridean tenor), 'states neither arise nor are legitimized by way of a logical deduction from universal norms . . . One can then say that the articulation of a concrete norm is not the result of a derivation, but the effect of a performative. Declarations such as "we the people"' – and here the ramifications for Brown's notion of popular sovereignty are clear – 'do not describe, they constitute the "we" and the "people" in their very utterance' (Rasch 2004: 24). This doesn't mean, as Rasch notes, that all such decisions are rendered arbitrary; rather, 'once the ineluctability of decision is acknowledged, the question of what regulates decision in the absence of logical necessity becomes pre-eminently political, contestable, and arguable' (Rasch 2004: 40). And this means, as he puts it succinctly, that 'politics cannot compensate for the lack of unity, but rather, by being its effect, *guarantees* this lack. It does not repress violence in the name of the good life; it structures and limits it' (Rasch 2004: 41).

I would only add here – and I have taken up the point in more detail elsewhere[10] – that the (il)logical form and 'violence' of the sovereign decision as a performative, regardless of its content, not only generates the lack of unity that politics cannot solve (indeed, another name for that lack of unity, if we believe Derrida, is 'democracy'); it also *prevents* the primacy of the political in Schmitt's sense by preserving – via Derrida, as it were – democratic and social antagonism as *not* being reducible to Schmitt's friend/enemy distinction, which for Schmitt grounds the priority of the political above all other social systems. This is so because, as Luhmann shows in his analysis of the autopoiesis of social systems, sovereignty is in fact not sovereign because the same paradoxical 'blind spot' of the performative is at work in the self-reference of *all* social systems, and in a context in which social complexity is always already exponentially greater than any system's attempt to reduce it via its own codes and protocols. It's this qualitative shift that Foucault is so interested in because of the challenges it poses to our assumptions about what the political is and how it operates. And so, to put it another way, we are back to the primacy of social complexity, figured as the radical complexity differential across the system/environment threshold, as that which *prevents* the political from being either an expression of sovereignty (of the people or otherwise) or of a social system that can overdetermine and steer all the others. Instead, social complexity and the paradoxical performativity that attempts to reduce it *short-circuits* sovereignty. And this, as Foucault tirelessly argues, makes things *more* political, not less, by keeping open the gap between 'the political' in its official, inherited semantics and the 'new schemas of politicization' that social complexity ceaselessly generates (Foucault 1996: 211).

NOTES

1. On his differences and affinities with Althusser, see Foucault's interview 'The Discourse of History' in Foucault (1996), p. 21. On determination in the last instance by the economic, see Althusser (1969), pp. 112–13; on structural causality and overdetermination, Althusser (1969), pp. 100–1 and Althusser and Balibar (1970), pp. 186–9, 310; on structure in dominance and overdetermination, Althusser (1969), pp. 204–6, 217.
2. For a characteristically illuminating discussion of the relationship between Foucault and Althusser from a Marxian perspective, one that emphasises the challenge of social complexity that I am foregrounding here, see Jameson (2002), pp. 63–8, 76–80. On Luhmann, Jameson (2002), pp. 88–94.
3. On this point, see Rasch (2004), pp. 22–3.
4. In this light, as Jeffrey Nealon has pointed out, the higher education system still retains a high degree of autonomy with regard to the economic system, even as we may rightfully decry, with Brown, its neoliberal bureaucratisation. And indeed, as he notes, by a strictly economic logic, the corporate university isn't nearly corporate *enough*, nor have attempts by various university enterprises to obey a completely economic rationale proven to be very successful (leaving aside the scandal of Trump University). See Nealon (2012), pp. 66–86.
5. As Gregg Lambert has pointed out, 'Foucault's own analysis might also be viewed as dated since it cannot account for significant divergences in neo-liberal doctrine that did not occur until the mid-1980s along with the rise of Thatcherism and Reagonomics; consequently, his analysis of American neo-liberalism, for example, extends only to the end of the Carter administration.' See Lambert (n.d.), p. 3.
6. Moreover, as Luhmann notes, 'On the basis of contemporary research one presumably has to declare that that which is experience and designated as reason, will, emotion, etc., is a subsequent interpretation of already present results of neurophysiological operations, and this to serve their further conscious treatment, but is by no means the decisive origin of human behavior' (qtd Moeller 2006, p. 231, n.3).

7. On the 'blind spot' of any observation that is constituted by unavoidable (and unavoidably paradoxical) self-reference, Luhmann writes: 'Cognitively all reality must be constructed by means of distinctions and, as a result, remains construction. The constructed reality is not, therefore, the reality referred to . . . One could say more precisely: The source of distinction's guaranteeing reality lies in its own operative unity. It is, however, precisely as this unity that the distinction cannot be observed – except by means of another distinction which then assumes the function of a guarantor of reality. Another way of expressing this is to say that the operation emerges simultaneously with the world, which as a result remains cognitively unapproachable to the operation. The conclusion to be drawn from this is that the connection with the reality of the external world is established by the blind spot of the cognitive operation. Reality is what one does not perceive when one perceives it' (Luhmann 1990), p. 76.
8. On this point, see Derrida's discussion of democracy and autoimmunity in Borradori (2004).
9. This point seems crucially misread to me by Brown (2015, p. 213). More generally, we can see the conundrum that Brown gets herself into when she writes that 'any demos could affirm one or more of the following: extreme inequality; invasive policing and surveillance; limited or nonsupervenient rights; nonuniversal rights; severe restrictions on speech, assembly and worship; conformism; intolerance; exclusions or persecutions of targeted peoples and practices; rule by experts or bureaucrats; war, colonialism, or a domestically militarized society. Many have done so. It will not do to say that such phenomena are undemocratic, if the demos willed or sanctioned them' (Brown 2015, p. 205). But on the other hand, she argues just a few pages later that 'democracy is an empty form that can be filled with a variety of bad content and instrumentalized by purposes ranging from nationalist xenophobia to racial colonialism, from heterosexist to capitalist hegemony . . . Even a radical or direct democracy . . . is capable of dark trajectories or simply of neglecting critical issues such as climate change, species extinction, or genocidal warfare beyond its borders. Thus, there are times when democracy may have to be intermixed with practices of nondemocratic stewardship or contained by moral absolutes' (Brown 2015, p. 209) – which only begs the question, of course: namely, the question of the priority of democracy as an expression of popular sovereignty.
10. Specifically, in Wolfe 2017.

BIBLIOGRAPHY

Althusser, Louis (1969), *For Marx*, trans. Ben Brewster, London: Verso.
Althusser, Louis and Etienne Balibar (1970), *Reading Capital*, trans. Ben Brewster, London: Verso.
Bateson, Gregory (1972), *Steps to an Ecology of Mind*, New York: Ballantine.
Borradori, Giovanna (2004), *Philosophy in a Time of Terror: Dialogues with Jürgen Habermas and Jacques Derrida*, Chicago: University of Chicago Press.
Brown, Wendy (2015), *Undoing the Demos: Neoliberalism's Stealth Revolution*, New York: Zone Books.
Burke, Kenneth (1984), *Permanence and Change: An Anatomy of Purpose*, 3rd edition, Berkeley: University of California Press.
Dawkins, Richard (1976), *The Selfish Gene*, Oxford: Oxford University Press.
de Rosnay, Joël (1979), *The Macroscope: A New World Scientific System*, trans. Robert Edwards, New York: Harper and Row.

Esposito, Roberto (2011), 'The Person and Human Life', trans. Diana Garvin and Thomas Kelso, in *Theory After 'Theory'*, ed. Jane Elliott and Derek Attridge, New York: Routledge, pp. 205–20.

Foucault, Michel (1996), *Foucault Live: Collected Interviews 1961–1984*, ed. Sylvére Lotringer, New York: Semiotext[e].

Foucault, Michel (2008), *The Birth of Biopolitics: Lectures at the Collège de France 1978–1979*, trans. Graham Burchell, ed. Michel Senellart, New York: Palgrave Macmillan.

Haraway, Donna J. (1991), *Simians, Cyborgs, and Women*, New York: Routledge.

Jameson, Fredric (2002), *A Singular Modernity: Essay on the Ontology of the Present*, London: Verso.

Lambert, Gregg (n.d.), 'On *Vitalpolitik*: Between "Raw" and "Cooked" Capitalism', unpublished manuscript.

Luhmann, Niklas (1990), 'The Cognitive Program of Constructivism and a Reality that Remains Unknown', in *Selforganization: Portrait of a Scientific Revolution*, ed. Wolfgang Krohn et al., Dordrecht: Kluwer.

Luhmann, Niklas (1995), *Social Systems*, trans. John Bednarz Jnr. with Dirk Baecker, intro. Eva. Knodt, Stanford: Stanford University Press.

Moeller, Hans-Georg (2006), *Luhmann Explained: From Souls to Systems*, Chicago: Open Court.

Moeller, Hans-Georg (2012), *The Radical Luhmann*, New York: Columbia University Press.

Nealon, Jeffrey T. (2012), *Post-Postmodernism, or, The Cultural Logic of Just-In-Time Capitalism*, Stanford: Stanford University Press.

Rasch, William (2004), *Sovereignty and its Discontents: On the Primacy of Conflict and the Structure of the Political*, London: Birkbeck Law Press.

Wolfe, Cary (2017), '(Auto)immunity, Social Theory, and the "Political"', *Parallax* 23:1, pp. 108–22.

CHAPTER 6

'That Path is for Your Steps Alone': Popular Music, Neoliberalism and Biopolitics

Jeffrey T. Nealon

Gilles Deleuze's 'Postscript on the Societies of Control' is short, and as the amount of scholarship dedicated to unpacking 'the control society' attests, the essay is highly overdetermined – which is to say, there's a lot of different ways to read and deploy it. And by the time the reader finishes perusing the present volume, he or she will surely have seen a lot of exegetical work done on Deleuze's essay. So rather than do extended hermeneutic work on the essay itself, I'm going to shift focus somewhat and delve into a specific cultural formation (the roles of popular music) within our contemporary control society. But as a kind of preface, let me just briefly lay out a few axiomatic things that I'm going to be taking out of Deleuze's 'Societies of Control' provocation; and by axiomatic I simply mean that I'm going to take these principles for granted, rather than arguing for them and deriving them from within Deleuze's work.

First, I'm going to take it for granted that the Deleuze's 'control society' is an attempt to translate Michel Foucault's sense of 'biopolitics' – which is to say, they're both attempts to diagnose the present (or at least the present that's emerging in the mid-1980s to early 1990s); and even more specifically they're both trying to give a name to a form of power that succeeds the Fordist disciplinary society of the mid-twentieth century in the West. If biopower is Foucault's name for the form that emerges after the reign of disciplinary power, Deleuze translates that emergence of biopolitical society as a shift towards '*societies of control*, which are in the process of replacing disciplinary societies' (Deleuze 1992: 5).

The second thing I'm going to take as axiomatic is that this movement from a socius saturated by discipline to a society of biopolitics or control likewise heralds a mutation in capitalism, from the Fordist factory capitalism of mid-century (dedicated to mass-producing objects in fixed settings), to the post-Fordist, neoliberal finance capitalism of our day (dedicated primarily to producing flexibly consuming subjects, updating their lifestyle portfolios everywhere all the time). Which is to say that money, especially the floating of currencies, is a crucial feature of the transition from discipline to biopower, from discipline to control. As Deleuze writes,

> Perhaps it is money that expresses the distinction between the two societies best, since discipline always referred back to minted money that locks gold as numerical standard, while control relates to floating rates of exchange, modulated according to a rate established by a set of standard currencies. (Deleuze 1992: 5)

So I'm going to take for granted that a loose quadrangle of terms – control, biopower, biopolitics, neoliberalism – are not exactly interchangeable, but largely co-evolving and overlapping. Obviously, one could contest this, or point out that these terms are highly disarticulated in some thinkers – for example, in Antonio Negri's work, a bottom-up biopolitics serves as antagonist and antidote to the top-down societal coercions of biopower (Negri 2015: 50). And neoliberalism has its own flabbiness as a term (it seems so everywhere these days that it's nowhere), but here I'm going to use these four terms more or less interchangeably, because I want consistently to highlight the role of capitalism in these mutations and emergences of biopower and control (after discipline).

The third thing I'm taking for granted is something that's implied in both Foucault and Deleuze, though maybe never stated outright: namely, if the terrain we inhabit has decisively mutated towards the biopolitical control societies of neoliberal capitalism, then the entrances and exits from that society will likewise need to be completely rethought. In other words, the ways individuals were interpellated into discipline, and likewise how something like freedom or resistance might be deployed in a disciplinary regime – both of these dramas need to be reconstructed from the ground up in a different type of non-disciplinary society. Which is to say it's implied here that interpellative norming and transgressive authenticity, those fetish concepts of the twentieth century, will need to be rethought, if not completely scrapped outright (the position I'll be defending). Foucault describes the biopolitical society as a world

> in which the field is left open to fluctuating processes . . . in which action is brought to bear on the rules of the game rather than on the players, and finally in which there is an environmental type of intervention instead of the internal subjection of individuals. (Foucault 2010: 259–60)

That being the case, the major difference between discipline and biopower is that in a biopolitical society, power no longer primarily has what we might call a 'mediated' relation aimed at confining or rigidly defining individuals (which is to say, it's not primarily doled out through institutional training as much as it is a question of direct access). The bearing area of disciplinary power is what you can do, and it's primarily invested in training at a series of institutional sites – clinic, factory, family, church, school, shopping centre, police checkpoint. Through a kind of intensification of discipline, the bearing area of biopower has morphed into your entire 'life' – your identity, your sexuality, your health, your internet searches, your artistic tastes – and thereby biopower's relation to any given individual tends to be less mediated by institutional factors, and instead constitutes a more environmental, diffuse, engulfing – one might even call it ambient – form of power.

So how is popular music related to the rise of biopower or the society of control? When it comes to linking the logic of biopower with the logic of popular music, the connection is perhaps nowhere more succinctly stated than in David Hesmondhalgh's *Why Music Matters*. He offers this concise response to his titling query:

> the fact that music matters so much to so many people may derive from two contrasting yet complementary dimensions of musical experience in modern societies. The first is that *music often feels intensely and emotionally linked to the private self* . . . Music is a set of cultural practices that have come to be intricately bound up with the realm of the personal and the subjective . . . The second is that *music is often the basis of collective, public experiences*, whether in live performance, mad dancing at a party, or simply by virtue of the fact that thousands and sometimes millions of people can come to know the same sounds and performers. (Hesmondhalgh 2013: 1–2; emphasis in original)

Much against the grain of his own highly optimistic humanist premises (the book argues that music matters because it helps facilitate what Hesmondhalgh calls 'human flourishing', a phenomenon that one might less generously dub the 'great extinction event that is the Anthropocene'), he does at least make it clear why music matters to a world where biopower is the dominant mode of power: if biopower strives to connect individual lives and identities seamlessly to mass demographic patterns, then we can see more easily music's privileged status as a kind of operating system for biopower. Music 'matters', as Hesmondhalgh so clearly shows us, because it's a set of intimately and deeply personal investments, yet at the same time it's a mass social phenomenon. In any case, that's the biopolitical magic:

> Music, then, represents a remarkable meeting point of intimate and social realms. It provides a basis for self-identity (this is who I am, this is

who I'm not) and collective identity (this is who we are, this is who we're not), often in the same moment. (2013: 2)

Insofar as 'music's special link to emotions and feelings makes it an especially powerful site for the bringing together of private and public experience' (2013: 2), that fact likewise makes music a privileged operator within a regime of biopower. In his essay on 'Music and Identity', Simon Frith restates the biopolitical claim succinctly: 'Identity is not a thing but a process – an experiential process which is most vividly grasped as *music*. Music seems to be a key to identity because it offers, so intensely, a sense of both self and others, of the subjective in the collective' (Frith 1996: 110).

STEAL YOUR FACE

There is no better way to illustrate the difference between a society of discipline and one of biopower than looking at the reception of popular music in the twentieth century. Specifically, I'd like to call attention to a 1967 CBS special report (available on YouTube)[1] hosted by the aptly named Harry Reasoner, where American viewers were warned about a growing youth menace in San Francisco, 'The Hippie Temptation' (the temptation there being the hippie lifestyle of sex, drugs and rock 'n' roll). Reasoner's prime examples for this special report were (who else?) The Grateful Dead, who are seen sitting around their Haight-Ashbury commune house, smoking cigarettes (and God knows what else), playing songs and talking peace, love and mind expansion – with the middle-aged CBS guy in a suit playing the straight-man heavy with real verve. I encourage you to watch the whole clip on YouTube, but I'd like to begin by zeroing in on the moment when the interviewer asks the Dead, 'What do you hope to accomplish?' by non-participation in mainstream social life as we knew it in the 1960s: Why not get with the disciplinary society? Get a job, get married, start a family, grow up dammit! Various members of the Dead reply by insisting they don't want to 'accomplish' anything – they just want to live free from interference by the Man, which will of course later become the mass-individualising mantra of biopolitics. As Reasoner notes, the hippies exemplified by the Dead 'do not want' the existing disciplinary identities (worker, family member, citizen, soldier) that 'our civilization' offers them, 'except on their own terms'; they recognise the immense problems of society, but 'their remedy is to withdraw into private satisfactions', which Reasoner concludes is the 'greatest waste of all'. The whole thing is pretty funny, in retrospect, and it even reminds us that Jerry Garcia didn't always have a beard (I'd always assumed he was born with one).

But what's most peculiar about 'The Hippie Temptation' is that its tone and demeanour – disciplinary power wagging its fingers at people who want only to be left alone to self-actualise – looks like something completely foreign to the American present, though it was only a half-century ago. If nothing else, watching the show today makes it crystal clear that the hippies, and their biopolitical sense that all revolution starts with and moves through the revolution of the individual, won the American culture war in a decisive manner. In the neoliberal world of radical, just-do-it individualism, all but gone are the imperatives of Reasoner's disciplinary world, where we're each supposed to sit down, shut up and do our jobs for the greater glory of society. (Even the US military, which would seem the last bastion of this kind of disciplinary thinking, sells itself these days as a biopolitical self-actualisation technique: 'An Army of One.')

Today, we have all succumbed to 'The Hippie Temptation'. Which is to say, our social world is no longer centred on docile, disciplined individuals working at their assigned roles to ensure more cohesive social wholes. Rather, we live in a biopolitical world of Deleuzean control, where constant innovation, resilience and disruption are the mantras du jour – where the modulating part is the constantly morphing whole, and vice versa. We've all transformed into what Deleuze has dubbed the constantly modulating 'dividual', rather than the in-dividual segmented and moulded by discipline (Deleuze 1992: 5). As Margaret Thatcher so elegantly put it in 1979, for neoliberal biopower

> there's no such thing as society. There are . . . men and women and there are families. And no government can do anything except through people, and people must look after themselves first. It is our duty to look after ourselves and then, also, to look after our neighbours. (Thatcher 2013)

Translated into Ronald Reagan's American idiom, the individualist sirens' song of neoliberalism goes like this: 'Government is not the solution to our problems. Government itself is the problem' (Reagan 1981). Likewise, if the fluid mutations of constantly updated lifestyles are the basic unit of everything for a biopower-based society, then neoliberal consumption capitalism is the logical organising principle or operating system for this discontinuous mass of dividuals, held together only by their quests to become who they really are, ceaselessly following Dead drummer Bill Kreutzmann's biopolitical prescription in 'The Hippie Temptation': always be 'expanding your consciousness, changing your life'. That biopolitical sentiment translated a decade later into Thatcher's refrain that it 'is our duty to look after ourselves'. Or as the Dead lay out the premises of biopower (the journey of life as the journey of the self) in 'Ripple', 'There is a road, no simple highway / Between the dawn and the dark of night / And if you go no one may follow / That path is for your steps alone' (Grateful Dead 1970).

Neoliberal consumption capitalism finally makes only one product: subjects, dividuals, selves. This is what Maurizio Lazzarato calls (following Félix Guattari) the 'machinic enslavement' of subjects to neoliberalism – enslavement here not signalling its disciplinary function, people subjectified or confined to a specific identity and forced to work as a cog in a machine of the social, but signalling our contemporary biopolitical 'enslavement' to the project of endlessly creating our own identities and subjectivities (Lazzarato 2014). Pindar's ancient wish – that we could all live by the dictum 'Become what you are'[2] – has morphed, as Lazzarato and Guattari suggest, into our contemporary biopolitical compulsion. And it's not only the Grateful Dead 'Drivin that train / High on cocaine'. Just think of the near state-funeral level of grief afforded in 2016 to biopolitical music pioneers David Bowie and Prince – both of whom showed us how to be ourselves . . . by imitating world-famous media superstars who are mutating constantly, always following their creative desires into uncharted subjective territory.

And while 'enslavement' to this project of constant self-creation is perhaps an inflammatory term (Lazzarato suggests the word enslavement is synonymous with Foucault's 'government', which is only to say we're worked on constantly by regimes of power that impel us to become ourselves), it is true that we really don't have any 'choice' in the matter. The only saleable commodity of the neoliberal present is your subjectivity, which is under constant reconstruction, deconstruction and modification by the machinic forces of capitalism. As Guattari puts it, 'Essentially, capitalism depends on asignifying machines' (Guattari 1984: 171). As Deleuze helpfully adds, these days 'the self does not undergo modifications; it is itself a series of modifications' (Deleuze 1995: 100).

So maybe the hardest thing to reconstruct looking back at 'The Hippie Temptation' is why anybody thought the hippie menace was something worth worrying about in the first place – any more than the dangers of jazz (now rebranded as 'America's classical music'), punk (the Clash song 'Pressure Drop' played under a 2007 commercial for the Nissan Rogue and 'Should I Stay or Should I Go' served as the 2016 jingle for Choice Hotels) or even hip-hop (which is now the official soundtrack of the affluent white suburbs) were in their respective days. While these musical-social formations were of course perceived as dangerous at their moments of emergence, it's harder to remember that from the vantage point of the biopolitical present, because the danger posed by hippie music only makes sense within a disciplinary society (where rampant do-your-own-thing-ism was a social problem or a 'temptation' – as opposed to today, where such self-obsession is the iron rule). As discipline becomes a residual formation and biopower ascends to the position of a cultural dominant, the function of cultural formations like popular music also changes drastically: within a generation, the directive 'Just Do It!' morphs from a slogan or practice challenging disciplinary norms (for example, when it serves as the title of Jerry Rubin's 1970 hippie manifesto) to an imperative that functions as an axiomatic confirmation of control society's biopolitical dictates (as in its reinvention as the Nike Corporation's official slogan). And subjective authenticity is thereby hoist on this petard of biopower, precisely because within a disciplinary apparatus, authenticity suggests individual subjectivity operating as a norm-busting transgression of the normative social dictates. In a biopolitical society, however, subjectivity as norm-busting transgression is the norm and rule, so the contemporary function of authenticity discourse – musical or otherwise – is largely left to push against an open door.

In short, the mutating landscape of twentieth-century popular music has coincided with the rise of biopower and the triumph of neoliberal society (wherein questions of individual subjective identity are directly connected to larger demographic shifts, a system where all we have in common is that we're all continuously trying to sculpt and modify our lives). Now surely other twentieth-century art forms found themselves saturated with biopower, economics and technology as well (say, novels and poetry with individual readers and the publishing industry; drama with the economics of patrons and falling demographics for live theatre; visual art with galleries and museums, and so on). But popular music has far deeper saturation into the socius (for example, a lot more people listen to music every day than read literature on a daily basis). However widespread popular music listening may be (one of the reasons why it's a privileged linchpin for understanding recent cultural production), in the end I'm just as interested in the residual disciplinary authenticity-logic that's remained so central to popular music practices. Of course, novels or poetry or film also depend on a certain kind of authenticity discourse. Any given person doesn't just read anything or go to see any old film; subjects choose (if that's the right word) according to certain kind of authenticity logic: you like historical novels or experimental poetry, while I like action films or romantic comedies.

To channel Pierre Bourdieu for a moment, the subjective uses and functions of all art forms depend to some degree on a mediating logic of 'taste', and taste is a category of discrimination based largely on the logic of authenticity and scarcity. As Bourdieu argues, in sizing up artistic practices, nothing offers *social* distinction to a subject more than the way he or she makes *cultural* distinctions among aesthetic objects or practices. And of course, popular music practices (of production, consumption and circulation) are where this logic is most intensely on display, and where the logic of 'mass authenticity' has to do a certain kind of heavy lifting in taking a ubiquitous commodity like popular music and making it a cornerstone of a very personal, individual identity statement. As Bourdieu insists in *Distinction: A Social Critique of the Judgment of Taste*, 'nothing more infallibly classifies than tastes in music' (Bourdieu

1984: 18). And it is precisely this biopolitical work – individual subjectivity sculpted on a mass demographic scale, with the two intertwined in a single set of practices – that makes popular music a singularly rich site for analysis of the biopolitical society.

NOT FOR SALE

When our old friends the Grateful Dead played their final 'Fare Thee Well' concerts over the weekend of 4 July in 2015, there was predictable grumbling from many Deadheads: the whole thing was a sell-out, a cash grab and a betrayal of the wandering roadshow ethos that had made the band a counter-culture icon for nearly half a century. For many of the faithful, the Dead were maybe the last vestiges of the 'old, weird America' that Jerry Garcia conjured when he suggested that in the late twentieth century, you could no longer plausibly run away to join the circus, but you could satisfy your wanderlust by following the Grateful Dead through a year of shows. Throughout the 1970s and 1980s, the Dead offered a steady diet of such shows, which in turn offered Deadheads around nine months per year of camping out, hitching rides, selling t-shirts and acid, trading tapes of shows, living below the radar of the taxman and the local cops. The Dead played a whole lot of concerts over those years, while they didn't really sell all that many records; and this in turn earned them additional underground cultural capital as 'anti-commodification' icons – in it for the authentic love of the music and the community, not the money.

Though of course there was always the other side of that coin, the sort of stuff that makes for books like Barry Barnes's *Everything I Know About Business I Learned from the Grateful Dead*: the Dead were authentic alright, but they were also routinely among the highest-grossing acts in any given year well through the 1970s and 1980s (because record sales tended only to make record companies rich, not necessarily the bands themselves). In fact, the Dead are now seen as avatars of the new media economy of shareware; they boldly gave away their content for free (not only encouraging but facilitating fans' taping of their live shows), and thereby the Dead solidified the authenticity of their brand with a fiercely loyal customer base. Whatever else they may have been, the Dead's decades as a travelling roadshow also constituted a long, strange graduate economics seminar in cross-platform niche marketing ('Do you like Dancing Bear LSD and bootleg cassettes of that killer 1977 Cornell show? Maybe you'd be interested in these tie-dye drapes for your VW microbus.') So the question remained hovering over those final shows: were the Grateful Dead authentic artists taking a final bow ... or money-grubbing sell-outs milking fans for all they were worth?

And thus is reconfigured yet again the 'way cool/sold out' dialectic that remains symptomatic of so many discussions concerning popular music. Is Kanye West really 'Not for Sale', as his logo proudly pronounced during his 2013 performance on *Saturday Night Live*? Or is the anti-commodification 'Not For Sale' stance simply a position you have to espouse if you want to be successful within the current landscape of popular music? When that discussion stalls (either Kanye is for sale, or he isn't for sale), then we can move on to endless similar discussions around and about musical authenticity – about my having liked Daft Punk before they went mainstream and became famous, or your insisting that the world has come to an end because you can hear Lou Reed's heroin-chic anthem 'Perfect Day' playing under a cell phone commercial, Iggy Pop's 'Lust for Life' being used to hawk luxury cruises ('that's like hypnotizing chickens') or a Taco Bell ad featuring Joe Jackson's 'One More Time' (conjuring his song 'I'm the Man', and its biting refrain 'I can sell you anything'). Or vice versa, you could argue that it's the height of authenticity for artists (or their estates) to take control of their songbooks and do whatever they want with them: why *wouldn't* a Ramones' song be featured in a 2017 commercial for a Peleton home workout bike? And round and round we go. In any case, this 'way cool/sold out' dialectic is undoubtedly another one of the myriad things that Lawrence Grossberg is referencing when he complains that nothing much has changed in the last half-century of critical thinking about popular music.[3] Wander into virtually any bar around happy hour on a Friday, and you can strike up this kind of authenticity conversation in a nanosecond.

Insofar as I'm looking to move beyond the sort of things that people routinely say about popular music, I somewhat ironically want to insist on – rather than try to apologise for – popular music's overdetermined status within such a commodity culture. And I'd also like to put 'authenticity' to bed as a critical or theoretical model for talking about music. The seeming centrality of musical authenticity is, as I've already suggested, one of the primary reasons why writing about music has become so hopelessly stalled and repetitive: you say it's authentic, I say it's sold-out crap. Music of course can and does produce meaningful cultural authenticity-affects for its listeners and producers, but you'll never find this representational thing called authenticity 'in' any music. Likewise, the jargon of authenticity may have deployed a certain capacity for resistance in a disciplinary society (allowing one perhaps to stand outside the normalising dictates of a Fordist factory society – we used to call it 'waving your freak flag'). But the mass authenticity compulsion of biopolitics offers very little friction to a post-Fordist, neoliberal control society, where we are all compelled endlessly to stand outside normative dictates, and constantly modulate our subjectivity.

In the end, popular music fans are less autonomous, taste-making, deciding subjects than they are dividual relays within a series of much wider flows – for example, flows of money, desire and technological innovation. Neither anti-commodity nor simply 'sold out' the discourse surrounding popular music is on the contrary a key factor in understanding how a whole matrix of practices can produce those authenticity-effects, so often associated with being 'not for sale', inside a wholly commodified context. Producing and maintaining this wonderfully oxymoronic mass-produced authentic individualism has been the primary cultural 'work' of popular music over the past half-century.

As such, the discourses and practices surrounding popular music production and consumption over the past few decades offer a skeleton key to understanding a larger shared American (indeed, increasingly global) phenomenon, the biopolitical importance of mass authenticity – the kind of thing that 70,000 people at the final Grateful Dead concert share with the demographically distinct throngs at Coachella or Bonaroo, not to mention those who attend the Big Barrel Country Music Festival, the Essence or Jazz and Heritage Festivals in New Orleans, the Alive Christian Music Fest, the season at Tanglewood, Festival Latino, the Full Terror Assault gathering of metal-heads, the Michigan Womyn's Music Festival, or the Brooklyn Hip-Hop Festival. Obviously, the demographic make-up of these audiences (in terms of race, ethnicity, class, age, gender, religion, sexual orientation) is widely disparate, but the biopolitical phenomenon of 'mass authenticity', accruing so powerfully to popular music discourses and practices, stitches these categories all together into a larger 'logic', one that will help us to understand how subject production and reproduction works – how it operates – in the biopolitical era of neoliberalism.

Of course, one could always argue, as Joseph Heath and Andrew Potter do in their *Nation of Rebels: Why Counterculture Became Consumer Culture*, that late twentieth-century American counterculture, and especially its soundtrack, never offered any kind of meaningful resistance to American capitalism. They argue that counterculture could hardly be 'co-opted' or 'sold out' because it was never in opposition to the economic mainstream values of American capitalist society to begin with:

> There simply never was any tension between the counterculture ideas that informed the '60s rebellion and the ideological requirements of the capitalist system. While there is no doubt that a *cultural* conflict developed between the members of the counterculture and the defenders of the older American Protestant establishment, there was never any tension between the *values* of the counterculture and the functional requirements of the capitalist economic system. The counterculture was, from its very inception, intensely entrepreneurial. It reflected ... the most authentic spirit of capitalism. (Heath and Potter 2004: 3)

While this argument tracks in some ways parallel to my own, especially in its attempts to end-run around talk of 'co-optation', I'm keen to make a distinction between them: for Heath and Potter, capitalism seems not to have changed at all over the past decades, and thereby capitalism's 'ideological requirements' have always-already been neoliberal or biopolitical, 'intensely entrepreneurial' at their core. However, I'm arguing that such widespread emphasis on biopolitical entrepreneurship was demonstrably *not* the case for American capitalism in its mid-century disciplinary or Fordist phase. Before the biopolitical, neoliberal revolutions of the Reagan–Thatcher 1980s, disciplinary capitalism didn't have much use for subjective authenticity. Having worked at a gum factory as a summer job in the late 1970s, I can attest that no one encouraged us to think of ourselves as entrepreneurs or rebels, nor were we implored to innovate anything at all on the assembly line. Disciplinary systems, as Foucault insists, want to fix subjects into certain moulded roles in order to assure the efficient production and reproduction of goods and services.

With the development and triumph of biopolitical capitalism, on the other hand, the question of value always needs to be run through the individual, and I'm sure that gum factory employees these days (the few who haven't been replaced by robots) are constantly called upon to innovate, share best practices, think outside the box, and parrot all the other noxious clichés of neoliberalism. But my point here is this: *American popular music's values of subjective rebellion and personal authenticity were not always coincident with the logic of mainstream American economic life.* In short, popular music's countercultural notions of personal authenticity as resistance to massification did perform an immense amount of useful work at the tail end of the disciplinary society in America: if the problem is subjective constraint, doing your own thing registers quite nicely as resistance. However, if several decades later the axioms of neoliberal capitalism dictate that you must be your own entrepreneur, that sense of '60s-style personal authenticity can only confirm, rather than contest, the normative practices of American economic life. In short, it's not that popular music sold out to the Man, or that musical rebellion and authenticity were always already a shill for the Man; rather, my argument is that the dominant logic of American capitalism has morphed into a biopolitical form that was presaged by twentieth century American popular music fandom and its intense investments in developing and maintaining your own personal authenticity within a wholly commodified field.

As the savvy reader will have noted, in forwarding this line of thinking, I'm also extending Jacques Attali's argument in *Noise: The Political Economy of Music*. Attali claims that the popular music of any given era doesn't merely *reflect* dominant economic discourses and practices, but music in fact *predicts* changes in economic regimes: 'music is prophetic', Attali insists, and 'social organization echoes it' (Attali 1984: 5) rather than vice versa. As Attali continues, music 'is neither an autonomous activity nor an automatic indicator of the economic infrastructure. It is a herald, for change is inscribed in noise faster than it transforms society' (1984: 5). As we've seen, music has functioned as a herald for widespread economic and social reorganisation, as in the US we've gone from a predominantly factory society of discipline to a neoliberal society of biopower – or in Attali's terms, from a disciplinary society of endless goods-based 'repetition' to what he sees in the mid-1970s as an emergent society of subjective 'composition'. He defines composition simply as any given individual's production-consumption' (1984: 144), or the (re)production of identity through consumption, what we now call the neoliberal 'prosumer'.

And as unlikely as the claim seems on the face of it, the practices that have sprung up around the past decades of popular music – as Attali reminds us, a powerful 'mode of immaterial production' (1984: 9) – have in fact presaged these decisive changes in the wider economy, for better or worse. Music is and has been a powerful apparatus of capture for values of all kinds; but it's also a powerful tool in subverting the present and/or carving out a livable future. So where do we go from here, having arrived on the territory of neoliberal biopower that was predicted for us by the discourses and practices surrounding American popular music? It is to that question that I now turn in conclusion, keeping in mind all the while Attali's clarion call (or is a siren's song?): 'Our music foretells our future. Let us lend it an ear' (1984: 11).

EVERYWHERE, ALL THE TIME

In the end, it's the 'mass culture' quality of popular music that primarily interests me; in other words, it's popular music's ubiquity (and maybe even its banality – the very reasons that someone like Adorno refused to take it seriously) that to my mind makes music the skeleton key to understanding changes in both cultural production and subject production over the second half of the twentieth century, and into the twenty-first. Just like everybody else, I'm not like everybody else.

But what exactly do I mean by saying that popular music is more central than other cultural forms for understanding the recent American cultural past and the present? Well, certainly in my lifetime, it has become very hard indeed to make convincing and sweeping cultural claims for literature or museum art as mass drivers of anything in particular, in terms of widespread cultural effects on contemporary subjectivity. Today, for better or worse, high art forms circulate in a niche market, like eBay collectibles, and as such are not really a mass pivot for diagnosing large-scale changes in contemporary subjectivity. But that doesn't stop art critics and literature scholars (people like me) from making all sorts of breathless mass cultural claims in the pages of academic journals – articles on 'The Environmental Politics of Jorie Graham' or 'Neoliberal Motifs in Jeff Koons'. Surely literature or museum art can perform cultural work, but if you're looking for a recent art form that's influential on a mass scale, you'd have to admit that most Americans don't read contemporary poetry, or really have much to say about art retrospectives.

But millions of people in the US still do have an iPod, and as of January 2017, around 90 per cent of Americans age 18–49 use a smartphone, most of them stocked with MP3s (organised into custom playlists).[4] Likewise, millions of people worldwide have Spotify, Pandora or other internet streams going much of the day (at work, on the bus and at home), as well satellite radio in the car for the commute. There's also popular music playing prominently within myriad other cultural forms that we encounter every day – TV shows and advertisements, video games, films, not to mention the ubiquitous pop soundtrack playing at the mall, the gym, the fast-food place, the dentist's office and the grocery store. Popular music presently enjoys a saturation level within everyday life that remains very much unlike any other contemporary art form. And as such, it's a particularly intense example of Guattari's 'machinic enslavement' (or government of dividuals) within the biopolitical control society.

In terms of its functioning, popular music's ubiquity allows it to operate at a largely subconscious level of the refrain – as you realise every time you find yourself humming some song you heard somewhere. At least for me, it's pretty easy to tune out the Fox News feed playing on the doctor's waiting room TV – often by throwing on the earbuds and listening to my own music. Or if you forgot your earbuds, you can just look away from the screen, because you have to pay a certain level of attention to be affected by visual media like television. However, it's much harder to tune out the soundtrack in the waiting room – precisely because you don't have to pay conscious attention to the music, but it continues to work on you nevertheless. Later in the day, you find yourself humming the words or toe-tapping the riff from some Motown song.

I wish neither to decry this functioning of popular music as sinister mind control, nor to find within it some hidden subversion. I have come before you neither to denounce nor celebrate the ubiquity of popular music, but to exploit and work with its everydayness – to see popular music as a privileged biopolitical operating system for examining cultural production and subject-formation in the twentieth and twenty-first centuries. The task I've set myself in this chapter is to take popular music seriously, not as a rarefied set of highly meaningful aesthetic objects, but as a common or everyday series of aesthetic practices, operations or forms of life. I've set out here not to discover what popular music means, but to examine how it functions, what kind of alternative 'cognitive map' it might offer through the cultural life of recent decades. And as such, I hope to meet everyday popular music fans and critics where they already are, in the midst of a sea of listening.

Of course, it's the actual practice of listening to music that has changed most substantially in the past twenty or thirty years, in the shift from discipline to biopower. Certainly musical taste continues to do some subjective sorting work through a kind of excorporative method that functions within music discourse and far beyond; but the thing that's really changed quite radically in recent decades is the function of popular music in everyday life (rather than the discourse that surrounds it, which hasn't changed substantially since its terms were set up by the Benjamin–Adorno debate in the 1930s). Over the past two decades, the disciplinary, analogue apparatus of listening to physical records or CDs (the immersive experience of listening to an entire album, consuming music on the analogy of reading a book) has been completely revolutionised by the MP3 playlist and the internet stream. And thereby music becomes less something to be consumed or interpreted, something that either positively or negatively offers our meaning to our lives. Rather, music becomes more something that is used by dividuals and other collective actors to create various scapes in our individual and social lives – the sleep scape, the gym scape, the study scape, the commute scape, the romance scape, the political rally scape, the shopping scape. All kinds of playlists or internet streams, for Saturday night as well as for Sunday morning.

Music theorist Anahid Kassabian calls this *Ubiquitous Listening*, an ambient redistribution of music across the surface of our entire biopolitical lives, as opposed to thinking of the song as an individualised art form (on the analogy of the book or visual art work) to which listeners pay particularly dense aural attention – huddled in front of the record player with some friends, decoding the hidden messages of Pink Floyd's *The Dark Side of the Moon*, or intently trying to identify all the samples in De La Soul's *3 Feet High and Rising*. That's not how the vast majority of listening happens today. As music has saturated our entire lives, the kind of attention we pay to it inexorably changes as well; and this, as Kassabian argues, should give rise to 'a whole new field of music studies, in which we stop thinking about compositional process, or genre, or industrial factors as the central matters' (Kassabian 2012: 19), and turn critical attention instead to the ways that the new listening technology 'modulates our attentional capacities, it tunes our affective relationships to categories of identity, [and] it conditions our participation in fields of subjectivity' (Kassabian 2012: 18). The ubiquitous, ambient music-scapes that Brian Eno dreamed of in the 1970s – in his *Music for Airports*, for example – have become the mundane reality of our MP3-packed lives only half a century later. And thereby the primary function of music has changed substantially – no longer primarily as something that offers group or individual meaning or identity through excorporative distinction, and more something that allows us to make our way through distributed fields of fluid subjectivity, surfing the modulations of late-late capitalist life, deploying just the right kind and levels of attention, focus and distraction.

'Well', the sceptical reader might reply, 'putting together a "killer workout playlist" isn't much of a form of resistance to multi-national capital'. Which is I suppose true enough, but it likewise seems to me that the whole category of resistance, like the sibling category of authenticity, may need to be updated in talking about and responding to present forms of capitalism. Or think of it this way, and this will be for me the final argumentative turn of the screw: when it comes to thinking about the legacy and history of cultural distraction, Adorno's beef with popular music was most definitively *not* that it merely delivered distraction from capitalist dictates. Rather, Adorno's critique is that music consistently *refused or failed to deliver* such distraction; as he writes in *Dialectic of Enlightenment*, it remains 'doubtful whether the culture industry even still fulfills its self-proclaimed function of distraction' (Adorno and Horkheimer 2007: 110). Which is to say, popular music for Adorno failed to offer its listener any kind of aesthetic zone at least temporarily twisted free from the most obvious and craven dictates of capitalist life (in Adorno's time, the iron command to conform). Ironically, however, today that's precisely one of the things that the MP3 or the internet stream offers to subjects, regardless of its artistic 'content' or whether anything in the playlist is intellectually challenging as music. That music would offer a subjectivity-twisting aesthetic challenge to the listener, Adorno's brass ring, is no longer quite to the point, simply because very few people are listening intently to the music anyway. People today primarily use music for things other than judging the excellence of music.

Maybe the problem with musical aesthetics since Adorno is not that music or music criticism is too bourgeois, but that music and its criticism largely failed to deliver any of the supposed gains of musical aesthetics (a momentary musical respite from the dictates of capitalist life) to anyone other than the bourgeois class (who could learn through aesthetic judgement to take its distance from the commodified banality of everyday life). And that more democratic offering of a momentary buffer from the dictates of what Jonathan Beller calls contemporary capitalism's 'attention theory of value' (Beller 2006: 4) may be what ambient listening could harness for the distracted consciousness of the twenty-first century.

As Dominic Pettman writes in *Infinite Distraction*, a renewed sense of ambient musical (dis)engagement might 'propose the possibility, or project, of fostering a more centripetal form of distraction (i.e., as something more enmeshed than sheer *dispersal*, allowing a self-reflexive type of engagement which avoids the overdetermined model of experience known as *attention*)' (Pettman 2015: 134). In the end, I can only second Pettman's sense that 'We should accept this challenge to rethink distraction as a potential ally' (Pettman 2015: 136) in the everyday fight against biopolitical capitalism and its all-the-time attention economy. Indeed, this harnessing of distraction as a weapon against the colonising forces of power has constituted an ongoing, but largely under-deployed, utopian possibility throughout the history of modern cultural studies. Think, for example, of Walter Benjamin's musings concerning the potential political upshot of modern 'reception in distraction': 'The sort of distraction that is provided by art represents a covert measure of the extent to which it has become possible to perform new tasks of apperception' (Benjamin 2003: 268). In short, what looks like mere musical distraction may be the beginnings of a potentially oppositional form of cultural practice, and one that helps us to understand attention and distraction as a mass cultural phenomenon, an ecology we inhabit rather than an individual disposition we choose.

As Yves Citton argues in *The Ecology of Attention*, a kind of distracted attention may be 'holding out the promise of an EMANCIPATORY DISTRACTION: if we cannot be attentive enough [because of sheer amount of cultural stuff that's out there], let us be attentive differently – and *make our distraction into an opportunity for a detachment which, freeing us from our voluntarist blinkers, will allow us to reconsider the problem in an entirely new way*' (Citton 2017: 117; emphasis and capitalisation in original). And that new way of thinking about attention and distraction may help us to think past the subjectivity traps of the twentieth century – the Adornian sense that it's only rare, authentic individuals who know how to rise above the fray of the shiny objects designed to draw the inauthentic attention of the masses. What we pay attention to in the internet age, as Jacques Lacan could have told us had he lived long enough, has everything to do with what the others are paying attention to. Thereby, we need to learn to pay attention to attention as a mass demographic or social phenomenon, not an individual choice. Insofar as we live in an environment of attention – we're soaking in it – Citton reminds us that,

> The detachment brought about by free-floating attention – whether it is rooted in a voluntary effort or in simple distraction through a lack of attentional resources – allows our joint (but unstuck) attention to discover new forms, properties and potentialities that were not previously available to any of the individuals in the group. (Citton 2017: 119)

Attention is a sea we live on and surf, rather than a scarce resource we need to hoard, and musical detachment (as well as renewed forms of musical focus) may offer us ways of speeding up or slowing down those constant flows of distributed, ambient cultural attention.

Or if that utopian thesis seems a bit far-fetched, consider Meaghan Morris's feminist plea, in her essay 'Banality in Cultural Studies', to rethink distraction as something other than a confirmation of the Adornian thesis that those distracted by popular art forms are 'cultural dopes'. As Morris counters, 'One could claim that this interpretation is only possible if one continues to assume that the academic traditions of "contemplation" really do define intelligence, and that to be "distracted" can therefore only mean being "dopey"' (Morris 2007: 129). Likewise, unless we rethink this relation between contemplation (understood as good, autonomous, resistant, meaningful) and distraction (bad, enslaved, hoodwinked, meaningless) when it comes to contemporary artistic production, about all we can do going forwards is to recycle the 'way cool/sold out' dialectic that, as we have seen, has become a cul-de-sac for thinking about popular music practices. As Morris insists, 'No matter which of the terms we validate, the contemplation/distraction, academic/popular oppositions can serve only to limit and distort the possibilities of popular practice' (Morris 2007: 129). And in the end, it is precisely through attending to the *practices* and *uses* of listening (rather than focusing on what popular music 'means' within our lives) that we might be able locate whatever hopes or fears accrue to the conflicted, everyday life of sound – possibilities or pitfalls for biopolitical subjects like us, who increasingly require practices that offer respite from our contemporary biopolitical enslavement to making and remaking our identities in every moment of our waking lives.

Or maybe what I'm arguing for here is, to borrow some lingo from Eve Kosofsky Sedgwick, a kind of 'reparative' (rather than 'paranoid') style of aesthetic engagement, one that looks to cultural productions for something other than depth, hidden meaning or large-scale significance. As Sedgwick puts it, summing up Melanie Klein's work on the paranoid and the depressive, 'the paranoid position . . . is a position of terrible alertness' (Sedgwick 2003: 128), always tasked with paying close attention so that one is not duped into playing the fool or making the same mistake over and over again. In listening parlance, the 'rockist' listener is resolutely paranoid, as he or she must always guard against being hoodwinked into investing in the wrong kind of 'inauthentic' music, thereby putting precious cultural and social capital at stake. But Sedgwick (perhaps counterintuitively) finds a kind of queer potential not within that paranoid mindset, but within a 'depressive' aesthetic engagement (what we're translating as a set of ear-budded practices to fight off attention capitalism): 'By contrast, the depressive position is an anxiety-mitigating achievement' that opens 'the position from which it is possible in turn to use one's own resources to assemble or "repair"' (Sedgwick 2003: 128) the paranoid space of constant subjective authenticity policing, or the contemporary overflow of way too many shiny objects vying for our attention. Though of course here I can see the paranoid retort coming back again strong for an encore, one . . . more . . . time: in short, the ultimate objection to such a position is that an ear-budded aesthetic space of involuted pleasure or mere escape is the *problem* rather than the *solution* in terms of the privatising neoliberal imperatives dominant of contemporary capitalist life. The revolution can't come about if everyone's walled off in an isolated ambient environment.

To that dismissal, Sedgwick offers a final (and to my mind definitive) rebuff, which is worth quoting at length:

> Reparative motives, once they become explicit, are inadmissible in paranoid theory both because they are about pleasure ('merely aesthetic') and because they are frankly ameliorative ('merely reformist'). What makes pleasure and amelioration so 'mere'? Only the exclusiveness of paranoia's faith in demystifying exposure: only its cruel and contemptuous assumption that the one thing lacking for global revolution, explosion of gender roles, or whatever, is people's (that is, other people's) having the painful effects of their oppression, poverty, or deludedness sufficiently exacerbated to make the pain conscious (as if otherwise it wouldn't have been) and intolerable (as if intolerable situations were famous for generating excellent solutions). (Sedgwick 2003: 144)

Amen, Eve. If they are to function as politically compelling, everyday cultural practices of whatever kind have to function first as a biopolitical bridge from here to there, rather than primarily being deployed as a cultural cover for the outsized demystifying claims of tenure-line intellectuals. In short, you have to follow how cultural practices function before you can talk about what they mean, and the functions of cover and momentary escape (so intensely bound up with the practice of listening to music) constitute the non-conscious and collective bases for those things called individual and group agency. And while it seems clear that 'The Revolution Will Not Be Televised' for all the corporate-media reasons that Gil Scott-Heron laid out for us in his 1970 song, in the future the revolution may be available for a free download. Or at least its soundtrack will be.

In any case, thinking about popular music as the operating system of biopower, or as a kind of cognitive map for charting the territory of neoliberal biopolitics, is following out the project that Deleuze offers in his control society essay – not so much a question of hope or despair, but a matter of looking for new weapons. So what tools does a biopolitical analysis offer us in terms of diagnosing the present? I would argue that the primary new tool on display here is one and the same with the new diagnosis – that the terrain of the disciplinary society has been permanently transformed, and that we live in a vastly different world from the disciplinary world of training, enclosure and confinement. We live instead in a world where we are enslaved to the very project of always modifying, updating and retooling our lives – the very thing that the disciplinary society fought to keep at bay. Hence, all the ways that we thought of ourselves as being confined and/or freed have given way to a kind of ubiquitous governmentality under contemporary capitalism. We are literally a series of dividual relays among a series of machinic flows. And listening is a privileged practice where we meet, resist and rework neoliberal social power, right on the surface of our everyday lives.[5]

NOTES

1. You can see 'The Hippie Temptation' here (the Dead come up at around the thirty-two-minute mark): https://www.youtube.com/watch?v=HlgRTlYZMIg
2. The full quotation – γένοι' οἶος ἐσσὶ μαθών – is most often translated as 'Become such as you are, having learned what that is': https://en.wikiquote.org/wiki/Pindar
3. Looking back on the field in his 2002 essay 'Reflections of a Disappointed Popular Music Scholar', Grossberg writes that especially where it pertains to critical theory, 'I do not think that writing about popular music has significantly changed (to say nothing of "progressed") in forty years' (2002: 28–9). From 'Reflections of a Disappointed Popular Music Scholar', in *Rock Over the Edge*, ed. Roger Beebee, Denise Fulbrook and Ben Saunders, Durham, NC: Duke University Press, 2002.
4. Check out the numbers from the Pew Research Center here: http://www.pewinternet.org/fact-sheet/mobile/
5. This chapter was originally given as a talk at the University of Stockholm. I'd like to thank Frida Beckman especially for inviting me, and Ulf Olsson for his insightful comments on that occasion. Parts of this chapter will reappear in my *I'm Not Like Everybody Else: Biopolitics, Neoliberalism and American Popular Music*, forthcoming from the University of Nebraska Press.

REFERENCES

Adorno, Theodor and Max Horkheimer (2007), *Dialectic of Enlightenment*, trans. Edmund Jephcott, Stanford: Stanford University Press.
Attali, Jacques (1984), *Noise: The Political Economy of Music*, trans. Brian Massumi, Minneapolis: University of Minnesota Press.
Beller, Jonathan (2006), *The Cinematic Mode of Production: Attention Economy and the Society of the Spectacle*, Hanover, NH: Dartmouth University Press.
Benjamin, Walter (2003), 'The Work of Art in the Age of its Technological Reproducibility (Third Version)', trans. Harry Zohn and Edmund Jephcott, in *Selected Writings, Volume 4 (1938–40)*, ed. Howard Eiland and Michael W. Jennings, Cambridge, MA: Harvard University Press.
Bourdieu, Pierre (1984), *Distinction: A Social Critique of the Judgment of Taste*, trans. Richard Nice, Cambridge, MA: Harvard University Press.
Citton, Yves (2017), *The Ecology of Attention*, trans. Barnaby Norman, Cambridge: Polity Press.
Deleuze, Gilles (1992), 'Postscript on the Societies of Control', *October* 59 (1992): 3–7.
Deleuze, Gilles (1995), *Difference and Repetition*, trans. Paul Patton, New York: Columbia University Press, 1995.
Foucault, Michel (2010), *The Birth of Biopolitics: Lectures at the Collège de France 1978–79*, trans. Graham Burchell, New York: Picador.
Frith, Simon (1996), 'Music and Identity', in *Questions of Cultural Identity*, ed. Stuart Hall and Paul du Gay, London: Sage.

Grateful Dead (1970), 'Ripple', *American Beauty*, Warner Brothers.
Guattari, Félix (1984), *Molecular Revolution*, trans. Rosemary Sheed, New York: Penguin.
Heath, Joseph and Andrew Potter (2004), *Nation of Rebels: Why Counterculture Became Consumer Culture*, New York: Harper Business.
Hesmondhalgh, David (2013), *Why Music Matters*, London: Wiley-Blackwell.
Kassabian, Anahid (2012), *Ubiquitous Listening: Affect, Attention, and Distributed Subjectivity*, Berkeley: University of California Press.
Lazzarato, Maurizio (2014), *Signs and Machines: Capitalism and the Production of Subjectivity*, trans. J. D. Jordan, Cambridge, MA: The MIT Press.
Morris, Meaghan (2007), ''Banality in Cultural Studies', in *The Cultural Studies Reader*, 3rd edition, ed. Simon During, New York: Routledge.
Negri, Antonio (2015), 'To the Origins of Biopolitics', trans. Diana Garvin, in *Biopower: Foucault and Beyond*, ed. Vernon W. Cisney and Nicolae Morar, Chicago: University of Chicago Press.
Pettman, Dominic (2015), *Infinite Distraction*, London: Polity Press.
Reagan, Ronald, First Presidential Inaugural Address, 20 January 1981, http://www.presidency.ucsb.edu/ws/?pid=43130
Sedgwick, Eve Kosofsky (2003), 'Paranoid Reading and Reparative Reading; Or, You're So Paranoid, You Probably Think This Essay Is About You', in Eve Kosofsky Segdwick, *Touching Feeling: Affect, Pedagogy, Performativity*, Durham, NC: Duke University Press.
Thatcher, Margaret (2013), 'A Life in Quotes', *The Guardian*, 8 April, https://www.theguardian.com/politics/2013/apr/08/margaret-thatcher-quotes

CHAPTER 7

Cinema in the Age of Control

Gregory Flaxman

THE TABLE OF INFORMATION AND THE SOCIETY OF CONTROL

On the face of it, the coupling of cinema and 'control society' is bound to seem awkward, perhaps even counterintuitive. Neither term is particularly easy to define, but their combination seems to fly in the face of manifest associations on both sides. Whereas the etymological and technical origins of cinema belong to an older pictorial, physiological and photomechanical history, control is inconceivable apart from the invention of a new generation of digital machines. In his 'Postscript on Control Society' (1990), the short essay which effectively launched the eponymous concept, Gilles Deleuze insists that 'information technology and computers' underwrite the emergence of our postdisciplinary regime of power (Deleuze 1995: 180). Thus, 'control' describes a political economy, a biopolitics and an episteme – with the understanding that the digital revolution transforms these categories in turn.

By these standards, cinema seems an anachronism. Media studies scholars have long argued that the so-called Seventh Art, often cast as the great mass medium of the twentieth century, actually culminates a technological lineage firmly entrenched in the opto-photo-mechanical tradition of the nineteenth century.[1] If anything, then, cinema demonstrates a tenacious capacity to adapt to the new era of electricity (by automating the camera, projector and even editing table, no less by embracing artificial light and the introduction of synchronised sound). For scholars like Friedrich Kittler, the wonder is that the cinema persists as long as it has, even surviving the challenge posed by the introduction of television, the electronic medium par excellence. The same cannot be said with respect to the digital age. Over the past twenty-five years, audio-visual 'entertainment' has been so profoundly – we might even say, *existentially* – transformed by new media and digital communications as to outstrip the material origins of 'film' (the celluloid or cellulous acetate film strip) and 'cinema' (the cinematographic machine). When we go to the movies, the film itself is increasingly shot digitally, quite possibly distributed digitally, and in all likelihood projected digitally. Moreover, the viewing experience itself is no longer reducible to the model of the movie-goer: we watch on televisions, PCs, tablets, phones, watches; we gaze at screens on refrigerators and gas pumps, in waiting rooms and aeroplanes. Finally, as if anyone need be told, the ostensible differences between cinema, television, and online entertainment are swiftly dissolving. No longer discrete media, all three are now contingent on digital information that exists irrespective of any single format: the device is contingent and the medium secondary before the all-encompassing abstraction of digital 'content'.

To put it bluntly, we're well past the point of adhering to a 'specificity thesis' of the cinema: the literality of film, the sensitive substance on which light was recorded ('like a decal', as Bazin said[2]), has been overwhelmingly replaced by the far less expensive means of digitally recording, animating, manipulating, storing and delivering audio-visual information. Has there been a moment in the past century of cinema as uncertain as our own, a moment when one is hard-pressed to say what cinema will look like or, better still, what it will *name* in the next decade, or two, or ten? This rhetorical question precipitates the real problem – the relation of cinema and control – that confronts us here, and in this respect Deleuze provides a particularly felicitous point of departure. After all, his elaboration of control sits alongside two 'cinema books' that, for all their philosophical ingenuity, seem decidedly film-specific and cinema-centric. Indebted to a legacy of film *auteurs*, hewing to a familiar film history, and oriented by a modernist sensibility, *The Movement-Image* (1983) and *The Time-Image* (1985) hardly seem suited to the protocols of control. Nevertheless, I would argue that in the final chapters of the second volume, where he weighs the current circumstances and uncertain futures of cinema, Deleuze ventures an analysis of control society *avant la lettre*. Though he never uses the phrase, the concept suffuses his elaboration of power sprung from centralisation, dispersed across a 'network', and insinuated into so many monads (Deleuze 1989: 265). We are entering a new age of machines, of 'automata', Deleuze says, and it's worth noting that, to describe this transformation, *The Time-Image* briefly takes leave of cinema (1989: 263–7).

Readers of the 'cinema books' are likely familiar with Deleuze's dedication to making film the means to frame political, historical and philosophical questions; but on this occasion, the relationship is reversed: cinema is framed by a 'technological and social evolution of automata' already afoot, 'a new computer and cybernetic race, automata of computation and thought, automata with controls and feedback' (1989: 264-5). It's on this basis that Deleuze poses the question that broadly concerns us here, namely: is there 'a new regime of images like that of automatism' (1989: 264)? In other words, is there a regime of cinematic images that corresponds to the emergence of computer technology, information science and digital media? To appreciate the question, no less Deleuze's hesitation to provide a definitive answer, it's worth considering the horizon of expectations within which he wrote. Published in 1983 and 1985, Deleuze's cinema books confront a social landscape dominated by 'electronic images, that is, the tele and video images' (1989: 265). There's perhaps no better measure of just how foreign the digital still seemed than the English translation of *The Time-Image* (published in 1989). The translators render Deleuze's phrase, '*images numeriques*', with 'numerical images' (1989: 265) rather than 'digital images' because this nomenclature did not yet exist.

Notwithstanding precursors, the digital era of cinema was still gestating. The release of *Terminator 2* (1991) and then *Jurassic Park* (1993) effectively mark the decisive emergence of CGI; it would be another five years before the first 'digital' films began to intermittently appear and another ten after that before they began to predominate. But if cinema has been assimilated to digital machines and digital information, I'd argue that the automatism that characterises the moving image remains irreducible to the technology of the computer or, more broadly, to the model of cybernetics. Even when the recording, editing and viewing machines are digital, the *déroulement* of images is oblivious to and unaltered by our reactions. We'd be foolish to deny the operation of other circuits of information, especially those available to a digital audience, but no matter how far one wishes to take this logic, I think we're forced to concede that between sender and receiver, image and perception, there is no immediate feedback loop: nothing alters the 'film' – the information – being transmitted. This *factum brutum* cannot be refuted, but it ought not to be regretted, as if it were a limitation or liability of the medium. On the contrary, and by dint of its anachronism, the cinema avails a unique vantage on digital technology and, more generally, on control societies. Naturally, particular film-makers and genres demonstrate a propensity for automata (Deleuze nods to Kubrick's *2001* and to science fiction more generally), but the concluding pages of *The Time-Image* concern a more subtle and yet more intrinsic 'mutation of form' that characterises a 'new regime of images' (1989: 264).

> The new images no longer have any outside (out-of-field), any more than they are internalized in a whole; rather, they have a right side and a reverse, reversible and non-superimposable, like a power to turn back on themselves. They are the object of a perpetual reorganization, in which a new image can arise from any point whatever of the preceding image. The organization of space here loses its privileged directions, and first

of all the privilege of the vertical which the position of the screen still displays, in favour of an omni-directional space which constantly varies its angles and co-ordinates, to exchange the vertical and the horizontal. And the screen itself, even if it keeps a vertical position by convention, no longer seems to refer to the human posture, like a window or a painting, but rather constitutes a table of information, an opaque surface on which are inscribed 'data,' information replacing nature, and the brain-city, the third eye, replacing the eyes of nature. (1989: 265)

This critical passage describes the attributes of a new image, the resulting reorientation of space, the revision of the screen, and thence the transformation of the spectator. While the film image no longer refers to the standing 'posture' corresponding to a window or painting (which is to say, *pace* Alberti, determined by pictorial perspective), the seated spectator has been transformed – or, better still, *in-formed* – by digital media. In contrast to the older, even classical conventions of the film screen, into the depths of which the eye ventured, the new digital (e.g., computer, television, tablet, smartphone) screen consists in what Deleuze calls an 'opaque surface' (1989: 265) on which windows are at once infinitely stackable and without depth. The image becomes a 'table of information' (1989: 265). We don't look through the image, nor even into it; rather, we look *at* it or *on* it. But inasmuch as we interact with the digital media, we now understand all too well that, in a sense, the image watches us: the data 'inscribed' is our own. Virtually everywhere we go, whatever we do, we are 'on screen' – captured by closed-circuit cameras, tracked by our GPS and IP address; submitted to facial recognition, thumbprints, retinal scans; recorded in financial transactions, logins, phone calls, web searches, etc.

Not surprisingly, it's in this context that contemporary Hollywood cinema (i.e., cinema of roughly the last twenty years) has reckoned with control society. Comparatively lucrative genres (action, espionage, sci-fi, the political thriller, etc.) and well-hewn plots (escape, manhunt, investigation, criminal procedural, conspiracy etc.) have been adapted to the pretence of a surveillance society. What so many of these instances share – and what we find articulated in popular culture more generally – is the acknowledgment and affirmation of a new objective, namely, getting 'off the grid'. The discussion to follow ultimately traces the cine-social emergence of control 'along the lines' of this phrase. In commercial American cinema and television, where getting off the grid has become commonplace, if not cliché, perhaps no films have more profoundly shaped the idea or envisioned the problem of the control-grid, as I'll call it, than the five instalments of the Bourne franchise. Looking back to the first instalment in the series, *The Bourne Identity* (2002), I argue that the film both wittingly diagnoses and unwittingly symptomatises the challenges of the control-grid.

THE CONTROL-GRID

Though Deleuze borrows the term 'control' from William S. Burroughs, the 'Postscript on Control Society' properly responds to Michel Foucault. Deleuze had published his monograph on Foucault only three years before (1986), and where the book left off, the 'Postscript' resumes – looking to the future.[3] Thus, Deleuze situates his intervention in the aftermath of what Foucault had called discipline. 'Foucault associated *disciplinary societies* with the eighteenth and nineteenth centuries', he writes, and while this diagram stubbornly persisted long into the twentieth century, Deleuze insists that his friend 'also knew how short-lived this model was' (Deleuze 1995: 177). In other words, control designates the emergence of a new regime of power (or 'model'), and if we entertain the notion of a corresponding regime of images, it rests on a corresponding precedent.

Notably, Deleuze's monograph is largely oriented by the institutional and discursive histories that broadly define Foucault's middle career. The sovereign power to punish and execute gives way to the modern institutions (the hospital, clinic, school, factory, prison, etc.), discourses, techniques and practices that Foucault calls discipline. Partitioned and distributed, selected and segregated, ordered and determined, the individual is subject to a new and more subtle kind of violence ('discipline, the gentle way . . .'). What makes Deleuze's analysis unique is that, among other things, he meets the challenge of analysing and expressing disciplinary society with an altogether cinematic reply. Not only does Deleuze envision discipline along cinematic lines, as the disjunction of the audio-visual ('So it is not surprising that the most complete examples of the disjunction between seeing and speaking are to be found in the cinema' [Deleuze 1988: 64]); he attributes to cinema a critical and cartographic capacity commensurate to disciplinary society itself.

Thus, Deleuze recounts an episode from Rossellini's *Europa '51* (*The Greatest Love*) in which the bourgeois protagonist, Irene (Ingrid Bergman), agrees to fill in at a factory job (1989: 46). At the end of a shift, she catches herself watching the workers filing out. In that brief moment, in that interval, an idea takes shape: as Deleuze suggests, both Irene's train of thought and the train of montage precipitate, in cinematic terms, a kind of 'reflective judgment' (Kant). Thus, 'instead of subsuming images which naturally belong' to a given genre and determining the scene according to the coordinates of familiar category – workers, factory, capital, etc. – the sequence 'constitutes the limit of images which do not belong to it but are reflected in it' (Deleuze 1989: 184). At that limit, where the lines and singularities are loosened, Irene's utterance – 'I thought I was seeing convicts' – grasps the very diagram of discipline: 'the factory is a prison, school is a prison, *literally, not metaphorically*' (1989: 20; emphasis added). Moreover, Deleuze returns to this moment from Rossellini's film in the first paragraph of the 'Postscript on Control Societies' to trace, *pace* Foucault, the logic that threads its way through disciplinary milieus (1995: 177). This argument, which effectively maintains that discipline is both analogical and literal, seems to run the risk of contradiction unless we recognise that Deleuze has effectively re-conceptualised these terms at hand. Analogic is not defined by common measure, nor by rhetorical device, but by dint of the variable diagram that traverses institutions and discourses. Thus, when he says the factory *is* a prison, Deleuze is careful to qualify that he is speaking '*literally, not metaphorically*'.

But if the analogue technology of cinema is equal to the analogical diagram of discipline, as he seems to suggest, what happens when the latter begins to break down? The 'Postscript' is set amidst the crumbling of the disciplinary institutions (prisons, factories, clinics, hospitals, etc.) that we have come to associate with the dismantling of the welfare state.[4] Beyond the unravelling of the social safety net, however, control induces a metamorphosis of the geometry of power – or, rather, the invention of a new geometry of power, a new topology, a new brain. In Deleuze's words, 'instead of converging on a single, mysterious leader, inspirer of dreams, commander of actions, power was diluted in an information network where "decision-makers" managed control, processing and stock across intersections of insomniacs and seers' (Deleuze 1989: 265). Rather than concentrate power (in a sovereign) or distribute it (in social institutions), control decentralises power into smooth spaces and disseminates power into supple, digital lines of force. The ambit of communication and information is extended along 'continuous range of different orbits' that give rise not only to a presentiment of open horizons but to a new sense of unimpeded mobility. '*Surfing* has taken over from all the old *sports*', Deleuze writes in the 'Postscript' (1995: 180). One suspects that Deleuze would have regarded 'surfing the internet', a phrase coined just two years later, as confirmation of control society. Whether in space or cyberspace, we are ostensibly liberated, released into a frictionless space of boundless movement that is extending along an endless wave of searches, agreements, purchases – of *choices*. In pointed contrasted to modern, disciplinary societies, which aggregated and segregated individuals in so many 'analogical' sites ('the factory is a prison, the school is a prison . . .'), control societies develop 'inseparable variations, forming a system of varying geometry whose language is *digital*' (Deleuze 1995: 178).

Under control, the moulds of discipline that had aggregated masses and individuated subjects give way to the smooth space of a digital domain on which we perpetually glide, 'moving among a continuous range of different orbits' (1995: 178). Segmentary functions cede to modulating surfaces of mobile milieu, and at first glance, naturally, control seems to offer the space in which to exercise limitless freedom. Control aspires to what we might think of as an open-floor plan: rather than 'operate by confining people' (1995: 174), control *promotes* circulation, inducing the movements with which freedom itself is increasingly identified – as the right to choose, to be oneself, an individual apart from all others. In space or cyberspace, uniqueness is encouraged and movement is induced. Why? In the first place, as we all know, movement is quickly monetised (e.g., toll roads, TSA pre-check, memberships, media access, internet speeds, digital roaming, etc.). But mobility has a secondary and arguably much greater cost inasmuch as it generates an endless fund of metadata. Phones, cars, computers, credit cards and countless 'smart devices' record our lives in real time, and now some corporations have begun to replace access cards and keys with digital chips that are implanted in one's forearm. With every movement, communication, purchase, text and choice – with every click – we contribute to the reservoir of metadata on which countless algorithms operate to produce search results, advertisements, offers, advance notices, payment reminders, traffic reports, weather alerts, etc. Today, the mobility makes us both the source of information and the object of analytics: our microhabits, inclinations, addictions – our metadata – form the basis on which algorithms work, predictive models are invented, and a fantastic new regime of *customised* power unfolds (the 'science' of marketing).

In this respect, I'd argue that the premise of control society is inextricable from the emergence of neoliberalism, and though Deleuze never uses the term, its post-Fordist logic suffuses the 'Postscript'. Surveillance, data harvesting and quantitative analytics have not been imposed (by governmental mandate) so much as they have been designed, marketed, incentivised and consumed under the auspices of a new brand of political economy. Significantly, Deleuze was largely unfamiliar with Foucault's lectures at the Collège de France, but I suspect he'd have been the first to acknowledge that Foucault's analysis of neoliberalism in the lectures from 1978–9 anticipates control society. In these lectures, collected as *The Birth of Biopolitics*, Foucault devises both a remarkable concept and equally remarkable process. This concept he calls a 'grid of intelligibility' (Foucault 2008: 252) – not a model but a modulating mould within which a given individual (Deleuze would say 'dividual' [1995: 182]) is calculated and configured. The corresponding process Foucault terms the 'optimalization of difference' (2008: 259). In relation to the framework within which the individual becomes legible, control encourages and even incentivises the expression of individuality and identity; the more refined the differences, idiosyncrasies and eccentricities, the more finely grained the grid of intelligibility. To those who would welcome the end of discipline and embrace control as if it offered unprecedented freedoms, Deleuze says, in so many words, be careful what you wish for. 'Compared with the approaching forms of ceaseless control in open sites, we may come to see the harshest confinement as part of a wonderful happy past' (Deleuze 1995: 175).

What do we mean by 'ceaseless control in open sites'? Both vast (even globalising) and capillary (even micro-political), control seems to envision a domain in relation to which there is no 'outside' (*dehors*),[5] and it's in this respect that we might understand the relatively recent ambition to get or go 'off the grid'. Over the past fifteen-odd years, the phrase has become a consistent refrain in popular culture and especially in Hollywood cinema. Notwithstanding its semantic range and valences, going off the grid is predominantly defined today by the prospect of disappearing without a trace – of slipping through the vast sieve (*crible*) of digital communications, surveillance and information. Thus, in action films, political thrillers, science fictions, comic book adaptions and countless procedural dramas, going off the grid has become *Zeitgeistig*. Beyond the obvious cases of action heroes on the run, the phrase now applies to geek hackers, criminal masterminds, witnesses in protective custody, gangsters, Mafioso, eccentric billionaires, compromised lawyers, spies and former spies, wanted individuals, abused spouses, and pretty much anyone falsely accused.

Still, this efflorescence represents a relatively recent turn in the context of a rather brief rhetorical history. As a recognised phrase, often marked by smart quotes, 'off the grid' first entered the lexicon in the early 1990s, when environmentalists and solar enthusiasts began to use it as shorthand for detaching themselves from the electrical grid. By the mid-1990s, the nomenclature had been co-opted by libertarians and fringe groups on the right whose distrust of government overreach charged the grid with paranoid significance. In detaching oneself from electricity, as well as other utilities and civic services, in moving to unpopulated areas and home-schooling one's children, and finally in severing the 'umbilicus' to the state, going 'off the grid' came to constitute an assertion of sovereignty and natural right.[6] The subsequent transformation – the digitalisation – of the grid owes, if not its origins, then surely its imagination, elaboration and popularisation to Hollywood cinema. As digital effects became increasingly common in commercial cinema of the 1990s, a number of Hollywood films (especially high-tech ones) began to channel anxieties about the scope and dangers of computer technology. This clever fusion, paranoia inspired by and envisioned with digital technology, had underwritten the earlier landmarks of digital effects, *Terminator 2* and *Jurassic Park*, and as the decade wore on the threat of technology was increasingly and specifically focused on the spectre of digital tyranny and totalising surveillance (e.g., *The Net* [1995], *Virtuosity* [1995], *The Truman Show* [1998], *Enemy of the State* [1998], *The Matrix* [1999], etc.).

Nevertheless, only with the release of *The Bourne Identity* (2002) did going off the grid acquire the sense to which we are accustomed today. Whether or not this is the first such instance in cinema (I haven't found an earlier one), the film and the franchise it launched have profoundly shaped the idea of the grid – in no small part by regarding it as an extension of the American security state. Deployed in all five Bourne films (and even more prominently in Tony Gilroy's scripts), the phrase describes the condition to which Bourne must aspire: 'All that matters is staying alive. You get off the grid, survive.' It goes without saying that getting off the grid no longer plausibly refers to the socio-physics of living apart but articulates the problem of making oneself vanish from the vast digisphere, the global recording milieu that is rapidly swallowing the earth. The premise ('going off') already implies a techno-social order in which the reach of media, communications and data processing has become immense and micro-political, immediate and invisible ('the grid'); the conceit is so frequently evoked, deployed and narrativised precisely because its plausibility is rapidly diminishing. In this vein, I'll suggest, the Bourne films produce a critical diagnosis of the control-grid at the same time as they symptomatise that same grid.

RE: BOURNE

'We don't have to stray into science fiction to find a control mechanism that can fix the position of any element at any given moment', Deleuze writes in the 'Postscript' (1995: 181), and we'd do well to keep this is mind as we consider the Bourne series. Loosely based on Robert Ludlum's best-selling novels, the Bourne saga effectively begins when the protagonist, unconscious and barely alive, is fished out of the Mediterranean by a passing trawler. One of the crew, a journeyman doctor, cuts away Bourne's wetsuit to find two bullets in his back and, later on, a microchip implanted in his hip. These matters are not resolved when Bourne wakes up: he cannot remember his name, his previous life, or even his tastes. More remarkable still, the amnesiac cannot explain his heightened faculties, physical capacities, martial arts, technical ingenuity and almost unfailing tactical intuition.

We soon learn that Bourne is the product of a secret CIA/DOD project to psycho-pharmacologically, biochemically and genetically engineer a new 'breed' of super-spies. In spite of the futuristic premise, or perhaps because of it, the Bourne films characteristically insist on depicting a world that, politically, culturally and technologically seems a great deal like our own. Admittedly, the fourth and fifth instalments – an abortive spin-off (*The Bourne Legacy*) and then Bourne's disappointing return (*Jason Bourne*) – have made more ample use of high-end digital technology, not only in the set design but also as the means to produce special effects. By contrast, the original trilogy succeeded, both critically and financially, by resisting the large-scale recourse to CGI that was already ubiquitous in Hollywood in the early 2000s. Even when the focus of the narrative shifts from the amnesiac's oblivion to the boardrooms, offices and data bunkers of Langley, where the search for the missing agent is already underway, the milieus are drab, nondescript and anonymous. Even by the standards of audiences in 2002, the film's representation of technology was familiar and underwhelming. Compared to the capacious war rooms, command centres and information processing units to which Hollywood has given rise since *Dr. Strangelove*, the operations bunker in *The Bourne Identity* is a low-ceilinged, windowless room crowded with bulky computer monitors, electronics, cheap book cases, stacked binders and scattered papers. Far from straying into futurism, *The Bourne Identity* is at once 'high concept' and seemingly 'low tech'.

For all that, *The Bourne Identity* unfolds something like the 'reticulation' (Simondon) of technologies – computers, databases, networks, cell phones, GPS, etc. – that begin to express the scope of this control-grid. The ostensible modesty of the operations bunker is belied by the assemblage to which it belongs, the instruments of communications, tracking and surveillance, of incomprehensibly vast data harvesting and data-mining, no less the computational power to process this wealth of information, to develop robust analytics and to make specific predictions. Thus, we return to *The Bourne Identity* because, apart from the series it launched, it's among the first films to reckon with the reality of the control-grid – not as a possible future or an alternate reality but as the world itself. Specifically, *The Bourne Identity* elaborates three discrete, albeit related, definitions of the grid with which we can trace the emergence of control. The grid is (1) a map qua strategic space of operations; (2) a unit of (access to) information or the integration of available units; and (3) a vast digital sieve within which one's life can be tracked, one's history – in space or cyberspace – can be accessed, and one's decisions can be predicted (or predictably manipulated). These three definitions of the grid are evoked at various points in *The Bourne Identity*, but in adumbrating this particular sequence we begin to grasp the techno-logic of control.

The first and most straightforward sense of the grid is cartographic. In pursuit of Bourne, the CIA operations officer who oversees Treadstone, Alexander Conklin, presses his team into action: 'Let's get a map up here. Come on, folks. Work it.' Notably, in Tony Gilroy's screenplay, the line reads, 'Let's get a grid map up here.' Likewise, later in the script (though not in the film), Conklin says, 'Our last sighting [of Bourne and his companion Marie] was forty-eight hours ago. Even if they stayed in the car, the grid is huge.' In these instances, obviously, map and grid are interchangeable terms, and this equivalence has a well-established precedent. The US military began the practice of gridding maps before World War II, and after the war the use of the grid became a piece of military vernacular. Needless to say, the nature of war has been radically transformed in the intervening years. Likewise, the idea of a delimited grid map, traditionally composed of surveillance, communications and strategy, eventually began to embrace the ambitions of global design. Satellite-based geo-location and navigation had been a strategic objective of the US military (in conjunction with DARPA) since the early 1960s, but when the Department of Defense embarked on the project, in 1973, the creation of a geosynchronous communications system began in earnest. The Defense Navigation Satellite System (DNSS) eventually comprised the twenty-four satellites that made the first generation of GPS operational (in 2000, the US made GPS commercially available; by 2020, four separate such satellite systems – American, Russian, European and Chinese – will be operative).

The earth is rapidly being gridded, cocooned by an invisible filigree of communications and surveillance in which Bourne now finds himself. Thus, when Conklin's group gets a bead on Bourne, we are introduced to a second, more technical sense of the grid: as the Treadstone analysts pore over the new data, one of them announces, 'We're getting grids. Airline, train, hotels.' The provenance of this usage is confirmed later on, in *The Bourne Ultimatum*, when a CIA task chief officer, Pamela Landy, is asked to resume pursuit of the rogue agent (she'd directed the operation against him in *The Bourne Supremacy*). Ushered into the 'grid room'[7] at the CIA, Landy brusquely asks the dozen or so analysts about Bourne's 'last fixed position' and 'status'. Their answers – he's alive, at large, possibly armed – leave her unsatisfied. 'Where are your grids coming from?' Landy asks. 'NSA Tactical', another replies. To appreciate what this means – indeed, to understand the second definition of the grid – we ought to acknowledge the degree to which the Bourne films mirror the contemporaneous consolidation of the security state. The films generally hew to the protocols, practices and nomenclature of what we know about national intelligence – above all, that the CIA, which is legally prohibited from undertaking massive data collection, relies in large part on National Security Agency ('NSA Tactical') for its surveillance data ('grids').

In this context, Landy's next question – 'You have an Echelon package?' – not only confirms the second meaning of the grid (i.e., access to a unit, or units, of data) but, in the same stroke, presages the third and final sense of the term. The reference to Echelon is borrowed from a long-standing and highly classified intelligence programme. Dating back to the 1960s, but only officially formalised in the early 1980s, Echelon designated a programme in signals intelligence (SIGINT), jointly operated by Australia, Canada, New Zealand, the UK and the US, to monitor the military and diplomatic communications of the Soviet Union and Eastern Bloc. Over the last thirty-odd years, especially with the end of the Cold War, the programme's directives have shifted and its reach grown. In 2001, a European Parliament report bluntly referred to Echelon as 'a global system for the interception of private and commercial communications',[8] and the Bourne films effectively adopt this definition. Thus, we arrive at the third sense of the grid – the one with which, rhetorically, most are familiar. Later in *The Bourne Identity*, when Treadstone discovers that Bourne has acquired a companion, a young bohemian named Marie, an analyst admits: 'It's tough, the girl's a gypsy. I mean, *she pops up on the grid here and there*, but it's chaotic at best.' As Treadstone begins a deep dive into Marie's past – bills, work history, taxes, cell phone records, the collateral records of anyone with whom she's been in contact, etc. – the full sense of the control-grid takes shape. No longer a map, nor even a volume of surveillance data, the control-grid aspires to 'comprehensive coverage' in which virtually everything will be recorded, archived and analysed. With its definite article, *the* grid asserts an authority that goes beyond any one grid (in the Bourne films, the CIA draws on several grids – most prominently, the NSA's, but the Defense Department and Liberty Crossing grids are also accessed) to designate what the head of cyber-ops at the CIA calls 'full spectrum surveillance', that is 'watching everyone all the time'.

The first intimations of the control-grid appear when Treadstone confirms that Bourne is alive and in Zürich. The bunker is dramatised in a flurry of camera movements that finally come to rest on a black and white image from a time-lapsed surveillance camera – Bourne, crossing the street, a bag slung over his shoulder. Quiet disbelief briefly fills the room (a voice off-screen gasps, 'unreal . . .'). The camera pans to frame Conklin, in the foreground and facing left, though the focus rests on his deputy; sitting in the recesses of the image, sitting in an adjacent office, the deputy emerges from a phone call to report: 'Zürich police are looking for an American man carrying a red bank bag.' In the sliver of a moment between this sentence and the next – 'He just tore up the embassy, and he put two cops in the hospital last night'– the world perceptibly shifts. When the film cuts back to Conklin, in the precise interval between the two sentences, we have already crossed a threshold: breaking the axis of action established to the point, the camera frames Conklin from the other side of the room, so that he appears to have literally reversed position. 'Get everybody up', he snarls. 'Do it now. I want them all activated.'

With a few keystrokes, we are shuttled into a critical montage sequence. The dialogue quickly becomes inaudible, yielding to the film's distinctive score, punctuated by an electric guitar's metallic reverberations to which the *décalage* of images is synchronised. Shots of an analyst, typing, give way to the screen itself, divided into tables of information. At the top, it reads:

AGENT VAN NOSTRUND/PASSWORD XX9891
ACTIVATE AGENT CONTACT: GRID SECTOR 43A
LOCATION OF ALL AVAI—

The film cuts to a close-up of the text, the remainder of the status report spilling out: '—LABLE AGENTS IN LOCATION'. The screen flashes to white, as if this were something between a cinematic dissolve and a web page reloading, to reveal: 'CODE: PROFESSOR 8933489CHIMP/INITIATED'. After Conklin and his deputy trade concerned looks, we return to the computer screen, which has now become a digital map of Europe, conveyed in quick cuts traversing the continent; at last, the widescreen map hones in on a red rectangle framing a coastal area in Northern Spain: 'LOCATING BARCELONA'. Thus, as if 'BARCELONA' had been clicked, the red rectangle expands, filling the frame like a window opened on a desktop. The digitally animated red tint quickly dissolves to reveal an aerial shot of the city (Gaudí's iconic cathedral in the distance), followed by increasingly specific location shots (each featuring the cathedral) until we are ushered into an expensively furnished apartment. A bespectacled man is giving a piano lesson. Amidst the film's score, which drowns out the student's practice, we nevertheless hear the teacher's phone buzzing. He pulls it out, revealing the text: 'PREP MODE AND ARM READY FOR TRANSPORT / HOLD PATTERN UNTIL FURTHER NOTICE'.

Surely the most obvious instance of digital effects in the trilogy, this sequence is, however, exceptional – both inevitable and endemic. Venturing to convey the digital reach of the grid, the film makes use of not only the resources of digital effects but, also, the model of the computer: the frame becomes a digital interface and, then, a film screen once more. Thereafter, with some degree of variation, the sequence follows the same message sent to the other two agents. In each case, the computer screen furnishes the artificial window of a windowless room, the digital aperture through which we pass, following the communiqué to its cellular destination, whereupon the agents – 'Professor' in Barcelona, 'Manheim' in Hamburg and 'Castel' in Rome – are activated. The sequence converts the distances – not merely the cartographic scope but the telemetry of the data – into aerial perspectives: these are not 'establishing shots' of the respective cities so much as they suggest the pathway of digital information, routed by satellite, directed at men in the midst of otherwise unrelated circumstances (a piano lesson, a business meeting and a man riding a moped).

In the course of this sequence, and in the context of *The Bourne Identity*, perhaps we can re-read the three designations of the grid, with which this section began, as aspects of control society ('control-grid'). Thus, we defined the grid as a (1) a map qua strategic space of operations; (2) a unit of (access to) information or the integration of available units; and (3) a vast digital sieve within which one's life can be tracked, one's history – in space or cyberspace – can be accessed, and one's decisions can be predicted (or predictably manipulated). In view of control, however, I think we begin to understand this logic inversely, so that we begin (3) with a hyper-receptive surface (*crible*) on which our movements, actions, addictions and habits are surveilled and recorded;

proceed to (2) an archive or aggregate of information that can be traversed, analysed and mined; and conclude with (1) a global tactical and communications network within which possibilities are entertained, risks assessed, predicates made, events orchestrated, orders conveyed and assets arrayed.

THE PHANTASM OF CONTROL

Nevertheless, we'd be foolish to deny that the success of the first three Bourne films consists in large part in the way that the resources of the CIA – and of the control-grid more broadly – are outwitted by material cleverness and overcome by old-school action. While Bourne possesses advanced technological expertise – sufficient, at least, to be able to get around walls of encryption – we're more likely to encounter his strokes of ingenuity in low-tech endeavours. In each film, as analysts search for signs of the rogue agent and labour to anticipate his next move, Bourne's strategy relies on an older, often audacious, kind of spycraft, on more rudimentary tools, and on a re-dedication to physical space. Whereas Treadstone and subsequent projects conduct business at a distance, with digital media and through proxies, Bourne unfailingly turns the tables by risking physical proximity and even *intimate* encounters with his adversaries. It's a narrative principle of the Bourne films that, in returning to the scene of past events or to the site of his genesis, the protagonist confronts his architects qua enemies in the flesh. The global scope of the trilogy is, as a rule, decided on a human scale.

The apotheosis of this logic, and arguably Bourne's signatory gesture, lies in turning the tables on his adversaries within the CIA – above all, it consists in those occasions when Bourne spies on those who purport to pursue him. In *The Bourne Supremacy*, as the CIA scours Berlin for the rogue agent, he calls Landy on a cell phone from a nearby rooftop. With a hand-held telescope he watches her, behind the anamorphic windows of a skyscraper, in the sudden stillness of the CIA's operation centre: the entire office pauses in silence as Landy negotiates with Bourne, Ward Abott gesticulating and muttering to her in the background. The presumption, of course, is that with respect to Bourne, the ostensible target, the CIA itself, is 'off-screen'; but when Landy stalls at the suggestion of a certain contact person, Nicky Parson (they'll need time to find her, get her on a plane to Berlin, etc.), Bourne's reply – 'Why? She's standing next to you' – confirms not only his perspective but the agency's unwitting exposure. Bourne pulls versions of this stunt numerous times over the series. Why? Even as the CIA determines to turn its digital resources on him, Bourne's success, in these moments of audio-visibility, lies in a more primitive (and entirely less expected) *modus operandi*. With a telescope and phone, Bourne becomes a kind of theatre in whom the wide-screen windows of the CIA offices and the soundtrack of the cell phone are synchronised. No doubt Bourne 'directs' a great deal of the action in the films, but at these remarkable moments Bourne assumes a kind of cinematic subjectivity.

No doubt, *The Bourne Identity*, *The Bourne Supremacy* and *The Bourne Ultimatum* were so satisfying because they ventured the futuristic conceit on the basis of a set design, style and ultimately a subject that seemed, cinematically, 'old school'. Critics hailed the first film as a refutation of the excesses of digital technology and the trilogy as a retort to the dominant logic of action blockbusters. *The Bourne Identity* was released in the wake of a wave of films – above all, *The Matrix* (1999) and *Crouching Tiger, Hidden Dragon* (2001), but also the first *Harry Potter* and the first *Lord of the Rings* instalment (both 2001) – that brought computer-generated imagery to bear on human movement, often in order to defy gravity itself. As if in response to this impulse, the Bourne trilogy compulsively returns to *factum brutum* of falling. The saga begins when Bourne plunges into the sea, and in the span of the first three films he plummets down a five-storey stairwell, crashes off a bridge, drives off an elevated parking structure, and finally dives from the roof of a multi-storey building into the East River.

But even if the Bourne trilogy roots its realism in the implacable violence of gravity, the action-images themselves are not in fact old school (or, rather, the term is both too simple and superficial to account for the action). Without entirely eschewing digital effects, the three films are nonetheless designed to give this appearance, that is to appeal to a visceral and kinetic authenticity. Admittedly, this quality became more pronounced when Paul Greengrass took over the franchise (he has directed every film after *The Bourne Identity*, with the exception of *The Bourne Legacy*). Whereas the original director, Doug Liman, established a formal economy commensurate to Bourne's lethal efficiency, Greengrass' style, marked by the immediacy of a hand-held camera and the disjunction of abrupt cuts, is at once more concrete and less meticulous; he depicts his protagonist's survival, investigation and vengeance with gritty, at time messy, and always violent sobriety. Of course, it's precisely at those moment when circumstances shift or plans go sideways, when Bourne is forced to improvise, that his programming kicks in, his array of faculties awaken, and his ingenuity – a resourcefulness that is as much strategic as it is athletic – snaps into action. Whatever ordinary objects are at hand (a pen, a magazine, a book, a dead body, toiletries, cars, etc.), Bourne makes them instruments equal to extraordinary situations.

In this respect, the Bourne films consistently juxtapose what Bourne can do, seemingly without reflection, and what he cannot remember, no matter how much he reflects. He can tie nautical knots ('I found the rope and I did it'), read and write, add and subtract, but he cannot say what kind of music he likes. Whereas Bourne's memories will take years (and, at present, four films) to return, his strategic abilities and innate expertise come back online almost immediately – it just remains for Bourne to discover what his body and brain can do. The first signs appear upon his arrival in Zürich. Sleeping on a park bench at night, he is accosted by two Swiss policemen who ask (in German) for his papers. Though disconcerted, he not only understands the request but, after replying in English ('I lost my papers'), he repeats himself in crisp German (over the course of the trilogy, Bourne also speaks French, Dutch, Italian, Spanish and Russian). The slight flash of surprise that crosses his face is replayed, a moment later, when one of the officers presses a nightstick against Bourne's chest. To say 'he' reacts would not be quite accurate: when he grips the end of the baton, something – some automatism – in him reacts. Once more, a glint of astonishment passes over his face before Bourne proceeds to decimate the policemen with furious grace. The affective interval, the moment of reflection between perceived situation and effective response, has been overridden by the protocols of the action-image that are internalised by Bourne and externalised by the film. The sensory-motor schema that traditionally governed action is not abandoned so much as it is 'upgraded'; reborn or rebooted, Bourne lacks long-term memory, but he retains a deeply ingrained programming, an automatism that vehicularises Bourne's brain and body, extending into knowledge, strategy, habit and instinct.

Thus, Bourne's is the story of a man who 'finds himself' in two different senses. The first is the sense in which, stricken with amnesia, he's compelled to recover his past and, thence, to confront it. Notwithstanding this narrative of discovery and redemption, however, *The Bourne Identity* also furnishes a second (less clichéd, more modest) sense of phrase inasmuch as the protagonist seems to constantly 'find himself' doing things that he did not know he could do at all. Notwithstanding the trauma from which he suffers, there's a sense in which Bourne seems to have been re-born, so to speak, on third base. He retains (re-discovers) his powers without having to pay their full price, to bear the full moral weight of what he's done: if anything, he exercises his powers in the course of moral vengeance. To be sure, *The Bourne Supremacy* depicts the protagonist's work of atonement: in images and fragments, Bourne begins to recall his first assignment, a botched assassination in which he killed both the Russian target and his wife. To remove suspicion, Bourne stages the scene to make it look like a murder-suicide, and it's in this context that he returns, years later, to tell the couple's orphaned daughter the truth about what happened. But inasmuch as he responds to the salience of this memory, the series tends to gloss the more far-reaching question of Bourne's complicity – to dissociate from a past whose enhancements he still enjoys. In a sense, Bourne is not responsible for his past because he never is, nor was, really 'himself'. Suffering from amnesia, he cannot remember his 'jobs' for Treadstone, but Treadstone itself was a mind-altering project. When he signed on, Bourne agreed to give up his past and even his real name (David Webb). He was re-conditioned, re-programmed and seemingly brainwashed before he ever suffered memory loss.

Moreover, the security state that creates Bourne is a much different assemblage than earlier generations of espionage networks. While spy novelists of the 1970s and 1980s such as Ludlum, John le Carré and Len Deighton were cynics of a sort, wary about the corporatisation of intelligence, their plots still revolved to a large extent around agents, handlers, spies, freelancers, mercenaries, etc. Espionage was still a 'trade' or 'craft' to be practised, and a network still principally referred to a constellation of individuals. Such 'human relations' stands in stark contrast to the conception of 'human resources'– the field of neoliberalism, human capital and risk assessment – in which the Bourne franchise travels. In the films, programmes (like Treadstone) compete for funding, answering not only to superiors and congressional committees but to cost–benefit analyses. Bourne himself is an 'asset', programmed to follow the 'protocols' of his 'behavioral software', but when he fails to fulfil his mission and disappears, his value (and potential liability) is quickly and coldly reappraised. What the intelligence community calls 'threat assessment' consists in weighing the risk Bourne poses, both locally and long term (i.e., the exposure of Treadstone itself), against the potential rewards of 'bringing him in'.

Far from diminishing over the series, however, the enticement to bring Bourne home actually increases with each film. Bourne is 'special', the programme's most successful agent, its acknowledged prodigy. Escaping the CIA and enacting his own revenge at their expense, Bourne is – ironically – the best possible advertisement for Treadstone. Indeed, the film delights in the very effects of a cause it is determined to critique: whatever has left Bourne an amnesiac has also endowed him with powers, at once physiological as well as intellectual, that make him capable of resisting control, going off the grid and even exposing military intelligence projects like Treadstone. In this light, Bourne's triumph ought to leave us suspicious – not because he succeeds but, rather, because success itself, getting off the grid, has become unimaginable apart from for those who are preternaturally gifted, 'more than human'.[9] Consider that, on the one hand, the films elaborate the increasingly pervasive and insidious systems of surveillance, information mining and analytics that paradigmatically define control societies. If anything, Bourne's experience compels us to confront how little space is beyond the reach of the control-grid. On the other hand, the premise of every last film in the series is that the protagonist is capable of evading and outwitting his adversaries. With respect to the control-grid, then, the Bourne films are at once diagnostic and symptomatic: while the elaboration of the control-grid offers a pointed critique of the security state, the films retain the fantasy of an outside. Bourne's exceptionalism secures the idea of going 'off the grid' even as it confirms that the objective is, if not impossible, then practically superhuman.

Thus, when Deleuze insists that '[w]e don't have to stray into science fiction to find a control mechanism that can fix the position of any element at any given moment', we should understand him to mean that, insofar as the present has become a kind of science fiction, the outside has effectively evaporated. Today, inasmuch as the coordinates of virtually anything on earth can be ascertained, going off the grid finally confronts something like its own impossibility. But where the Bourne trilogy retains the fantasy of an outside, we might conclude by turning to the fitting (if unofficial) sequel to these three films – *Citizenfour*. Laura Poitras' riveting documentary, devoted to NSA contractor Edward Snowden, begins (eerily enough) when the film-maker herself is contacted. Snowden introduces himself not by giving his own name and references but, instead, by providing Poitras with frighteningly detailed accounts of her life. But if the information legitimises Snowden and suggests the stakes of his potential revelations, the vast extent of the surveillance also dictates the altogether paranoid precautions that one must *reasonably* adopt ('assume your adversary is capable of one trillion guesses per second'). Minutes later, we're shown a computer screen on which a 'GPG' – an email and file encryption program – is run. At first the encrypted (or 'PGP') text rapidly unscrolls, after which it appears, decrypted, as Poitras reads the message. As she continues, this text gives way to 'U.S. Customs and Border Protection logs' describing Poitras' own travel (where she went, why, what was in her bags, what did she say). One log reports that 'DURING QUESTIONING SUBJECT POITRAS TOOK EXTENSIVE NOTES AND RECORDED THE NAMES OF INTERVIEWING OFFICERS' – only to add that these same documents were photocopied by authorities. Over these logs, she reads Snowden's sobering warning:

> For now, know that every border you cross, every purchase you make, every call you dial, every cell phone tower you pass, friend you keep, article you write, site you visit, subject line you type, and packet you route is in the hands of a system whose reach is unlimited but whose safeguards are not.

As we now know, in part as the result of Snowden's leaks, the NSA surveillance programme in question, 'Stellar Wind', relies on data-sharing agreements with telecommunications corporations; what ought to be added is that those corporations, and countless others, are collecting and analysing our metadata (indeed, with the end of net-neutrality in the US, internet providers will be able to *sell* that data). Political campaigns now appeal to us for contributions using roughly the same algorithms with which Amazon makes personal recommendations, or Google selects particular ads, or the NSA flags particular phone calls. Indeed, the control-grid is already so deeply woven into the fabric of existence that we're bound to return to Deleuze's conclusion: 'It's not a question of worrying or hoping for the best, but of finding new weapons' (1995: 178).

NOTES

1. See, for instance, Kittler's *Optical Media* (2010).
2. See André Bazin's essay, 'The Ontology of the Photographic Image', in *What Is Cinema?* (2005: 16).
3. See, especially, the appendix to *Foucault*, 'On the Death of Man and Superman', where Deleuze delivers a discourse on posthumanism (Deleuze 1988: 124–32).
4. In spite of this, Deleuze is never nostalgic. In his 'Postscript' he writes: 'We ought to establish the basic sociotechnological principles of control mechanisms as their age dawns and describe in these terms what is already taking the place of the disciplinary sites of confinement that everyone says are breaking down' (Deleuze 1995: 182).
5. See Deleuze 1989: 265.
6. The phrase, appearing in Philip Weiss' important article, 'Off the Grid' (1995), is attributed to James (Bo) Gritz. A libertarian and self-styled supremacist, Gritz casts himself as a kind of spokesman for a predominantly right-wing movement (Weiss is primarily writing about Northern Idaho). 'Off the umbilical' is, for Gritz, synonymous with off the grid.
7. The term is coined in Gilroy's script for *The Bourne Ultimatum*.
8. See http://www.europarl.europa.eu/sides/getDoc.do?pubRef=-//EP//NONSGML+REPORT+A5-2001-0264+0+DOC+PDF+V0//EN&language=EN
9. Beyond the Bourne films, the roster of those who have been forced to go off the grid includes John McClane (*Die Hard*), Ethan Hunt (*Mission Impossible*), Evelyn Salt, Lucy, Batman, Catwoman, Optimus Prime, James Bond, and virtually all of The Avengers.

BIBLIOGRAPHY

Bazin, André (2005), *What Is Cinema?*, trans. Hugh Gray, Berkeley: University of California Press.
Deleuze, Gilles (1986), *Cinema 1: The Movement-Image*, trans. Hugh Tomlinson and Barbara Habberjam, Minneapolis: University of Minnesota Press.
Deleuze, Gilles (1988), *Foucault*, trans. Seán Hand, Minneapolis: University of Minnesota Press.
Deleuze, Gilles (1989), *Cinema 2: The Time-Image*, trans. Hugh Tomlinson and Robert Galeta, Minneapolis: University of Minnesota Press.
Deleuze, Gilles (1995), *Negotiations*, trans. Martin Joughin, New York: Columbia University Press.
European Parliament Temporary Committee on the ECHELON Interception System (2001), *Report on the Existence of a Global System for the Interception of Private and Commercial Communications (ECHELON Interception System) (2001/2098(INI))*, http://www.europarl.europa.eu/sides/getDoc.do?pubRef=-//EP//TEXT+REPORT+A5-2001-0264+0+DOC+XML+V0//EN

Foucault, Michel (2008), *The Birth of Biopolitics: Lectures at the Collège de France, 1978–79*, trans. Graham Burchell, Basingstoke: Palgrave Macmillan.
Gilroy, Tony, *The Bourne Identity* (script draft), http://www.dailyscript.com/scripts/bourneidentity.html
Gilroy, Tony, *Bourne Supremacy* (script draft), http://www.dailyscript.com/scripts/bournesupremacy.pdf
Gilroy, Tony, *Bourne Ultimatum* (script draft), http://www.imsdb.com/scripts/Bourne-Ultimatum-The.html
Greenwald, Glenn (2014), *No Place to Hide: Edward Snowden, the NSA, and the U.S. Surveillance State*, New York: Metropolitan Books.
Keefe, Patrick Radden (2006), *Chatter: Uncovering the Echelon Surveillance Network and the Secret World of Global Eavesdropping*, New York: Random House.
Kittler, Friedrich (2010), *Optical Media*, trans. Anthony Enns, Cambridge: Polity.
Libicki, Martin (2001), *Who Runs What in the Global Information Grid: Ways to Share Local and Global Responsibility*, Santa Monica: Rand Publishing.
Ludlum, Robert (1981), *The Bourne Identity*, New York: Bantam Books.
Milner, Greg (2016), *Pinpoint: How GPS Is Changing Technology, Culture, and Our Minds*, New York: W. W. Norton & Company.
Simondon, Gilbert (2017), *On the Mode of Existence of Technical Objects*, trans. Cecile Malaspina and John Rogove, Minneapolis: Univocal Publishing.
Weiss, Philip (1995), 'Off the Grid', *The New York Times Magazine*, 8 January, pp. 24–33, 38, 44, 48–52, http://www.nytimes.com/1995/01/08/magazine/off-the-grid.html?pagewanted=all

CHAPTER 8

Towards a 'Minor' Fascism: Panoptic Control and Resistant Multiplicity in TV's *Spooks*

Colin Gardner

INTRODUCTION: VELVET FASCISM

In 'The Book', Season 4, Episode 5 of television's *Spooks*, journalist Gary Hicks (Douglas Hodge) witnesses the murder of Clive McTaggart (Andrew Burt), a retired high-ranking intelligence officer who was about to publish his memoirs, which contain highly sensitive government secrets. Determined to see the book published but fearing that unnamed members of British intelligence may be attempting to suppress it, Hicks turns to Harry Pearce (Peter Firth), an old friend of McTaggart's and the current head of Section D, MI5's counter-terrorism unit. Their conversation provides a concise summary of the show's perspective on contemporary control culture and its relation to both Foucault's biopolitics and Deleuze and Guattari's analysis of post-World War II micro-fascism as a maintenance of peace based on perpetual fear, 'giving any and everybody the mission of a self-appointed judge, dispenser of justice, policeman, the neighborhood SS man' (1987: 228):

> Hicks: He was getting more and more despondent about the way our political system's degenerated, you know. The lies, the spin, Iraq, the whole 'politics of fear' thing. Dirty bombs and all the other fantasies this government keeps coming up with to justify their existence and make themselves look like self-righteous heroes. He called it . . .
> Pearce: '. . . Velvet Fascism'. I know. Although I doubt the people of Manhattan would necessarily agree with you.
> Hicks: Please! 9/11 was the best thing that ever happened to you people.
> Pearce: The line between fear and complacency is a thin one.
> Hicks: But fear's much better when it comes to getting votes isn't it?

One is immediately reminded of Deleuze's oft-quoted statement on contemporary fascism in *Two Regimes of Madness*. Discussing accusations of anti-Semitism in Daniel Schmid's film, *Shadow of Angels*, Deleuze notes that old-style fascism (historically associated with Nazi Germany, Franco's Spain and Mussolini's Italy) looks positively quaint and folkloric in comparison to the current model:

> The new fascism is not the politics and the economy of war. It is global agreement on security, on the maintenance of a 'peace' just as terrifying as war. All our petty fears will be organized in concert, all our petty anxieties will be harnessed to make micro-fascists of us; we will be called upon to stifle every little thing, every suspicious face, every dissonant voice, in our streets, in our neighborhoods, in our local theaters. (Deleuze 2006a: 138)

Created by David Wolstencroft for Kudos Productions, the eighty-eight episodes of *Spooks* (a.k.a. *MI-5* in the US) aired on the BBC over ten seasons from 2002–11. Centred upon MI5's headquarters at Thames House in London (and more specifically Section D's secure suite of quarters known as 'The Grid'), the show habitually followed a 'Terror Threat of the Week' formula, whereby hostile forces from both outside the UK (Russia's Federal Security Service or FSB, Israel's Mossad intelligence network, Al-Qaeda, radical Muslim groups from Iran, Iraq, Syria, Turkey, Serbia and the former Soviet republics) and inside its borders (IRA remnants, right-to-lifers, eco-terrorists, anti-immigration racists and rogue military officers) pose a threat to British citizens through various devices, from dirty bombs and nuclear threats to political assassination and cyber-terrorism. Usually the main crisis, which stretches MI5, government and police resources to the limit, is a carefully planned diversion for another more serious attack that is disclosed in the final ten minutes, activating a race against time before all hell breaks loose. Significantly, the series makes little or no attempt to discriminate between terrorism and progressive anti-government resistance. Thus, potentially sympathetic left-liberal causes – with their affective and ethical (in a Spinozist sense) potentialities – such as environmental activism, post-human animal rights and anti-globalisation organisations, are tarred with the same 'anarchist' and 'terrorist' brush, framing them as one more dissident threat to be feared and eradicated. The show's writers thus place the audience in an uncomfortable position: we are encouraged to root for our MI5 heroes while at the same time deploring their complicit cooperation with panoptic government surveillance and global capitalist exploitation of the world's natural resources.

My aim in this chapter is not to work through this seeming contradiction dialectically (for example through a Brechtian distanciation of control culture through the use of MI5 as an affirmative alienation device) but rather to explore the complexities of this Velvet Fascism as a series of interlocking lines through which Section D acts as a kind of 'minor fascism' in relation to a majoritarian surveillance and security culture represented by both its so-called 'allies' – MI6, the CIA and government agencies such as The Joint Intelligence Committee (JIC) and the Government Communications Headquarters (GCHQ) – and by its traditional enemies – most notably the FSB, Russia's post-Cold War successor to the KGB. *Spooks* is a particularly rich example of the fluidity of these relationships and the show takes great pains to use the television medium itself as an expressive and analytical parallel to the surveillance technologies used by both sides. Thus, the framing effect of our home monitor sets up a *mise en abyme* with the multiple layers of surveillance screens within the diegesis itself, while watching the show on DVD gives us the ability to freeze frame, rewind and fast forward to observe details more closely, much like the computer-driven gadgetry used by the tech wizards at The Grid. The key question of course is whether this multiplicity of images is giving us the whole picture or just what 'they' (in terms of both the diegetic characters and the show's writers) want us to see – a key part of how Velvet Fascism's fear strategy works in the first place.

'MINOR' FASCISM AND FOUCAULT'S *DISPOSITIF*

My use of the term 'minor' fascism is, of course, an adaptation of Deleuze and Guattari's concept of minor literature in reference to the work of Franz Kafka and Samuel Beckett. According to Deleuze and Guattari, 'A minor literature doesn't come from a minor language; it is rather that which a minority constructs within a major language' (1986: 16). It is defined by three major characteristics: (1) A high degree of deterritorialisation: for example, Prague German (in the case of Kafka), or Irish English via French (Beckett); (2) Everything in minor literature is political: every individual or subjective intrigue connects immediately to politics, so that, for example, the Oedipal family triangle connects to other triangles – commercial, economic, bureaucratic, juridical (as in Kafka's *Metamorphosis*); (3) Everything takes on a collective value and enunciation so that literature is always the concern of the people, a pack or a multiplicity, whether literal or yet to come. 'We must be bilingual even in a single language', argues Deleuze in his *Dialogues* with Claire Parnet, 'we must have a minor language inside our own language, we must create a minor use of our own language' (Deleuze and Parnet 1987: 4).

Daniel Smith takes this even further, arguing that:

Minor languages are not simply sublanguages (dialects or idiolects), but express the potential of the major language to enter into a becoming-minoritarian in all its dimensions and elements. Such movements, to be sure, have their own political ambiguities, since they can mix together revolutionary aspirations with reactionary and even fascistic tendencies (archaisms, neoterritorialities, regionalisms). (1997: xlvii)

Following this literary model, MI5 would act as a kind of minor fascism – deterritorialising, becoming-minoritarian by connecting lines from a variety of societal milieu in order to create a fluid multiplicity of political and informational forces – against rigidly structured hierarchies of control that serve more majoritarian (read: reterritorialising) interests, such as strident nationalism (including the US), jihadist religious fundamentalism and the 'Controlled Holocaust' of limited nuclear war. Foucault's analysis of biopower and modern-day security systems is extremely relevant in understanding these reterritorialising tendencies and suggests how a minor fascism might be used to disclose and limit their more nefarious objectives from within.

In his series of lectures published as *Security, Territory & Population: Lectures at the Collège de France 1977–1978*, Foucault defined biopower as:

> the set of mechanisms through which the basic biological features of the human species became the object of a political strategy, of a general strategy of power, or, in other words, how, starting from the eighteenth century, modern Western societies took on board the fundamental biological fact that human species are a species. (Foucault 2007: 1)

Biopower works as a set of procedures which operate through three basic modalities of security. First, we have the legal or juridical mechanism, an archaic form of the penal order which was operable from the Middle Ages to the eighteenth century. This consisted largely of laying down a law and fixing a punishment, creating a binary division between what was permitted and what was prohibited. This was overcoded (note that it's not a successive and chronological sequence but rather an overlapping stratum) by the modern disciplinary mechanism, the main subject of Foucault's *Discipline and Punish*, whereby law comes to be framed by mechanisms of surveillance and correction. Finally, and this brings us into the realm of *Spooks* and control culture, we have the contemporary apparatus/*dispositif* of security, marked by new penal forms and a re-calculation of the advantages and costs of penalties and punishment. As Foucault explains, the dispositif is 'a thoroughly heterogeneous ensemble consisting of discourses, institutions, architectural forms, regulatory decisions, laws, administrative measures, scientific statements, philosophical, moral and philanthropic propositions – in short, the said as much as the unsaid. Such are the elements of the apparatus' (1977: 194). Instead of the old binary opposition between the permitted and the prohibited, the dispositif constructs an optimal mean or average alongside 'a bandwidth of the acceptable that must not be exceeded. In this way a completely different distribution of things and mechanisms takes shape' (Foucault 2007: 6). Under this regime the new equation is surveillance + diagnosis + classification = discipline as security.

Foucault outlines three main spatial features of the dispositif: sovereignty, discipline and security; whereby '... sovereignty is exercised within the borders of a territory, discipline is exercised on the bodies of individuals, and security is exercised over a whole population' (2007: 11). For our purposes it's important to note that Foucault sees the people not as a series of individuals or subjects but as a multiplicity, so that the specific space of security is largely concerned with setting up a milieu where a series of possible events might unfold and circulate within a given time and space, allowing for an open field of possibilities (and thus minimal damage to the *status quo*). Thus, for Foucault, 'it was a matter of organizing circulation, eliminating its dangerous elements, making a division between good and bad circulation, and maximizing the good circulation by diminishing the bad' (Foucault 2007: 18). In short, Foucault collapses the milieu into the dispositif to allow for maximum political contingency. His philosophy is thus pragmatic, functional and multiplicitous.

Spooks follows this Sovereignty–Discipline–Security triad quite faithfully although, as we shall see, it allows for a number of overlapping lines between them through an ever-changing network of macro- and micro-fascisms. Thus, Sovereignty is represented by HM Government, specifically in the form of the Home Secretary who, with the exception of the traitorous Nicholas Blake (Robert Glenister), usually represents official government policy and works in close liaison with MI6 and MI5's Section D. There are also ultra-paranoid extra-governmental secret organisations code-named 'Yalta' and 'Nightingale', molar fascisms geared towards future contingencies based on worst-case disaster scenarios. Discipline is meted out by GCHQ, the JIC – which, since the end of World War II has included the chief of the London station of the CIA, and the National Security Coordinator at the Cabinet Office. In addition to MI5, which is in charge of domestic surveillance, security in *Spooks* is divided between MI6 (overseas) and the CIA which, as far as the writers are concerned, is indistinguishable from the US Government's sovereignty and, through plausible deniability, is more than willing to carry out Washington's dirty work. As Foucault summarises the main elements of the dispositif:

> let's say then that sovereignty capitalizes a territory, raising the major problem of the seat of government, whereas discipline structures a space and addresses the central problem of a hierarchical and functional

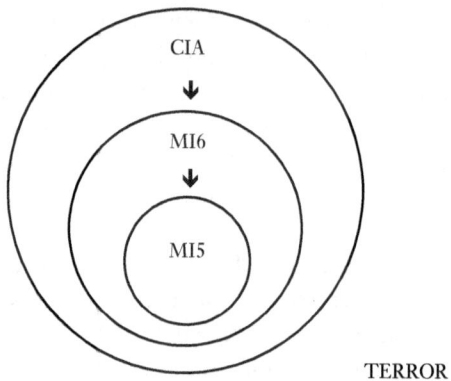

Figure 8.1

distribution of elements, and security will try to plan a milieu in terms of events or series of events or possible elements, of series that will have to be regulated within a multivalent and transformable framework. (2007: 20)

While MI6 condescendingly thinks of MI5 as junior league amateurs, the CIA are the show's ostensible villains as they ride roughshod over British territorial jurisdiction, kidnap British agents and extradite British nationals through extraordinary rendition. Indeed, in Season 8, rogue CIA agents are shown to be the prime movers behind 'Nightingale', a US-led plot to level the terrorist playing field through strategic nuclear war.

In this sense, we might diagram *Spooks*' security hierarchy as follows, with MI5 circumscribed and outranked by the larger spheres of influence of MI6 and the CIA as they take on global terror organisations, but acting as a minor resistance to both (Figure 8.1). However, it's important to note that these are fluid, not rigid demarcations lines. Deleuze is enormously helpful here in understanding Foucault's dispositif not only as lines of sedimentation but also in terms of fissures and fractures. In 'What is a Dispositif?' he describes his own idea of an apparatus:

First of all, it is a skein, a multilinear whole. It is composed of lines of different natures. The lines in the apparatus do not encircle or surround systems that are each homogenous in themselves, the object, the subject, language, etc., but follow directions, trace processes that are always out of balance, that sometimes move closer together and sometimes father away. Each line is broken, subject to *changes in direction*, bifurcating and forked, and subjected to *derivations*. Visible objects, articulable utterances, forces in use, subjects in position are like vectors or tensors. (2006b: 338)

The apparatus, through the distribution of variables by different curves (and the regimes of utterances they engender), thus makes provision for lines of flight, for minoritarian deterritorialisations, as part of its very nature. In this way, MI5's Section D is able to exploit cracks, breaks and ruptures as a means of mutating its own role within the assemblage. As Deleuze puts it, 'Untangling the lines of an apparatus means, in each case, preparing a map, a cartography, a survey of unexplored lands – this is what he [i.e. Foucault] calls "field work"' (2006b: 339) – a not inapplicable term for what spooks more generally call 'spycraft'.

CLASS AND DESIRE IN CONTROL CULTURE: FOUCAULT'S 'GOOD' AND 'BAD' CIRCULATION

One of the main strengths of *Spooks*' analysis of control culture is that although the show is committed to presenting the people as a fluid multiplicity, like the spy novels of John le Carré, it doesn't ignore traditional issues of class difference. This follows two separate but complementary lines. On the one hand, the show plays lip-service to a vertical, stratigraphic Marxist approach (MI5 as the poor cousin to MI6, the CIA and controlling government agencies). On the other it also follows Deleuze and Guattari's more libidinal analysis in *Anti-Oedipus*, where they raise the key question of why groups always tend to act against their own class interests. They correctly state that it's not a question of being fooled ideologically but rather that,

> It is a problem of desire, and desire is a part of the infrastructure. Preconscious investments are made, or should be made, according to the interests of the opposing classes. But unconscious investments are made according to positions of desire and uses of synthesis, very different from the interests of the subject, individual or collective, who desires. (1983: 104)

In other words, control culture doesn't lend itself well to a Marxist analysis – i.e., that the masses act against their own interests because they have been ideologically deceived – whereby false consciousness can always be cured by systematic consciousness raising. For Deleuze and Guattari, politics isn't a matter of ideology but of libido:

> We see the most disadvantaged, the most excluded members of society invest with passion the system that oppresses them, and where they always *find* an interest in it, since it is here that they search for and measure it. Interest always comes after. (1983: 346)

The key is to recognise the character of libidinal investments and then make them more revolutionary, a solution that *Spooks* makes manifest through the notable *absence* of the people as a libidinal agency so that MI5 must, in effect, 'speak' for them.

Let's explore a straightforward Marxist class analysis first, the better to undermine and complicate it later. Despite (or perhaps because of) its overseas intelligence role, MI6 has far more intimate ties with the government and seems to have a privileged status with the JIC. In 'Traitor's Gate' (Series 1, Episode 4), for example, we are introduced to Jools Siviter (Hugh Laurie), the MI6 Section Chief, who is conducting a joint operation with MI5's Section D through their shared asset, Peter Salter (Anthony Head), who has infiltrated anti-globalisation demonstrators linked to an anarchist terrorist group. The casting of Laurie, who had earlier co-starred with Stephen Fry in *Jeeves and Wooster*, brings out Siviter's Old Etonian, Oxbridge elitism and his condescension towards Harry Pearce and his team is clearly built on Wodehouse-ian class lines. Indeed, Laurie combines Bertie Wooster's propensity for being a hapless 'upper class twit' with Jeeves' more calculating, behind-the-scenes shrewdness to provide MI5 with a formidable foe with considerable reach into the corridors of power. In one scene, Siviter meets Pearce and his Senior Case Officer, Tom Quinn (Matthew Macfadyen) alongside the Thames by MI6's Central Headquarters at Vauxhall Cross. In the first two seasons, Tom Quinn is the show's leading character and holds a position of considerable responsibility. Siviter's flippant condescension towards him (as well as MI5 in general) is thus all the more remarkable given the official parity between the two organisations:

> Siviter [to Pearce]: And you've brought little terrier Tom along with you as a surprise. Good to see you Tom [. . .] I thought it might be rather jolly if we walked about a bit. Always gives one a bit of a frisson don't you find, going amongst the plebs talking of high state secrets. And if you're very good, I've got a bit of a treat for you.

At this point Siviter reprimands Pearce for bringing 'little Tom' along in the first place. 'It is my decision to use whatever officers I want', responds Pearce.

> Siviter: With respect, it is not your decision to make. Are we going to have to come over the river and potty-train all you people? MI6 runs operations abroad, MI5 at home. English Channel, Calais, foreign bods and Johnnies south, we take care. White cliffs of Dover, all British, Irish and assortments North, your concern.

Pearce argues that Salter is an MI5 undercover officer and therefore under his command. Siviter insists Salter was seconded to MI6.

Siviter: The operation concerns a foreign national, so we are *prima mobile*.
Quinn (uncomprehending): What?
Siviter: Oh Tom, you spoke. So good to see you working on your skills.

Significantly, in Season 1, Siviter's MI6 (which one case officer later refers to as the 'supercilious officer class') is less concerned with keeping MI5 in its place as a security 'underclass' than protecting its own interests against incursions by the CIA (who would be its natural 'enemy', as both are concerned with overseas security operations). However, once again the molecular lines are crossed as Siviter's men use Pearce's Section D for their own ends to unseat an 'undesirable' government minister. Thus in 'The Rose Bed Memoirs' (Season 1, Episode 5), a disgraced MP, Hampton Wilder (Tim Pigott-Smith) is released from prison after serving a sentence for embezzlement. However, Pearce quickly learns that while inside Wilder wrote his memoirs, which include details of a potential political bombshell: he and his fellow MP, fast-rising political star Richard Maynard (Nicholas Farrell) once performed illegal arms deals with the Arabs. To make things worse, the memoirs have mysteriously disappeared. Section D eventually discovers that MI6 stole the memoirs and Siviter reluctantly hands them over. It turns out that everything is a lie and that the memoirs are trash, concocted by MI6 in order to force Maynard's resignation. The latter, it turns out, is a CIA asset and as a government minister constitutes a severe security risk. So much for the so-called 'special relationship' – i.e., shared intelligence – between the US and Britain.

MI6 is a far more serious adversary in the opening two episodes of Season 5 ('Gas and Oil', Parts 1 and 2), necessitating a far more libidinal approach to class politics. Here, the social field is infused by an incommensurable desire as well as by commercial vested interests, so that Velvet Fascism and capitalism play on a diffuse network of unconscious complexes. In this case, Michael Collingwood (Nicholas Jones) joins forces with the former Ambassador to Russia, Sir Jocelyn Myers (John Castle), newspaper tycoon Paul Millington (Roger Allam) and other members of big business to stage a coup to take over the government, thereby re-aligning security, economic and informational micro-fascisms with an overcoding political sovereignty whereby the government and control society join forces. Using the rallying cry 'Djakarta is Coming', the group deliberately misdirects MI5's Section D into suspecting an Al-Qaeda connection. Their outrageous plan is to take over air traffic control and cause a mid-air collision between two passenger planes over central London, an act of terror so outrageously provocative that it would give the group the necessary leverage to coax the Prime Minister into giving them emergency powers (as well as garnering public support) for extreme security measures, including detaining citizens without trial and allowing armed police officers to shoot any protestors opposing the new policies.

The ideology of the plotters is made clear in an ultimatum showdown at a military intelligence bunker in Whitehall with Pearce, new Senior Case Officer, Adam Carter (Rupert Penry-Jones), National Security Coordinator Juliet Shaw (Anna Chancellor) and the Home Secretary, Nicholas Blake. For Pearce, who knew of MI6 involvement all along, the former Ambassador Jocelyn Myers is the final piece in the jigsaw: corporate power.

> Myers: The rules are different now, Harry. They changed the day a British government accepted Guantanamo Bay and admitted the torture chamber as an instrument of state policy.
> Juliet Shaw: But that wasn't enough for you?
> Myers: Britain needs a new kind of leadership.
> Collingwood: Sea levels are rising, oil's running out, terrorists are going nuclear. Do you really think this current system is capable of dealing with that?
> Pearce: Spare me the Four Horsemen of the Apocalypse. This is nothing to do with national security. Nothing to do with Al-Qaeda, either. This is a coup d'état, pure and simple.

Millington, the newspaperman, then plays the affect card, that extreme measures are necessary to protect our children's future. 'But there's no reason to dismantle our democracy', responds Shaw. Then it's a battle between macro- and micro-fascisms:

> Myers: I wonder why we fetishise democracy so much. It's a system that's a blink in the eye of history.
> Pearce: It's a system that better men than you have died to protect.
> Collingwood: Well I haven't seen anyone taking to the streets to defend it yet. And the argument against civil liberties has been fought and lost.
> Pearce: That's not for you to decide.
> Millington: You're assuming that people will notice the difference. You're assuming the British people actually care about abstract principles. They'll put up with anything as long as you serve it up with a picture of Will Young in the shower.
> Pearce: You insufferable snob. You're pronouncing on the national character while warming your feet at the club.

Just as Pearce underscores the class conflict at the heart of the crisis, Myers delivers his final ultimatum: the Prime Minister has a week to accept the new terms of government.

Millington's cynical observation that the people won't notice the difference between democracy and fascism when push comes to shove reinforces the key point, noted above, of why groups always tend to act against their own class interests, even in the extreme context of a coup d'état. 'Hence the goal of schizoanalysis', argue Deleuze and Guattari,

> to analyse the specific nature of the libidinal investments in the economic and political spheres, and thereby to show how, in the subject who desires, desire can be made to desire its own repression – whence the role of the death instinct in the circuit connecting desire to the social sphere. (1983: 105)

In the case of a revolutionary unconscious investment, desire cuts across the interests of both the exploiting *and* exploited classes and causes flows to break apart rigid segregations and reductive Oedipal applications. As a minor fascism, MI5 thus has the *libidinal* option of taking on the role of a deterritorialised outsider, a generator of micro-lines and breaks, nomadic and polyvocal. In short, it becomes a question of *circulation* rather than territory.

We see the beginnings of this more affirmative role in Section D's relations with the CIA These are altogether more complicated as the agency has no legal jurisdiction on British soil yet it persistently interferes in both MI5 and MI6 activities. This may be justified in 'Without Incident' (Season 2, Episode 6) when the CIA, in the form of MI5 liaison officer Christine Dale (Megan Dodds) must override Section D's authority in order to protect the president during George W. Bush's unscheduled visit to Britain. However, the writers have a largely jaundiced view of the so-called 'special relationship' between the US and the UK, which is made clear in 'The Deal' (Series 6, Episode 5) during a blunt conversation between Harry Pearce, Adam Carter and Bob Hogan (Matthew Marsh), the CIA's London station chief. Hogan is furious that an Agency investigation has been compromised by MI5 meddling:

> Hogan: You think we're stupid? You can steal classified CIA intel from under our noses with no repercussions?
> Pearce: We wouldn't have to steal it if you'd let us know what was going on.
> Hogan (laughs): You've been letting the politicians get to your head, Sir Harry. There is no special relationship. When you're useful you're useful, when you're not you're in the way.

Little has changed by Season 10. CIA Deputy Director Jim Coaver (William Hope) is kidnapped by MI5 under suspicion of attempting to derail trade talks between Russia and the UK. The Grid also suspect him of instigating the murder of Section D's Data Analyst, Tariq Masood (Shazad Latif), using a known CIA asset as their assassin. Coaver denies the accusation, but because the CIA have been painted as the 'bad guys' throughout the show's extended run we doubt his veracity. Because of this, the Agency becomes a useful blind or misdirection for other lines of flight and Coaver is later proved to be on the level: it turns out that a faction of Russian nationalists led by former MI6 asset (and Pearce's ex-lover) Elena Gavrik (Alice Krige) is behind the attacks and Tariq's murder. Nevertheless, Coaver's interrogation gives the writers a chance to sound off against US foreign policy:

> Coaver: Who do you think formulates CIA policy? Scooby-Doo? The only reason we give a rat's ass about your country is because you let it be a breeding ground for fanatics. Are we happy that you're cuddling up to the Russians? No, it's one more foothold in Europe for them. But if we wanted to stop you, we wouldn't have to resort to scare tactics to do it. That includes taking out your office boy.

Perhaps the most interesting episode involving the CIA is 'The Sting' (Season 4, Episode 9) because it discloses fracturing micro-lines and fissures within the Agency itself, a rare occasion when it is not uniformly tied to *official* Washington policy. Pearce is under direct pressure from the Foreign Office (via Juliet Shaw) to sanction the CIA's forced extradition of Louis Khurvin (Philip Arditti), a suspected Iranian terrorist who also happens to be a British citizen. Pearce, fed up with the government's pandering to CIA demands and convinced that MI5 has no interest in Khurvin as a potential risk, refuses to comply. This leads to a showdown between Section Chief, Adam Carter and the CIA's field officer, Alex Roscoe (William Armstrong) at a landing strip, just as Khurvin is about to be airlifted to Guantanamo:

> Carter: You're not taking him, Alex. As long as you're standing on this soil, you're under UK law.
> Roscoe: No, I'm under US law. And that allows us to pick up anyone who we believe to be a threat to our national security, anywhere in the world.
> [Pearce calls Roscoe to stop the extradition:]
> Pearce: You're missing the point. Whatever you're accusing him of, he's a British citizen, he still has rights.

After Kurvin is released, Pearce places him under surveillance, just to be on the safe side, but when he kills two MI5 surveillance officers the CIA and the Foreign Office are understandably incensed. Juliet Shaw places Pearce under suspension and takes over Section D herself, urging Carter to find Khurvin before he commits another act of terror.

At this point, the British Government and the CIA are acting in joint sovereignty over the country's own security forces. However, the CIA overplays its hand by providing photographic evidence that Khurvin attended a terrorist training camp the previous summer, but Carter doubts its veracity and it proves to be an extremely sophisticated Photoshopped fake. Eventually, the team discovers a direct link between Khurvin and an American businessman, Nick Pollard (Peter Vollebregt), who turns out to have expert counter-intelligence skills. Pearce contacts an old CIA cohort who believes that Pollard is a 'black ops' independent contractor: 'Nixon used to call them "The Horribles". Howard Hunt and Gordon Liddy [. . .] Freelancers. Deniables. You want something dirty done, you don't want to get bit on the ass down the road . . .' Does he have a CIA connection? 'They may have trained him but they don't own him anymore.'

This rogue line of flight is a useful asset with the US and Iran on the brink of war, especially if Washington wants British support for a pre-emptive strike. It turns out that Pollard is grooming Khurvin as his patsy, his very own Lee Harvey Oswald presented to the world's media, 'gift-wrapped in an Iranian flag'. Khurvin is to fire a surface-to-air missile against an inbound flight heading for Heathrow, the Iranians will be blamed and both the US and UK will have an excuse to go to war. Khurvin is shot in the nick of time, and Pollard is arrested. The episode ends with a return to the airstrip where Roscoe awaits the official extradition of Khurvin. Only this time the tables are turned. When Carter tells him that Khurvin is dead, having tried to commit a terrorist attack, Roscoe says it would never have happened if the CIA had been able to extract him in the first place. Yet Pearce explains that the real ringleader is Pollard, an American citizen held under the Prevention of Terrorism Act. 'If you want him back you'll have to go through the proper channels. In the meantime Alex, inform your superiors to put their own house in order before they even think about messing about in mine again.'

This episode is an excellent example of the overlap (and overcoding) of the old binary opposition between the permitted and the prohibited, represented by Section D's upholding the rights of Khurvin's British citizenship against extraordinary rendition by foreign powers, and the CIA's adherence to a more flexible 'bandwidth of the acceptable', Foucault's open field of possibility in which a series of uncertain elements unfold (2007: 6). The CIA (or, more specifically, its unofficial 'black ops' contingent in the form of Pollard), with its deliberate criss-crossing of boundaries and jurisdictions, thus operates in a way much closer to Deleuze's non-stratified space:

> 'When the outside collapses and attracts interiority,' the interior presupposes a beginning and an end, an origin and a destination that can coincide and incorporate 'everything.' But when there are only environments

and whatever lies between them, when words and things are opened up by the environment without ever coinciding, there is a liberation of forces which come from the outside and exist only in a mixed–up state of agitation, modification and mutation. (Deleuze 1988: 87)

Thus, while Pearce and MI5 attempt to control all circulations based on sovereign rights, the CIA uses its adopted milieu (London) as a classic dispositif, to promote what is generally desirable to the population (good circulation) while eliminating what is uncertain in a given situation (bad circulation). The apparatus/dispositif is thus invoked as a problem of security but it is also applicable to the problem of war: extraordinary rendition as the extension of war by other means (to paraphrase Clausewitz).

THREE FASCIST LINES: MOLAR, MOLECULAR AND SUICIDAL LINES OF FLIGHT

In terms of Deleuze's theory of lines, Pearce's commitment to the opposition between the permitted and the prohibited constitutes an attempt to return to the binary machine of the first of three lines, which is defined by molar segmentarity based on social classes, sexes, ages, territories and jurisdictions, 'In short, all kinds of clearly defined segments, in all kinds of directions, which cuts us up in all senses, packets of segmentarized lines' (Deleuze and Parnet 2007: 124). Deleuze's example of 'You're not at school anymore . . .' as a segmented rite of passage from adolescence into adulthood would in this case be something like, 'You're not on American soil anymore' or 'You're out of your league.' Of course it's not as simple as that because the overcoding objectives of the first line are constantly modified and criss-crossed by the other two lines, as the messy nature of modern espionage and its reliance on surveillance technology and computer codes makes clear. Thus, we have lines of molecular segmentarity (what Deleuze calls supple modifications), 'proceeding by thresholds, constituting becomings, blocs of becoming, marking continuums of intensity, combinations of fluxes' (Deleuze and Parnet 2007: 130). On this line, fluxes of deterritorialisation shoot between binary segments. There is never any synthesis as this molecular line disrupts all binarisms. Like Gregory Bateson's plateau, it traces another line that's always in the middle, or, thinking geopolitically, it's the North–South line of the Middle East and Africa that disrupts the old Cold War East–West axis, Deleuze's 'little crack coming from the South'.

Finally, we have the line of flight, an abstract molecular line with a tendency to always escape both segmentarity and becoming, creating mutant flows that defy ordering, as if something carried us away, across our segments, but also across our thresholds, towards a destination which is unknown, not foreseeable, not pre-existent. This line is simple, abstract, and yet is the most complex of all, the most tortuous: it is the line of gravity or velocity, the line of flight and of the greatest gradient . . . (Deleuze and Parnet 2007: 125)

Although the line of flight appears to arise in the wake of, and detached from, the other two lines it actually gives rise to them as a creative force. Lines of flight are primary: they constitute the social field to the point that the other lines are always derivative (on the one hand) but also immanently caught up with each another. 'What we call by different names – schizoanalysis, micro-politics, pragmatics, diagrammatism, rhizomatics, cartography', notes Deleuze, 'has no other object than the study of these lines, in groups or as individuals' (Deleuze and Parnet 2007: 125).

For our purposes, the key part of Deleuze's complex classification of lines is its relation to fascism and how *Spooks* plays out these characteristics as part of its mapping of control culture. In his Preface to *Anti-Oedipus*, Foucault lists the book's three main adversaries, pointing the finger at (1) Political ascetics – defenders of a pure order of politics; (2) Bureaucrats of the revolution, civil servants of Truth and poor technicians of desire – psychoanalysts and semiologists – subjugators of the multiplicity of desire to a law of structure and lack; and

> Last, but not least, the major enemy, the strategic adversary is fascism (whereas *Anti-Oedipus*' opposition to the others is more of a tactical engagement). And not only historical fascism, the fascism of Hitler and Mussolini – which was able to mobilize and use the desire of the masses so effectively – but also the fascism in us all, in our heads and in our everyday behavior, the fascism that causes us to love power, to desire the very thing that dominates and exploits us. (Foucault 1983: xiii)

However, it's important to acknowledge that Deleuze and Guattari's take on fascism evolves considerably in the passage from *Anti-Oedipus* to *A Thousand Plateaus*. In *Anti-Oedipus*' original diagnosis, 'The choice is between one of two poles, the paranoiac counterescape that motivates all the conformist, reactionary, and fascisizing investments, and the schizophrenic escape convertible into a revolutionary investment' (1983: 341). In *A Thousand Plateaus*, the paranoia-schizz binary has been replaced by a key distinction between totalitarianism and fascism. The former, which is quintessentially conservative, is always a state affair (typified by Stalinist Russia), constructing a relation between the state as a localised assemblage and the abstract machine of overcoding it effectuates. In contrast, fascism involves a war machine taking over the state which, when it has war as its sole aim, is inherently self-destructive. In this sense their theoretical source is 'a bizarre remark by Paul Virilio', whereby, as they put it, 'in fascism, the State is far less totalitarian than it is *suicidal*. There is in fascism a realized nihilism' (Deleuze and Guattari 1987: 230). Whereas the totalitarian state tries to seal off all lines of flight, fascism is constructed on an intense deterritorialisation which it transforms into a pure line of destruction.

Spooks is largely concerned with the inherent dangers of the second and third lines of fascism – the molecular and suicidal lines of flight – although its final season returns to a more macro (albeit modified), Stalinist Cold War model. However, it is important to note that it's not a question of examining these lines in isolation as they constantly connect, break and slip over into each other in multiplicitous ways. For example, the first, molar line of rigid segmentarity defines our relations with the state as a whole and all the devices of power working constantly on our bodies, particularly the abstract machines which overcode us in order to control our ways of perceiving and acting, our affects and the various regimes of signs and codes through which we make sense of the world. Most states oscillate between two extremes: the liberal state is an apparatus that directs and controls the abstract machine, while the totalitarian regime becomes indistinguishable from it. It's not a question of destroying the line because that would entail destroying ourselves. Instead, it must be made more supple:

> The prudence with which we must manipulate that line, the precautions we must take to soften it, to suspend it, to divert it, to undermine it, testify to a long labour which is not merely aimed against the State and the powers that be, but directly at ourselves. (Deleuze and Parnet 2007: 138)

In theory, this should be the role of the second, molecular line which sets up more mobile relations of force rather than concrete devices of power; using cracks and fissures instead of segregations. However, this line also contains an inherent danger, which Deleuze calls 'the black hole phenomenon':

> it is the supple lines themselves which produce or encounter their own dangers, a threshold crossed too quickly, an intensity become dangerous because it could not be tolerated. You have not taken enough precautions. This is the 'black hole' phenomenon: a supple line rushes into a black hole from which it will not be able to extricate itself. (Deleuze and Parnet 2007: 138)

Significantly, as Deleuze explains to Parnet, Guattari calls these micro-fascisms:

where each embeds himself in his own black hole and becomes dangerous in that hole, with a self-assurance about his own case, his role and his mission, which is even more disturbing than the certainties of the first line: the Stalins of little groups, local law-givers, micro-fascisms of gangs ... (Deleuze and Parnet 2007: 138–9)

There are numerous examples of black holes in *Spooks* and in most cases, as we shall see, they quickly slip over into the suicide line. A typical example can be found in the aforementioned 'Traitor's Gate', where Peter Salter, working undercover on a joint mission for MI5 and MI6 inside an anti-globalisation anarchist group, falls in love with Andrea Chambers (Bronwen Davies), one of the 'terrorists'. After his defection has been revealed, Salter is debriefed by Section Chief Tom Quinn, who inquires as to his motives. Salter, it seems, has fallen victim to the nihilistic 'black hole phenomenon', citing:

Salter: Boredom. Crippling, chest-tearing, bum-clenching boredom. With what this country's become. Buy. Sell. Image. Credit card nirvana. When the Soviet Union was crap we thought, yeah, we got something. My father died for it. Democracy. Now there's nothing. It's all gone, it's dead. No one believes in anything anymore. Then there was Andrea. This posh girl turning herself inside out for what she believes. A passion for a new life. It nearly broke her, but she's in good faith. I've always thought that about you, Tom. You're in good faith.

Although Quinn is convinced that Salter's 'new anarchist faith' was a strategic feint to go further undercover, his motives are based on genuine affect, a certainty for the cause that ultimately leads to an inexorable line of flight to oblivion. As Deleuze points out, it's okay to have the prudence of the experimenter, 'but it is a disaster when they slip into a black hole from which they no longer utter anything but the micro-fascist speech of their dependency and their giddiness: 'We are the avant garde,' 'We are the marginals' (Deleuze and Parnet 2007: 139). In the world of *Spooks*, the only outlet for true affect is the suicide line, and Salter complies, stringing himself up in the men's room in front of a horrified Quinn.

'Diana' (Season 4, Episode 10) is an even more complex example, as it entails a fluid movement across all three lines, setting the stage for the attempted coup of Jocelyn Myers and Richard Collingwood that opens Season 5. In this case, former MI5 officer Angela Wells (Lindsay Duncan) shows up at The Grid and holds the whole team hostage, locking down all communications to the outside. She believes she has evidence that British security services killed Princess Diana in a plot hatched up by 'The Contingent Events Committee' chaired by

Harry Pearce. She plans to detonate a bomb and kill everyone unless Pearce reveals the truth. Wells has a personal stake in the investigation as her then fiancé, Peter Haigh (James Scales) was part of Diana's security detail and committed suicide as a result of his failure to save her. The crisis also affects The Grid on a personal level as Senior Intelligence Analyst Ruth Evershed (Nicola Walker) was Peter's step-sister and, it seems, one-time lover. What is clear is that the contagion of Peter's black hole and suicidal line has passed inexorably over to Wells who combines it with a religious self-righteousness: 'You know what this country lacks?' she muses. 'A culture of death. We used to have one, of course. When we were Christian.' She kisses the detonator button as if they were the beads of a rosary.

Although Wells is well trained in all of MI5's attempts to trick her, Ruth Evershed eventually breaks her by lying about her affair with Peter, stating that he was never in love with Wells, only her. Incensed, Angela presses the detonator button but it turns out to have been a dummy all along. Wells was never suicidal, only caught up in a dangerous intensity. Pearce subsequently explains that the committee was formed to concoct worst-case scenarios in order to work out contingency plans to forestall them (yet another 'bandwidth of the acceptable'). Interestingly (and not surprisingly), MI5 has a provision for black hole micro-fascist burn-out called 'Victim in the Field'. As Adam Carter explains, 'It's a spooks tradition. If one of us goes to pieces during an op in the field we get them out of trouble but never tell.' Although one can argue that this wasn't strictly an op, Wells clearly thought it was. However, there are conditions for Wells' release: silence, leave the country, we never see you again or we throw you to the wolves.

But there's a macro-fascist sting in the tail. Wells' siege was a misdirection designed to cover up her real object: to steal a report on the new security measures at Buckingham Palace. She plans to blow up the Royal family! As Pearce puts it, 'It's the Coriolanus nightmare: the greatest fighter in your army turns against you and tries to destroy everything you stand for.' Again, there's a race against time to defuse the bomb and of course the Royals are saved in the nick of time. The problem is the 'Victim in the Field' code itself: it doesn't allow for its inevitable line of flight into the suicide machine. Wells knew that she would have the 'out' and exploited it to the full. The episode ends on a cliffhanger with Wells on a rooftop, sniping at Pearce and Carter on the street below. Season 5 opens with Wells sparing Pearce, who is in her direct line of fire, and jumping to her death but not before shouting 'Jakarta is coming', thereby linking her suicide to the macro-line of the planned coup d'état that follows. As Deleuze and Guattari put it, 'Suicide is presented not as a punishment but as the crowning glory of the death of others' (1987: 231), as a macro-fascism to come.

Season 8, which focuses largely on the 'Nightingale' plot, explores the molar line's attempts to re-segment the molecular line's tendency towards self-destruction, despite the risk of an even greater macro-fascist 'Controlled Holocaust'. For Deleuze and Guattari, power and impotence are alternating currents between the molar and molecular. Indeed, all forces of power shift from one line to the other, from the petty and lofty, the rogue and the grandiloquent, the demagogue and high-ranking imperialist. However, as they point out:

> this whole chain and web of power is immersed in a world of mutant flows that eludes them. It is precisely its impotence that makes power so dangerous. The man of power will always want to stop the lines of flight, and to this end to trap and stabilize the mutation machine in the overcoding machine. (1987: 229)

'Nightingale' is a direct manifestation of this desire and it is here where MI5's role as a minor fascism pays its greatest dividends as a counter force. 'Nightingale' consists of a global network of clandestine groups, including rogue CIA officers, the DeWitt banking network, Chinese hardliners and high-ranking members of the British government (including former Home Secretary, Nicholas Blake) who are attempting to exploit a diplomatic showdown between India and Pakistan after an Indian submarine is seized in Pakistani waters. Current Home Secretary Andrew Lawrence (Tobias Menzies) arranges a summit between the Indians and moderate Pakistani President Mudasser (Nicholas Khan) to help defuse the situation, but nuclear war is a clear and present danger as India gives Pakistan one week to release the submarine. Appeasement is highly unlikely given that the head of the Pakistani army is a bellicose general, Azim Ali, who is looking for any excuse to initiate a war. 'Nightingale' has already transferred 6 billion US dollars from a secret CIA account in DeWitt's Bank to bolster Ali as the future Pakistani leader and they plan to assassinate the appeasing Mudasser so that the deadline will pass and nuclear war will become inevitable.

Senior Case Officer Lucas North (Richard Armitage) investigates 'Nightingale' through his intimate affair with CIA agent and MI5 liaison Sarah Caulfield (Genevieve O'Reilly), who is also a secret 'Nightingale' asset. Caulfield's revelations indicate a clear intention to re-segmentarise escalating global terror by eliminating minor fascist elements such as the Taliban, Al-Qaeda and ISIS and return the world to strict nuclear jurisdictions:

North: Why is Nightingale provoking a war between India and Pakistan?
    [. . .]
Caulfield: Because I've seen what happens when the Taliban take control of a state. I was in Kabul, remember?

North: And you think that a war will solve that? Nuke the Swat Valley?
Caulfield: It's only a matter of time before they take Pakistan. And there won't be any peace talks if or when the Taliban get their hands on nuclear weapons.
North: *This* confrontation will also go nuclear. You know that.

It's at this point that Sarah asserts the molar return to binary demarcations, filling up the 'little crack from the South' and restoring the old East–West geopolitical axis on new lines:

Caulfield: No we can control it. Goodbye Al-Qaeda high command, goodbye Taliban.
North: And India?
Caulfield: Down, but not out. It suits China, who hold most of our debt. Only connect, Lucas. Yeah, wars are bad, but they're like forest fires, seeds grow from the ashes.

'Nightingale' thus represents the ultimate move towards macro-fascism as global suicide: risking total annihilation as the war machine appropriates the state and takes on peace–war as its sole end. As Deleuze and Guattari put it, the war machine absorbs a smooth space that surrounds and envelops the whole earth, absorbing all of its lines:

Total war itself is surpassed towards a peace more terrifying still. The war machine has taken charge of the aim, worldwide order, and the states are no more than objects or means adapted to that machine. This is the point at which Clausewitz is effectively reversed; to be entitled to say that politics is the continuation of war by others means, it is not simply enough to invert the order of the words so that they can be spoken in either direction: it is necessary to follow the real movement at the conclusion of which the states, having appropriated the war machine, and having adapted it to their aims, reimpart a war machine that takes charge of the aim, appropriates the state, and assumes increasingly wider political functions. (Deleuze and Guattari 1987: 421)

CODES AND SURVEILLANCE: TV AND 'FALSE MOVEMENT' AS A MICRO-FASCISM

As we noted earlier, *Spooks* is very adept at metacommunicating the television medium itself as an intrinsic part of control culture, whereby the home viewer is positioned as equal parts culpable participant, distanced observer and critical analyst. The series is dominated by mediated surveillance imagery (so that even when we witness events 'at first hand' we always wonder if it is not a hidden observer's point of view); multiple split screens that show simultaneous action (often incorporating members of The Grid so that we are watching security people monitoring suspects or assets); swish pans, vertical and horizontal wipes and freeze frames. In almost every case, narrative and character is reduced to pure information, pure code, for as Deleuze explains:

> In the societies of control [. . .] what is important is no longer either a signature or a number, but a code: the code is a password, while on the other hand disciplinary societies are regulated by *watchwords* (as much as from the point of view of integration as from that of resistance). The numerical language of control is made of codes that mark access to information, or reject it. We no longer find ourselves dealing with the mass/individual pair. Individuals have become '*dividuals*', and masses, samples, data, markets, or '*banks*'. (1992: 5)

An excellent example of this reduction of bodies to '*dividuals*' can be seen in an extended four-minute surveillance sequence from Season 8, Episode 5. Before being uncovered as a 'Nightingale' agent by Lucas North, Sarah Caulfield murders her CIA London station chief, Sam Walker (Brian Protheroe), who was getting dangerously close to blowing her cover. However, Caulfield still needs a patsy to take the rap for her traitorous act. When she learns from North that retired MI6 agent Jack Colville (Stephen Boxer) is targeting former field agents who he believes were responsible for the torture and death of his lover, Mina Baranova, during a botched operation in Serbia years earlier, she sees her opportunity. Colville has planted a bug inside The Grid so that he is able to access all their data, including the names and locations of his intended targets, and also listen in on their surveillance chatter. Next on his hit list is Roger Maynard (Andrew Havill), former MI6 Station Head in Belgrade, who is scheduled to make a television appearance later that day. If Caulfield can steer Colville towards assassinating Maynard and then show that the latter – painted as a rogue agent – was responsible for killing her CIA boss, Sam Walker, she's off the hook and 'Nightingale' can continue its machinations.

The sequence is preceded with a shot of Colville parked outside the GBN 24 Television studios, pointing a surveillance camera at the front door of the building. He records the key pad as a visitor punches in the access codes ('the code is a password') which he will duplicate to gain access himself. We then see Maynard – an expert on war crimes – being interviewed on a television screen (which doubles our own TV monitor as spectators of the show within a show), so he is immediately reduced to a virtual image that can be easily manipulated, fragmented and reconstituted by surveillance technology. Just as

Lucas North is sent in to intercept him at a safe liaison point, we cut to a split screen: on the left, Caulfield is at the front desk trying to gain access to the TV network's building ('Just make the call'), while on the right, Colville is seen approaching from the outside. Caulfield is then briefly replaced by Maynard's TV interview before we cut back to her gaining entry, just as Colville punches in the security code at the front door. As Caulfield says, 'OK, I'm in' to her unseen 'Nightingale' controller in the left screen, we immediately cross-relate it to Colville (who is acting 'under the radar') in the right. We then cut to a three-way split as North enters the building and we now see a series of close-ups of Tariq (MI5's surveillance whizz) as he feeds North information as to Maynard's whereabouts from his desk back at The Grid.

As Maynard's interview ends, he dominates the screen as an 'actual' body (i.e., he is not mediated through a monitor) and sips from a glass of water. His mobile phone vibrates: 'Code Red Alert'. We follow him in a single shot as he leaves the studio and checks in to MI5: 'Maynard. Code 378.' We cut to a close-up of Tariq: 'Confirmed. Exit 19. Repeat, Exit 19.' Maynard: 'Copy. Exit 19.' Suddenly, the screen splits again and as Maynard continues towards Exit 19 in the left frame, Caulfield re-appears in a smaller frame to the right as an American-accented voice-over says: 'Intercept from MI5. Target to Exit 19. Check back route.' Clearly the intercept is a 'Nightingale'-sanctioned 'go'. Caulfield's frame enlarges (as if to codify her increasing agency in the cat and mouse game), but Colville replaces Maynard in the left frame as he is also stalking the same quarry. Caulfield's right frame then drops down and is replaced by Lucas North, headed for Exit 19.

Michael J. Shapiro's analysis of anti-fascist aesthetics in two film adaptations of Philip K. Dick stories – Richard Linklater's *A Scanner Darkly* (2006) and Steven Spielberg's *Minority Report* (2002) – is extremely useful here as he shows how the surveillance body is innately fractured but also resistant to conventional narrative and spectatorial scopic 'control' (2013: 27–41). First, Shapiro notes a marked turn towards a spatial analytic, whereby the split screens and multiplicitous surveillance codings mimic the micro-fascism of securitisation: thus Maynard, Colville, Caulfield and North's real-life bodies are collapsed with the panoptics of security surveillance as intersecting micro-lines. Second, their bodies and movements are noncompliant with the exigencies of the narrative (what Deleuze calls the sensory-motor action image). Shapiro cites an excellent passage from Jérôme Game on this point, with specific reference to the films of Robert Bresson, Buster Keaton and John Cassavetes:

> the cinematographic body is no longer an object of film or knowledge; rather, it is a model of knowledge via the editing. The latter is no longer conceived as the restitution of a world, but as its invention, the composition of an identity. Editing [. . .] is indeed what allows the unveiling of

the body as fragmentation, in direct opposition to the Platonic body implicit in any linear script-based editing. Thus promoted as a unit of perception, the body nevertheless remains everything but unitary; on the contrary, it precipitates a diffracted perception [. . .] [T]he body is simultaneously that which is filmed and that which (re)organises the film in the mind/body of the spectator. In this way, the spectator's body receives the film (and is affected by it), and the filmed body, when screened, reappropriates its own destiny, it becomes source rather than object of cinema; it is no longer just filmed, it is reconfiguring the already-filmed. (Game 2001: 50–1)

In this sequence, all four diegetic bodies are inherently fragmented, fuelling the phantasmagoria of the cinematic narrative but at the same time baring the device (through split screens) of its own artifice. Everything ends up split: the diegetic body, the viewing body, the scopic screen.

As the sequence progresses, Caulfield eventually makes contact with Maynard and, passing herself off as a Section D operative, offers to lead him to Exit 19 and apparent safety. Instead, she takes him to a large, empty, glassed-in room and tells him that there has been a change of plan: it's not safe to proceed and they are to wait for further instructions. We then cut to a wide-angle 2-shot as both are silhouetted against the windows, sitting ducks for an assassin's bullet. But we know that the danger is much closer to home, for we quickly return to a series of split screens as our characters-as-'*dividuals*' are once again taken over by the 'knowledge model' of editing. Caulfield exits, leaving Maynard unprotected in the left frame while North checks in with Tariq to the right: 'Something's wrong. He's not here. Make contact again. I'm gonna go look for him.' The affective ramifications of this misinformation/misdirection are revealed as we return to a full-frame image of Maynard, shot from the rear. Tariq calls him on his cell, wondering why he isn't at the exit as planned. Before Maynard can explain Sarah's 'change of plan', Colville enters and shoots Maynard through the throat. Colville is about to apply the coup de grâce when Caulfield walks in, aiming a gun at him. The film returns to conventional cross-cutting and shot-reverse-shot editing as Colville lays down his gun, and Caulfield plans how to both exploit and kill off her 'get out of jail free card'. Before she can act Lucas North walks in, Colville escapes and Maynard dies in North's arms, but not before uttering Mina Baranova's (Colville's dead lover's) name. We then cut to Sarah in the corridor, talking to her unseen handler:

Sarah: Colville got away.
American VO: That's unfortunate, Sarah. You better re-think your Walker cover.
Sarah: I'll deal with it.

In conclusion, it's interesting to note how far this analysis of '*dividuals*' and action-images as perceptual data evokes Deleuze's discussion of the time-image in *Cinema 2*, particularly his analysis of false movement as the opening-up of a progressive space for a 'people yet to come':

> Time ceases to be derived from the movement, it appears in itself and itself gives rise to *false movements*. Hence the importance of *false continuity* in modern cinema: the images are no longer linked by rational cuts and continuity, but are relinked by means of false continuity and irrational cuts. Even the body is no longer exactly what moves; subject of movement or the instrument of action, it becomes rather the developer of time, it shows time through its tirednesses and waitings . . . (1989: xi)

As we just saw in the Maynard assassination sequence, the surveillance-image creates a vertigo of spacing, injecting voids, slippages, misdirections and false continuities as part of the very fabric of the narrative. As spectators we see and hear far more than Tariq, who is attempting to choreograph everything from The Grid, because we see both Caulfield's and Colville's machinations at work outside of the CCTV matrix. On the other hand, we never see the whole picture because the split screens cover up more than they reveal: the interstices *between* the frames on-screen are far more pregnant with meaning-as-information than the edits between actions that unfold in succession. As Deleuze puts it in a famous passage:

> the actual is cut off from its motor linkages, or the real from its legal connections, and the virtual, for its part, detaches itself from its actualizations, starts to be valid for itself. The two modes of existence are now combined in a circuit where the real and the imaginary, the actual and the virtual, chase after each other, exchange their roles and become indiscernible. (1989: 127)

However, far from being a progressive cinema (tied in *Cinema 2* to post-war neorealism; Jean-Luc Godard's focus on the itinerant *balade*, opsigns and sonsigns; and non-Western paradigms such as the work of Glauber Rocha or Ousmane Sembène), this is now the cinema of surveillance, of control culture. The 'people' is no longer missing: it has returned not as a revolutionary formation but as a multiplicity, *the* subjectivity of the dispositif. Which is why the acceptance of a minor fascism may be the only form of viable resistance to Velvet Fascism and why spooks become our heroes as well as our enemies: our very own 'abstract machine'.

BIBLIOGRAPHY

Deleuze, Gilles (1988), *Foucault*, trans. Seán Hand, Minneapolis: University of Minnesota Press.
Deleuze, Gilles (1989), *Cinema 2: The Time Image*, trans. Hugh Tomlinson and Roberta Galeta, Minneapolis: University of Minnesota Press.
Deleuze, Gilles (1992), 'Postscript on the Societies of Control', *October* 59, Winter, pp. 3–7.
Deleuze, Gilles (2006a), 'The Rich Jew', in *Two Regimes of Madness*, trans. Ames Hodges and Mike Taormina, ed. David Lapoujade, New York: Semiotext(e), pp. 135–8.
Deleuze, Gilles (2006b), 'What is a Dispositif?', in *Two Regimes of Madness*, trans. Ames Hodges and Mike Taormina, ed. David Lapoujade, New York: Semiotext(e), pp. 338–48.
Deleuze, Gilles and Félix Guattari (1983), *Anti-Oedipus: Capitalism and Schizophrenia*, trans. Robert Hurley, Mark Seem and Helen R. Lane, Minneapolis: University of Minnesota Press.
Deleuze, Gilles and Félix Guattari (1986), *Kafka: Toward a Minor Literature*, trans Dana Polan, Minneapolis, University of Minnesota Press.
Deleuze Gilles and Félix Guattari (1987), *A Thousand Plateaus: Capitalism and Schizophrenia*, trans. Brian Massumi, Minneapolis: University of Minnesota Press.
Deleuze, Gilles and Claire Parnet (1987), *Dialogues*, trans. Hugh Tomlinson and Barbara Habberjam, New York: Columbia University Press.
Deleuze Gilles and Claire Parnet (2007), 'Many Politics', in *Dialogues II*, trans. Hugh Tomlinson and Barbara Habberjam, New York: Columbia University Press, pp. 124–47.
Foucault, Michel (1977), 'The Confession of the Flesh', in *Power/Knowledge: Selected Interviews & Other Writings, 1972–1977*, ed. Colin Gordon, New York: Pantheon Books, pp. 194–228.
Foucault, Michel (1983), 'Preface' to Gilles Deleuze and Félix Guattari (1983), *Anti-Oedipus: Capitalism and Schizophrenia*, trans. Robert Hurley, Mark Seem and Helen R. Lane, Minneapolis: University of Minnesota Press, pp. xi–xiv.
Foucault, Michel (2007), *Security, Territory & Population: Lectures at the Collège de France 1977–1978*, trans. Graham Burchill, ed. Michel Senellart, New York and Basingstoke: Palgrave Macmillan.
Game, Jérôme (2001), 'Cinematic Bodies: The Blind Spot in Contemporary French Theory on Corporeal Cinema', *Studies in French Cinema* 1:1, April, pp. 47–53.
Shapiro, Michael J. (2013), 'Anti-fascist aesthetics', in *Deleuze & Fascism*, ed. Brad Evans and Julian Reid, London and New York: Routledge, pp. 27–41.
Smith, Daniel W. (1997), '"A Life of Pure Immanence": Deleuze's "Critique et Clinique" Project', 'Introduction' to Gilles Deleuze, *Essays Critical and Clinical*, trans. Daniel W. Smith and Michael A. Greco, Minneapolis: University of Minnesota Press, pp. xi–liii.

CHAPTER 9

Species States: Animal Control in Phil Klay's 'Redeployment'

Colleen Glenney Boggs

Cartoon animals are inescapable. With recent titles ranging from *Penguins of Madagascar* (2014), a spin-off from the *Madagascar* movies (2005, 2008, 2012), to *The Secret Life of Pets* (2016) and *Zootopia* (2016; in the UK, *Zootropolis*), they are everywhere. They are also inescapable in another sense. We cannot get away from cartoon animals, no matter how much we and they may want to go our separate ways: the movies revolve around animals trying to escape their human bondage. Likewise, the films depict humans abandoning their responsibilities to domesticated animals who then try to fend for themselves. Even in films that remain devoid of human characters, animal whereabouts are a key concern: investigating animal disappearances launches the career of a police bunny in *Zootopia* and helps her befriend an outlaw fox and recruit him for the police force. Whereas the key plot of previous pet movies such as *Lassie Come Home* (1943) revolved around the trauma of inadvertent separation and the triumph of reunion (a plot element that does persist in *The Secret Life of Pets*), the current movies have more in common with the genre of prison-break narratives. Celebrity-voiced cartoon creatures perform antics-with-an-attitude and recall Steve McQueen's cool. Only now and then do the escape movies venture towards the more gut-wrenching noir of *The Shawshank Redemption* (1994), for instance when we encounter a group of pets-rendered-refuse in the sewers of New York and get a very different appreciation of the dirty secret that makes up *Life of Pets*. One thing these cartoon creatures all understand is that they are dispensable – the abandoned pets but even the special ops *Penguins of Madagascar* share this knowledge, though their affective response differs and ranges from horror to an acceptance that verges on the nihilistic.

Current animated movies collectively seem like an elaborate pun on the notion of 'animal control', a word that euphemistically describes the life and death decisions municipalities make about the non-human creatures in their midst. What makes this pun all the more poignant is the fact that – even when a film overtly rejects human beings from inclusion in animal life-worlds – the movies rely on human beings in two ways. For one, the movie-goers are human and – two – the talking, singing, car-driving, uniform-wearing and high-tech-gear-operating cartoon creatures are themselves human, all too human. Cartoon animals eliminate the possibility of becoming-animal with their insistent narratives of becoming-human that reinforce the species boundaries they appear to unsettle. Their exaggeration of human characteristics makes these films laughable as forms of self-recognition for adults and children alike. In this sense, the cartoon animals become proxies for control narratives whose subject is ultimately human.

The laughter of self-recognition is a feature of cartoons going back as far as *Scooby-Doo* (1969–1970), with the comic-foil double of teenager Shaggy and his dog Scooby-Doo. However, that earlier kind of animated silliness had a countercultural bent to it that made the 'Mystery Van' a version of flower-power, anti-Vietnam and anti-Nixon sentiment, critical of rather than complicit with state control. Scooby-Doo himself is the show's ultimate countercultural hero. In a symbiotic relationship with Shaggy, he remains intelligible mainly by expressing his libidinal energy, specifically his gluttonous drive; Scooby-Doo's voracious appetite keeps the 'gang's' detective work from falling into complicity with states of control, and keeps it separate from the control of the state. With Shaggy himself as the prototypical stoner, the cartoon's central characters indulge their appetites and remain beyond the pale of physical or emotional control.

Scooby-Doo also reminds us of an ingredient that is largely missing from most of the contemporary films: inter-species camaraderie. While there are several instances of enemies becoming frenemies and even friends, earlier animal narratives' reliance on the species-line-crossing odd couple is largely absent: the penguins of Madagascar stick together in a para-military group that forms command structures but does not befriend others. What makes the absence of the odd couple curious is not just the fact that animal narratives, by and large, have depended on the human–animal bond as a staple – again, *Lassie* comes to mind – but also the fact that concurrent with this wave of popular animal narratives, the scholarly field of animal studies has emphasised cross-species bonds. Variously characterised as the 'autre-mondialisation' that 'companion species' produce (Haraway 2008: 22), the species kinship that 'kissing cousins' share (Bartkowski 2008: 4), or the reframing of posthumanism as a post-species condition (Wills 2008), the field has been unsettling the species lines that popular movies ultimately reaffirm. There is very little in these movies that resembles the companionship emphasised in animal studies.

Cartoon animals want to get away, and yet that attempt at autonomy reanimates the control apparatus they are trying to escape in the first place. As I said in the beginning, cartoon animals are inescapable.

Where might we look, then, for theoretical paradigms and cultural contexts that help us make sense of this pervasive oddity? The short answer to this question is announced by this book's title: we are pushed into a *control culture* that configures itself in postdisciplinary terms. The shift from discipline to control goes hand in hand with the rise of biopower that understands the regulation of populations as its proper domain. The longer answer to this question requires us to probe into the definitions and definitional limitations of current scholarship on biopower.

To a large extent, scholars have understood the domain of biopower to be civilian and in line with state power, not military power. However, biopower brings to the forefront a vision of social order that emerged concurrently with the so-called Enlightenment model of the state of reason and nature. As Michel Foucault argued,

> Historians of ideas usually attribute the dream of a perfect society to the philosophers and jurists of the eighteenth century: but there was also a military dream of society; its fundamental reference was not to the state of nature, but to the meticulously subordinated cogs of a machine, not to the primal social contract, but to a permanent coercion, not to fundamental rights, but to indefinitely progressive forms of training, not to the general will but to automatic docility. (Foucault 1979: 169)

Arguing that scholars have long overlooked the 'military dream' of society, Foucault called for an engagement with non-civilian forms of control in their own right and in relation to civilian social formations. But how exactly that would work remained a bit obscure in that Foucault hedged his bet on the relation between the state and the military; what exactly does it mean that there was 'also' a military dream of society, and that he described that dream via a set of negations ('not' . . . 'but')? This begs two questions. One, how did the military apparatus and state relate to or differ from one another? And, two, is there a way of describing the military state constructively and not just via negations?

Gilles Deleuze and Félix Guattari take up these questions. In their 'Treatise on Nomadology: The War Machine' in *A Thousand Plateaus*, they differentiate the state apparatus from the war machine, arguing:

> It will be noted that war is not contained within this [State] apparatus. *Either* the State has at its disposal a violence that is not channeled through war – either it uses police officers and jailers in place of warriors, has no arms and no need of them, operates by immediate, magical

capture, 'seizes' and 'binds,' preventing all combat – *or*, the State acquires an army, but in a way that presupposes a juridical integration of war and the organization of a military function. As for the war machine in itself, it seems to be irreducible to the State apparatus, to be outside its sovereignty and prior to its law: it comes from elsewhere. (Deleuze and Guattari 1987: 352)

For them, the war machine is a space of becoming-animal. As Irving Goh explains, 'The affinity between becoming-animal and the nomadic war machine is undeniable' (Goh 2006: 228) He explains that becoming-animal 'is not the anthropomorphic mimesis of animals', such as we see in the cartoon creatures that populate current cinema (2006: 228). Instead, Goh explains that becoming-animal 'is about the adjacent space between the human and the animal [. . .] in which a molecular anti-anthropomorphism at the edges of the human departs and communicates with the molecular particles of the animal that have likewise left the frays of its form' (2006: 228). This becoming generates a multiplicity, a pack, and sets aside the pets that Deleuze and Guattari deride as Oedipal. The pack itself, however, is not a final 'communitarian outcome', according to Goh, but an intermediary step towards 'new nonorganic social relations' (2006: 229).

If this becoming-animal is premised on the difference between the state and the military, and if the state and the military are understood in their distinction from one another, then what happens when the distinction between the two collapses? We need to ask that question in the context of the contemporary United States, where the cultural production of the films I have referenced has occurred alongside the so-called 'War on Terror' which began around 2002, is ongoing, and currently has no end in sight. Fought on multiple fronts, it is most often associated with the 'War in Iraq', often with little reference to the so-called home front of American civilian life. A book that breaks this barrier is Phil Klay's short-story collection *Redeployment* (2014), which by its very title indicates the deep imbrications, the back-and-forth of US soldiers repeatedly sent home and stationed abroad. It posits a linkage between the state apparatus and the war machine. For Klay, developing an understanding of that linkage directly involves an engagement with animal beings and animal becomings. The collection's eponymous opening story frames the book in relation to animals – dogs in particular – and offers a contemporary version of human–animal relationships that may on the surface seem in stark contrast to contemporary cartoons' portrayals of animals. Yet the work is deeply in dialogue with the larger question of how a culture of control expresses and exerts itself via fantasies of species. Klay makes horrifically clear that 'animal control' remains deeply tied to human agency yet exceeds that agency and becomes a modality for biopower more broadly speaking.

In the process of controlling animals, human beings subject themselves to control structures. Impacting physical bodies on the one hand, this 'animal control' is also an affective modality. That affective modality makes species itself contingent: far from a fixed category, species is rendered fungible for strategic purposes of exerting control, physical as well as emotional. Becoming animal is no longer an alternative to state formations, but a direct result of the fusion between the state and the military, and itself a form of control that closes off possibilities for alterity. What the cartoon landscape and *Redeployment* ultimately have in common is an understanding that species states are subject to definition, and that those definitions of species are a core mechanism for how control culture operates in our current moment.

I

'We shot dogs' (Klay 2014: 1). The opening lines of Phil Klay's story 'Redeployment' are shockingly unsentimental. But the fact that they are shocking to readers, and noticeable for their seeming lack of sentimentality, tells us something about the expectations we already bring to animals in literature. In being shocked by the violence against dogs and in noting the seeming absence of an affective engagement, we are reading the text through a particular cultural and political legacy that dates back to John Locke and reflects a specific vision of civil society.

First published in 1693, John Locke's *Some Thoughts Concerning Education* reflected on how to use childhood pedagogy to cultivate good citizens. Offering a model of child-rearing that relied on rational as well as emotional training, Locke turned his attention to animals in two respects – one, as literary characters and, two, as living creatures. Examining the landscape of texts available to children, Locke lamented the fact that no appropriate literature existed, with the possible exception of Aesop's *Fables* (Locke 1968: 298). Harkening back to a text from antiquity that linked – albeit often loosely – animal fables with moral instruction, Locke's choice established a connection between species and order. His call for more children's literature resulted in the development of the genre in general, and its reliance on animal representations in particular (Boggs 2013: 138–43). Locke also turned his attention to children's direct interactions with animals and insisted that children needed to be taught kindness. Claiming that 'Children love *Liberty*', he warned his readers that 'they love something more; and that is *Dominion*' (Locke 1968: 204). They exercise such dominion in their treatment of animals, Locke argued, that:

> the Custom of Tormenting and Killing of Beasts, will, by Degrees, harden their Minds even towards Men; and they who delight in the

Suffering and Destruction of inferiour Creatures, will not be apt to be very compassionate, or benign to those of their own kind. (1968: 226)

To cultivate compassion towards others, he advised that children be given animals and taught to practise responsibility towards them. Locke explained that the cultivation of compassion was crucial for turning children away from despotism to good citizenship, which required a sense of care for others. Laying the basis, then, for the boom in sentimental literary texts that extolled that virtue, Locke linked the relationship between species to the education of citizens.

Despite the opening line's appearance to the contrary, the narrator of Klay's story has learned this lesson well. 'I'm a dog person', he says in the same paragraph (Klay 2014: 1). Defining himself in relation to species and via the affective bond to dogs that marks him as a person, the narrator creates a stark juxtaposition between the violence of the opening line and the creaturely compassion that the Lockean frame expects him to exercise towards dogs. It is that juxtaposition that he himself strains against, and in which he positions his readers. Here is the full opening passage: 'We shot dogs. Not by accident. We did it on purpose, and we called it Operation Scooby. I'm a dog person, so I thought about that a lot' (Klay 2014: 1).

While his assertion that he's a 'dog person' would make the narrator a good citizen of the society Locke envisions, that citizenship is here set up dialectically against the martial vision of a society that undercuts such self-definitions. Beginning with the plural 'we', and repeating it three times before arriving at the first person singular, the passage stages a collective, group formation. That collective asserts a sense of purpose: it does not shoot dogs 'by accident' but 'on purpose', and thus lays claim to the volition of the reasoning subject. The reasoning subject in Locke's vision is first and foremost the individual, but, here, volition remains collective and is operationalised. The opening sets up the parameters of Lockean subject- and social-formation, but also undercuts them by an emphasis on a collective that strains against individual volition in its emphasis on violence. The violence that is enacted here is directed against dogs. It also expands into violence against personal sensitivities and the social structures that cultivate and rely on compassion. That association is made all the more poignant by the fact that American soldiers stationed in the war zones wear what are known as dog tags; the military marks them as dog persons, and so even the narrator's seeming self-identification is co-opted. In emphasising a collective 'we', the story temporarily opens up a space of becoming animal. But the animal becoming that is invoked also turns into a form of self-violence and self-destruction in that it animates an apparatus of animal control that fuses the military with the civilian state. In upending Locke's dictum that human beings ought to learn via other creatures to be 'benign to those of their own kind', this violence becomes directed not only at the dogs but at the 'dog person' of Klay's story (Locke 1968: 226).

The fact that the group identified its action and 'called it Operation Scooby' indicates that it is not the military per se that gives rise to this operation. As much as this group is troping on Lockean education, it is also parodying military order. The militarisation of cartoon character Scooby-Doo ridicules the nomenclature of military command structures and appropriates it for humorous purposes. But the humour seems misguided – naming the shooting of dogs for a cartoon dog is inappropriate at best, and it is that friction which the following sentence augments. Shooting dogs on purpose and being a dog person are antithetical in Locke's logic, but, clearly, that logic does not apply to the military society that the group's 'operation' and shooting of animals already set up. The dream of the military society that Foucault invoked here runs alongside the dream of civilian society. Subject to both civilian norms and military orders and yet beholden to neither, the 'we' of this opening paragraph exercises a form of control that tropes on but operates beyond disciplines. It also forecloses the possibility that this collective 'we' could turn into a pack. Becoming-animal is cut off in that the paragraph establishes a collective in violent opposition to animals; it asserts a form of being, and of being human, that stems from two acts of violence, the violence against animals and a violent rejection of becoming a 'dog person' in *either* the Lockean or Deleuzian sense.

The story's opening establishes the postdisciplinary realm as one of biopower. Focusing on the plural 'dogs' that turns these creatures into a collective and a species, it differs from the narrator's insistence in the singular: 'I'm a dog person.' Defining his subjectivity in the first person singular via the relation to the singular 'dog' and 'person', the narrator performs an act of individuation that runs counter to the collective and collectivising action of shooting dogs in the plural, that is of shooting at a larger number but also – at least metonymically – at a pack.

II

Biopower occupies a complicated position in scholars' reflections on the relation between sovereignty and governmentality. On the one hand, Foucault historicises it as the form of power that succeeds structures of sovereignty that decided over life and death, and focuses on life as such, that is on the conditions of living and on population as species. At the same time, in Giorgio Agamben's adaptation of the term, biopower generates new forms of sovereignty: Agamben explains that the so-called 'homo sacer' who is banished from legal protection occupies a position similar to the sovereign who adjudicates over which forms of life count as *bios*, that is as legally protected, and as *zoë*, that is as outside the realm of the law (Agamben 1998: 8). The collective 'we' aggregates that power to itself when it decides to inhabit the sovereign position of deciding over life and death, and also turns that sovereignty into a form of biopower by establishing which life forms do – or in this case do not – count as *bios*. As Jennifer Parker-Starbuck has argued, 'the controlled use and mastery of animals creates an Agambenian "animalization" of humanity, allowing similar disregard for those considered not fully human' (Parker-Starbuck 2006: 654). She points out that 'Agamben's concern is not to protect the animal per se, but to expose humanist traditions and politics that have sought to control and regulate forms of life as "animalistic" so as to retain the privileged status of (selected forms of) humanity' (2006: 654).

For the narrator, Lockean identification in a post-Lockean frame causes an insurmountable gap. The dog becomes the site of a gap of social visions that map onto a sense of cognitive dissonance: 'I thought about that a lot' (Klay 2014: 1). Exemplifying the so-called Enlightenment subject, the narrator defines himself as a rational being engaged in the key act of reasoned assessment. But that reasoned assessment occurs outside of the structures it is meant to create and reflect. It is a social construct outside of the social norms and disciplines that give it meaning. That dissonance is cognitive but also affective: there is a gap between the emotional statement 'I am a dog person', and the amount of thinking this emotional response elicits. The opening shows the friction that the war on terror produces in the Lockean subject: caught in a conflict that tropes on civil society and military order, the very parameters of species interaction, subject formation and civil society are simultaneously activated and undercut. The categories that enable social structure and subjectivity are themselves at risk.

But in what sense, and for whom? To what extent can the narrator, who is serving in the military and deployed to the war zone in Iraq, stand in for the Lockean subject more generally speaking? The question becomes especially relevant given the imbalance between American military spending and American military personnel. According to *The Military Balance* for 2016, 'the US remains the world's most capable military power' (*The Military Balance* 2016: 38). In terms of personnel, that means 1,381,250 active servicewo/men, 14,850 civilian employees and 840,500 reserves for a total of 2,236,600 (2016: 38). The US population on 26 February 2016 was officially calculated at 323,063,587, which means roughly 0.7 per cent of the population was in the military (http://www.census.gov/popclock/; accessed 27 February 2016). What significance can we attach to this relatively small percentage? Klay's story takes up precisely that issue in that it weaves the dream of military society together with the civil society that the military nominally protects. Instead of reading the figure to show that a small number of people serve the military in a civilian society, we could also read the figures to reveal that a large number of civilians belong to military society. The overarching theme of 'Redeployment' indicates an imbrication of the one with the other. In that sense, the crisis of the Lockean subject in the war zone becomes paradigmatic of the crisis that the so-called state of exception inaugurated by the war on terror initiates for liberal subjectivity as such.

Explaining how the sight of a dog drinking blood led to the killings of Operation Scooby, the narrator performs important distinctions and slippages. Pointing out that 'it wasn't American blood, but still', he indicates that the violence against animals takes place within the context of violence among human beings (Klay 2014: 1). But those human beings themselves have a precarious relationship to biopower and its willingness – or lack thereof – to recognise them as *bios* or *zoë*. Stating that watching the dog drink blood was 'the last straw, I guess, and then it's open season on dogs', the narrator begins the next paragraph: 'at the time, you don't think about it . . . and you're killing people' (2014: 3). The suspension of thought indicates a break in the subject's reasoning. That break takes the form of suspending the distinction between dogs and people. It lumps dogs and people together as the enemy of a war machine that advances 'block by block' (2014: 3). And yet that lack of discrimination is itself crucially important: in lumping human beings and dogs into the same category of *zoë*, it asserts one of biopower's most crucial functions, namely the ability to make determinations about species as such. In suspending the difference between dogs and people, this war machine effectively asserts its power over all life. It reflects the fungibility of species lines in making dogs and human beings alike in their designation as killable with impunity. It exercises a control of life as such that articulates control as its own raison d'être; it exercises control as such, removed from purposes of distinction and discipline.

That form of species-blurring control emerged as one of the hallmarks of the so-called war on terror in the use of animals and animal imagery at Abu Ghraib. Having written at length about this matter elsewhere, I will here only summarise my findings, namely that the depiction of detainees as dogs via the use of leashes, and the use of guard dogs to intimidate the detainees, created categories of what Cary Wolfe and Jonathan Elmer have termed the 'humanized animal' – that is, the guard dog – and the animalised human – that is, the leashed detainee (Wolfe and Elmer 1995: 146). Both are subject to control by the so-called 'humanized human', the soldier, who allots himself the power to designate species (1995: 147). That 'humanized human' inhabits the position of the sovereign who is himself exempt from the biopower he exercises. Klay's narrator draws this connection to Abu Ghraib and to forms of power that exercise control via species designations. The soldier is unable to get his thoughts into 'any kind of straight order' (Klay 2014: 2). Interweaving different memories, he tries 'to think about home, then you're in the torture house. You see the body parts in the locker and the retarded guy in the cage. He squawked like a chicken' (2014: 2). Associating torture with animal cruelty, the narrator likens the prisoner to a caged 'chicken'. The association is made all the more poignant by the fact that one of the perpetrators of the abuse at Abu Ghraib, Lindy England, worked in a chicken factory (Singer and Dawn 2004). That factory was convicted of cruelty in workers' treatment of the animals. Combining the sense of home with torture and the fungibility of the species line, the narrator implicates the two in each other. The narrator's depiction of this logic outside of the prison setting indicates that the species logic practised at Abu Ghraib might be paradigmatic for the larger war on terror.

What such a charge does not yet account for is the distress and trauma that the narrator himself undergoes. The narrator describes how on the aeroplane back, it was his own dog 'Vicar and Operation Scooby, all the way home' (Klay 2014: 3). The narrator introduces this juxtaposition by a mini-portrait of how he and his wife adopted their dog, Vicar, from the 'shelter'. Although the narrator does not state so explicitly, he implicitly invokes the fact that such shelters are also known as humane societies. In fact, they are alternatively known as animal control and humane societies, and it is the friction between those two that resonates in him juxtaposing Vicar and Operation Scooby, taking that friction 'all the way home' (2014: 3). The narrator associates domesticity with his wife and dog, even animalising his wife when he reflects on the 'fine dark hairs' on her arms, and indicates that his wife is 'ashamed of them, but they're soft, delicate' (2014: 2). The narrator's depiction of his wife's hairs pivots from the descriptive to the intimate when he reveals that his relation to them is not just one of sight but also of touch – they're soft. That touch of the hairs creates a relationship between them that makes her his pet. It strangely animalises her and turns that animalisation into a moment of intimacy between them. By extension, then, their shared adoption of a dog brings a non-human creature into a domestic setting that revolves around the sense of touch and a process of becoming-animal in an intimate relationship. There is a slippage in this description between the dog and the wife, and while that slippage here revolves around affection and intimacy, it also recalls how such slippage can be violent. This realisation leads the narrator to an impasse, where he reflects that 'you're prepared to kill people', that the target on which you practise are 'man shaped', but are called 'dog targets' even though they 'don't look like fucking dogs' (2014: 3). The association between the literal and the symbolic slips around the image of the dog, and part of the violence that the passage captures is not that of killing but of categorising. The brutality lies in the way in which structures of affection and of violence no longer remain separable when it comes to the slippage between the human and the animal. To the extent that affect is subject-forming, this impasse also marks a crisis in the subject that amounts to a conceptual crisis of subjectivity.

The relationship to animals structures the narrator's affective economies, but the fungibility of who or what is an animal makes those affective economies illegible. Sarah Ahmed argues that emotions are not 'a private matter', but 'circulate between bodies and signs' and thereby create the 'effect of the surfaces or boundaries of bodies and worlds' (Ahmed 2017: 1312). The 'man shaped . . . dog targets' that 'don't look like fucking dogs' locate us precisely in this tangle, where the soldiers are not in a private but in a public-military realm in which the circulation between bodies and signs creates yet unsettles a sense of boundaries that confuse and conflate bodies and worlds (Klay 2014: 3). In shooting at targets, the soldiers are trained to anticipate a sense of danger, yet that danger is rendered amorphous or – as a variation on multiplicity – polymorphous. To the extent that the danger is amorphous, the soldiers themselves are rendered amorphous: in the narrator's account, the ability to distinguish friend from foe is invoked and then rendered illegible by the training nominally meant to provide that legibility. In Ahmed's account, the 'negative attachment to others is redefined simultaneously as a positive attachment to the imagined subjects brought together through the repetition of the signifier' (Ahmed 2017: 1313). But in Klay's account, the constant slippage of the signifier undercuts these cohesions. Klay's story goes yet a step further than Ahmed's analysis: whereas Ahmed demonstrates how legibilities are produced to created identitarian positions, Klay ponders how illegibility generates uncertainties that put the attempt to control in constant overdrive because it cannot definitively alight on the cohesion of a repeating signifier. It is the slippage of that signifier which produces what we might consider a sheer control mechanism, in which the objects of control are subject to but ultimately irrelevant to the control apparatus.

Biopower no longer operates as control of a specified or specifiable other; control becomes an infinite process in and of itself that is constantly reanimated by the slippages that it, in turn, reanimates. If power produces the subject, then the correlative here is that control produces the objects of control, which are subjected to constant species slippage. Along the species line, this produces a sense of control over life as such, which no longer resides in the specificities of species but in the fungibility of the species line. Put in Ahmed's terms, the affective economy has morphed into the control economy in the biopolitics of the war on terror. The indeterminacy of the object also explains something crucial about the experience of the war on terror as one that is not about fear but about anxiety. As Ahmed writes, 'when the object of fear threatens to pass by, then fear can no longer be contained by an object. Fear in its very relationship to an object . . . is intensified by the loss of its object . . . The slide between fear and anxiety is affected precisely by the "passing by" of the object' (2017: 1318).

The anxiety produced by the passing of the object is played out in the narrator's homecoming. Driving back to Fort Lejeune from the landing field, he notes that 'I sort of knew where I was, but I didn't feel home. I figured I'd be home when I kissed my wife and pet my dog' (Klay 2014: 5). The passage sets the narrator and the reader up for a sense of the uncanny. Arguing that he didn't 'feel' home, and that the feeling of home would come in the physical encounters with his wife and dog, he indicates that marriage and pet ownership define domesticity. Even as he anticipates a reunion with his wife and dog, the narrator experiences a strong sense of tactile disorientation when he hands in his rifle:

> That was the first time I'd been separated from it in months. I didn't know where to rest my hands. First I put them in my pockets, then I took them out and crossed my arms, and then I just let them hang, useless, at my sides. (Klay 2014: 6)

Companionship for him has become defined by his relationship to the objects of war, and with the 'passing by' of that object comes his sense of disorientation. Imagining a return from the companionship of his rifle to the companionship of wife and dog, he implicitly weaponises both in that they fill the gap left by his rifle's absence. His companionate relationships have been with the objects of war, and in imagining their replacement by his wife and dog he marks both the anxiety of their passing by and the rendering martial of his spouse and dog.

The narrator explains the way in which this tactile disorientation is exacerbated rather than alleviated by his re-entry into civilian life. When his wife takes him on a shopping trip, he muses that consumption is 'how America fights back against the terrorists' (2014: 11). Unable to shake the literal habits of military protocols, he muses that walking thought the mall, 'you startle ten times checking for it [your rifle] and it's not there. You're safe, so your alertness should be at white, but it's not' (2014: 12). The double realisation of his safety and of his feeling unsafe indicates the ways in which his sense of physical control has become imbricated with his sense of psychological control.

The narrator embeds this account of the shopping trip within his depictions of watching television on the couch with his ailing dog. When he and his wife return from shopping, the dog has thrown up and is too shaky to rise from the couch. He takes the dog to a natural setting to shoot him and remembers being unable to shoot at an 'insurgent' he encountered in Fallujah (2014: 15). He explains:

> Staring at Vicar, it was the same thing. This feeling, like, something in me is going to break if I do this. And I thought of Cheryl bringing Vicar to the vet, of some stranger putting his hands on my dog, and I thought, I have to do this. (2014: 15)

The earlier scenes have set up this reaction: The narrator's sense of home revolved around him petting his dog, that is around him literally putting his hands on his dog. The idea of someone else doing so disrupts his definition of home. If he is not the one to put his hands on his dog, not only is he losing his sense of home, he is losing his sense of control which gives him that sense of home. That control has come to define not only his sense of home but also his sense of personhood. He describes a feeling that 'something in me is going to break' (2014: 15). Tied up in his tactile relationship to his dog is not just his sense of self-control, but his sense of self as such. The control structures that he himself is a part of have come to control him, and the species line that enables those control structures has become something that controls him. Because affect has become tied for him to military objects, if forecloses companionship in the sense that Donna Haraway and other have identified, and also seals off the possibility of becoming-animal, when such becoming-animal itself simply reanimates control mechanisms.

In her introduction to this project, Frida Beckman poignantly asks: control of what (see p. 1)?. Like the characters that recognise their own dispensability alongside that of others, alongside the soldier who shoots dogs at home and abroad, the current moment seems to offer a frighteningly nihilistic answer. That answer at times takes the form of answering the question 'control of what?' by saying 'control of everyone and everything', where such control extends to actions and emotions, bodies and brains, species in the singular and plural. Cumulatively, it takes on an even more nihilistic form. It eliminates the 'of what' from the question, so that control stands alone and has become separate from concrete objects. It is hard for us to theorise control in the abstract. Even when we eliminate specific actors in favour of, say, actor-network theory, there is still something there that is exerting control. But Phil Klay's story opens the possibility that control becomes a mechanism in and of itself – that the control that is exerted in turn exerts control, and that a deeply dystopian spiral comes into existence, generating control as such, without an object beyond itself. That is also what makes contemporary cartoons so disturbing: in operationalising Scooby, they foreclose the alternatives they might once have opened.

BIBLIOGRAPHY

Agamben, Giorgio (1998), 'Homo Sacer: Sovereign Power and Bare Life', trans. Daniel Heller-Roazen, in *Crossing Aesthetics*, ed. Werner Hamacher and David E. Wellbery, Stanford: Stanford University Press.
Ahmed, Sara (2017), 'Affective Economies', in *Literary Theory: An Anthology*, ed. J. Rivkin and M. Ryan, Malden, UK: Blackwell Publishing, pp. 1312–29.
Bartkowski, Frances (2008), *Kissing Cousins: A New Kinship Bestiary*, New York: Columbia University Press.

Boggs, Colleen Glenney (2013), *Animalia Americana: Animal Representations and Biopolitical Subjectivity*, New York and London: Columbia University Press.
Deleuze, Gilles and Félix Guattari (1987), *A Thousand Plateaus: Capitalism and Schizophrenia*, trans. Brian Massumi, Minneapolis and London: University of Minnesota Press.
Foucault, Michel (1979), *Discipline and Punish: The Birth of the Prison*, New York: Vintage Books.
Goh, Irving (2006), 'The Question of Community in Deleuze and Guattari (I): Anti-Community', *symploke* 14:1/2, pp. 216–31.
Haraway, Donna (2006), 'Encounters with Companion Species: Entangling Dogs, Baboons, Philosophers and Biologists', *Configurations* 14, pp. 97–114.
Haraway, Donna (2008), *When Species Meet*, Minneapolis and London: University of Minnesota Press.
Klay, Phil (2014), *Redeployment*, New York: Penguin Books.
Locke, John (1968), *The Educational Writings of John Locke: A Critical Edition with Introduction and Notes*, ed. James L. Axtell, Cambridge: Cambridge University Press.
Parker-Starbuck, Jennifer (2006), 'Becoming-Animate: On the Performed Limits of "Human"', *Theater Journal* 58:4: pp. 649–68.
Singer, Peter and Karen Dawn (2004), 'Echoes of Abu Ghraib in Chicken Slaughterhouse', *Los Angeles Times*, 25 July 2004, M. 5.
The Military Balance (2016), 'Chapter Three: North America', *The Military Balance* 116:1, pp. 27–54.
US and World Population Clock. United States Census Bureau, http://www.census.gov/popclock/
Wills, David (2008), *Dorsality: Thinking Back through Technology and Politics*, Minneapolis: University of Minnesota Press.
Wolfe, Cary and Jonathan Elmer (1995), 'Subject to Sacrifice: Ideology, Psychoanalysis, and the Discourse of Species in Jonathan Demme's *Silence of the Lambs*', *boundary 2* 2:3, pp. 141–70.

CHAPTER 10

Control and a Minor Literature

Frida Beckman

No, I didn't want freedom. Only a way out – to the right or left or anywhere at all. I made no other demands. (Kafka 2015: 83)

While Gilles Deleuze's control theories have been gaining attention within fields such as philosophy and political theory, their possible effects on and in relation to the field of literature is if not an undeveloped then certainly an underdeveloped mode of enquiry. Deleuze writes in his 'Postscript' that there is no need to worry about the increasingly all-encompassing control mechanisms that he outlines, but that we must nonetheless search for 'new weapons'. Here, I would like to point to how Deleuze himself, especially in his collaborations with Guattari, can help us develop such 'weapons' in a specifically literary context and thus help us read and understand literature in control society. Because I see this as the beginning of what I hope to be a broader engagement by literary scholars with Deleuze's conception of control, I will address what seems to be an obvious question to ask literature within such theoretical parameters: the relation between the history of the novel and discipline. The emergence of the novel in the Western world is intimately associated with the emergence of industrial capitalism and, in turn, with the focus on the individual but well-trained bourgeois subject, and it could be interesting, therefore, to think about ways in which the novel as a form and our novel reading as interpreting subjects might be affected by the continued development of disciplinary society towards the somewhat different structures and mechanisms of control society.

Theories of the development of the novel have in common an emphasis on the connection between its form and its focus on the individual. The hero of earlier literary forms, such as the epic, was never strictly speaking an individual, as György Lukács points out, but rather a representation of the relation between the parts and the whole (Lukács 1971: 66). Indeed, the focus on the general and the universal was, Mikhail Bakhtin observes, so central to the epic that it disintegrates as a form as the individual perspective increases (Bakhtin 1981: 34). Ian Watt notes that the novel's focus on this perspective fundamentally challenged the formal demands of earlier literary forms since capturing the unique experience of the individual meant a departure from the predetermined and the general (Watt 2000: 30). But unlike the heroes of the epic, who had cosmic possibilities, Guido Mazzoni points out, this individual is also represented as inevitably shaped by laws and institutions (Mazzoni 2017: 222–5). This feature is underlined by new historicists such as D. A. Miller and Jeremy Tambling who point to the close relations between the novel and constructions of the subject in industrial capitalism (see Miller 1988 and Tambling 1995). In other words, it is an ambivalent and ambiguous individual who emerges through and with the novel. On the one hand, the integrity of individuals as thinking subjects with a right to themselves is forwarded and supported. Cartesian theories of the subject are significant as are Locke's and Hobbes' theories of the individual's possession of the self as property that will have enormous influence on the modern society and the novel building that emerges with industrial capitalism. What C. P. Macpherson later comes to theorise in terms of 'possessive individualism' lays the ground for what Watt sees as an increasingly strong focus on 'economic individualism' as the novel takes shape as a mode of literary expression. With the middle class, in other words, and as we already know, grows a focus on the individual and the liberal subject is ascribed a considerable role in the development of society. On the other hand, the construction of the individual in the novel is affected by the civil society of which it constitutes a part. The ambition of the novel to capture ordinary people and ordinary life is reflected exactly in how the individual is recurrently circumscribed by state policy, the law, labour specialisation and other restrictions of the individual subject (Mazzoni 2017: 225).

This aspect has also been developed in Foucauldian readings of how the novel form is shaped by, but also constitutes a part of, the power structures of disciplinary society. During the nineteenth century, Foucault notes, the more spectacular and hierarchal forms of power that had previously shaped the West are increasingly replaced by discreet and continuous techniques of power. Surveillance, training and normalisation take place via societal institutions; the family, the school, the factory, the army barracks and the prison come to constitute major instruments and functions of power. In disciplinary society, people are no longer controlled as a great and anonymous mass but by being individualised as subjects. Correct training, Foucault shows, is enabled by observation, normalisation and examination. The role of the institution is to measure, differentiate, examine, analyse, divide and train individuals and thus to ascertain a normative behaviour. The individual, he insists, is not an elementary nucleus that can be exposed to or protected from power; what disciplinary society makes clear is how the construction of 'bodies, gestures, and desires' in terms of individuals is itself an effect of this modern construction of power (Foucault 2003: 29–30). As Michael Hardt puts it, disciplinary society thus comes to constitute the underside of civil society (Hardt 1995: 33).

In *Discipline and Punish*, Foucault notes a connection between these shifting power structures and developments in literature. While the epic constructs unique heroes and depicts their great and honourable deeds, the novel both accounts for and creates individual subjects that, through precisely this process, can be objectified as well as normalised. In other words, the novel becomes part of the 'correct training' of disciplinary society. Miller places the emerging novel form in this context and underlines how disciplinary power becomes part of both its form and its function. Characters of the novel go through disciplinary training and normalisation and through this the class divisions of society become clear. This happens, Miller insists, via the novel's 'double plot'. For example, he shows how Dickens' novels put into contrast the more overt police form of power that keeps the poor and the working class under control with the more discreet and disciplinary power that takes place via the social training of the middle class – a Foucauldian micropolitics. According to this reading, not only the characters of the novel but also the readers of the novel are shaped by discipline – the novel form becomes part of the internalisation of the functions of disciplinary society. In a similar fashion, Tambling explores the extent to which the novel form is not just influenced by but also very much aware of the power structures growing strong during this period. Both Miller and Tambling thus suggest, in slightly different ways, that the novel form does not just happen to coexist with or reflect disciplinary society but is actually deeply imbricated in its forms of power.

In this light, and by clarifying and emphasising the gradually changing role of institutions and individuals in society after World War II, Deleuze's control texts impel us to pose questions regarding the current status of such relations between discipline and literature. Alongside various developments, not the least technological, subtler forms of control emerge, as Deleuze shows. These forms are not primarily dependent on institutions or on normalised individuals. Deleuze's starting point is specifically in Foucault's theories of disciplinary society as well as in his indications, in his late lectures at Collège de France, towards gradual changes in its power structures. In *Discipline and Punish*, as we have noted, Foucault theorises the emergence of disciplinary society during the eighteenth and nineteenth centuries and its characteristics – how the subject and the individual are shaped and trained via the many institutions of society. But in his later lectures at Collège de France, later collected as *'Society Must be Defended': Lectures at the Collège de France 1975–76* (2003) and *The*

Birth of Biopolitics: Lectures at the Collège de France 1978–79 (2004), he notes how these power structures continue to develop – the influence of institutions decreases and control begins to take different shapes. The individual as such takes on less importance as a mode and target of control as the biopolitics Foucault describes here focuses rather on life itself in all its shapes and forms, from cells to species. After a technology of power that focuses on the body as an individual, he explains, follows another which is not individualising but rather 'massifying', that is, 'directed not as man-as-body but at man-as-species' (Foucault 2003: 243).

When Deleuze starts developing these theories at the end of the 1980s and beginning of the 1990s, he sees how such control is increasingly replacing disciplinary society (Deleuze 1995a). While disciplinary mechanisms are analogous, control society is digital and its individuals, if they can still be called that, are in continuous change in relation to different irregular points of contact. In this context, it is no longer the individual and its training and normalisation as a unit that constitutes a central focus. Through the more free-floating and all-encompassing modes of power characteristic of control society, it is smaller components that matter. Control is less of individuals and more on a more minute level of detail – of affects and desires. Deleuze brings out the concept of the 'dividual' to illuminate how the components of life that are controlled and manipulated in control society no longer can be reinscribed in the context of the individual. Instead of signatures or numbers designating individuals in disciplinary society, control society is characterised by codes and data. Where disciplinary society is compared with a mole and its burrows, control society is a serpent, the coils of which 'are even more intricate' (Deleuze 1995a: 182).

As I note in my introductory chapter to this book, Deleuze gives Burroughs the dubitable honour of having named this 'new monster', but while he is careful to refer to Burroughs repeatedly regarding nomenclature – in 'Postscript' as well as in 'Control and Becoming' – Deleuze does not offer a developed analysis of what exactly Burroughs' literature does to illuminate such control mechanisms. The most concrete articulation he makes in relation to this can be found in a letter to Serge Daney where he recognises how Burroughs takes the problem of control to the very heart of literature by replacing authors and authority with control and controllers (Deleuze 1995b: 75). Other small pointers can be found in other places in his philosophical works where Burroughs is mentioned more or less in passing, like for example in *Francis Bacon: The Logic of Sensation* (Deleuze 2003) where he compares Bacon's and Burroughs' ability, in art and literature, to see how the body works to 'escape through a point or through a hole that forms apart of itself or its surroundings' (Deleuze 2003: 17) or where he and Claire Parnet, in *Dialogues*, want to show how 'pick up' as a method is more useful than Burroughs' cut up (Deleuze and Parnet 2007: 10) or where he and Guattari read Burroughs' *Naked Lunch* as a schizoid body in *A Thousand Plateaus*. But it is clear that Burroughs not only formulates control as a concept but also struggles with ways of adjusting and relating to the ever-present control – by and via information and communication – that he has identified and that he counters them by means of formal experimentation. Later researchers have followed this up more closely than Deleuze did and so we see, for example, how Timothy D. Murphy, Nathan Moore and Christopher Land work to further develop Deleuze's control theories in widely different contexts – from literature to organisational theory to law – while repeatedly returning to Burroughs' literary texts (see Murphy 1997; Land 2005; Moore 2007).

Compared to the short reference to Burroughs in 'Postscript' and 'Control and Becoming' the attention to Kafka in 'Postscript', which includes no less than seven lines, seems almost detailed. Deleuze points specifically towards Kafka's *The Trial* as a novel which captures the gradual transition between discipline and control that Deleuze works to theorise. Kafka's novel, he suggests, shows how the disciplinary system – where the individual, as a seemingly free agent, moves from one institution to another – is breaking down to make room for a control society in which control is exercised through constant change and postponement (Deleuze 1995a: 179). In their book about Kafka, Deleuze and Guattari develop readings of his work in relation to the machinic and to minor literature, but here, in the control essay, Deleuze thus presents Kafka as an example of how the breaking point between discipline and control is signalled within the framework of the novel. This brief reference makes for a concise example of how literature works with these transitions of power and also gives an indication of how Deleuze's and Deleuze and Guattari's earlier theories on literature may help us approach the challenges literature generally and the novel especially may face in control society. Because, naturally, it is to Deleuze and Guattari's *Kafka: Toward A Minor Literature* (1986) that we must turn to continue developing Deleuze's control theories in a literary context. Deleuze's reference to Kafka in his control texts has, of course, been noted before and analyses of Kafka from a political perspective are hardly uncommon, and neither are readings of his work within the framework of biopolitics more specifically, but few have stopped to look at how Deleuze and Guattari formulate, via Kafka, what could be a strategy for reading literature in the era of control.[1]

In *Kafka* we see how Deleuze and Guattari are sceptical of the possibilities of the novel to break free from the economy of the individual. Becoming remains highly limited, at least within the novel tradition to which I have referred above and which Deleuze and Guattari would undoubtedly have called a major literature. A major literature is constructed by genres, shaped by traditions and inflected by long-term structures. It puts faith in representation and interpretation. It is thus a part of an economy of molar structures where the individual is central and the narrative representational. Characteristic of a major literature is that it makes space for the drama of the individual 'in the light of day' while consigning the political to the basement (Deleuze and Guattari 1986: 17). Even if it from a literary perspective can be worth noting that the novel form is historically one of the least formally bound modes of literary expression and that we also need to acknowledge its experimental side, it is clear, as I have suggested earlier, that this loose and experimental form nonetheless seems inevitably centred on the development of the individual with the context as background. This can be connected to the earlier mentioned ambivalent individualism characteristic of the emergence of the modern novel, and that is shaped both by strong theories of the individual and by the power mechanisms of industrial capitalism. It can also be compared to the civil society that, Hardt suggests, is shaped by two sides – an upper side that can be seen to reflect Gramsci's belief in the ultimate goal of democracy existing beyond the state and within the self-determination of the individual – and a disciplinary underside, that makes clear how power cannot be separated from the individual, as Foucault insists (Hardt 1995: 33). Hardt reads Deleuze's texts on control society in this context and expands on how the new control mechanisms that Deleuze describes cause the gradual perishing of civil society. Gramsci's and Foucault's theories no longer suffice to analyse this emerging 'postcivil' society. Deleuze's brief interpolation on control society can, according to Hardt, be seen as constituting a first attempt at developing a new theory (Hardt 1995: 34). And, of course, Hardt himself, as well as Negri and others, continue to develop such a theory within the frames of political theory.

But also exactly from a literary perspective, and if we take a closer look at how Deleuze and Guattari analyse the novel form's intimate connections with the economy of a major literature, we can see how Deleuze's brief sketches on control society can be further developed within the framework of his own production. Discussions of this kind are held in the Kafka book. Apart from novels, Kafka also wrote short stories and letters and while much if not most of this – and especially the letters and the novels – were never intended for publication, these different forms of writing give some insight into Kafka's writing processes. It is mainly the contrast between the novels and the shorter stories that Deleuze and Guattari are interested in.[2] And here becoming-animal comes to constitute a fault line. Unlike the short stories, which are densely populated with animals and animal-becomings, Deleuze and Guattari note that there are very few animals in Kafka's novels and definitely no becoming-animal. It is, they suggest, as if becoming-animal cannot be developed within this format 'as though the becoming-animal was not rich enough in articulations and junctions'. By toying with the idea that Kafka would have written about 'the bureaucratic world of ants or about the Castle of the termites', they realise that this would have resulted in science fiction and a form of descriptive symbolic writing that has little in common with Kafka's project (Deleuze and Guattari 1986: 38). This is what makes them look at the tensions and differences between the short stories and the novels in Kafka's oeuvre. The differences between the two can, as they admit, be questioned considering the fact that some of the stories consist of the beginning of unfinished novels and the novels constitute unfinished stories (Deleuze and Guattari 1986: 38). But ultimately, this strengthens rather than weakens their argument. The short stories show how becoming-animal functions to resist the mechanisms of major literature. And in the three novels that were actually published[3] – *The Trial* (1925), *The Castle* (1926) and *America* (1927) – inhuman violence and desire are effected 'through the use of human parts and cogs' (Deleuze and Guattari 1986: 39). This way, becoming-animal appears also in the novels, even if it is never developed, and the novels thus come to point to new assemblages.

Five points are noted in Deleuze and Guattari's attempt to explain why the novel struggles to break free from the structures of major literature. In a first point they note that a text that includes animal-becomings cannot be developed into a novel. Here, they give 'The Metamorphosis' as an example, where Gregor's reinscription into Oedipal family structures lead to his death. In point two, they see how a text about animal-becomings cannot be developed into a novel unless it includes enough machinic connections beyond the animal, connections that constitute seeds for the novel exactly because they go beyond the animal. This, they suggest, is the case in 'The Investigations of a Hound' where the investigations themselves create potential frameworks for development but where the project ultimately fails. The third point explains how Kafka comes to abandon a text that seems like a seed to a novel if he sees the seed as a possible escape route, 'an animal escape that allows him to finish with it' (Deleuze and Guattari 1986: 38). So for example the temptation of letting the traveller become-animal in one of the versions of 'The Penal Colony' is greater than the prospect of following up on the concretely machinic and thus construct a novel. The fourth and, according to themselves, only positive point underlines how a novel cannot become a novel unless the machinic connections are organised into real and independent assemblages. This happens in each of Kafka's three novels as the machinic, the human and the social make up the cogs that bring the novels into being. In the fifth point, we see how a text that includes machines will not be developed unless it manages to couple up to a concrete sociopolitical assemblage, as in for example 'The Cares of a Family Man', where the machine becomes too abstract (see Deleuze and Guattari 1986: 38–40 for a discussion of all five points).

Deleuze and Guattari thus emphasise the formal difficulties and limitations that the novel form has in creating a minor literature. Kafka, they suggest, has many reasons to abandon his texts before they turn into novels and each failure constitutes a success. But at the same time as they illuminate the difficulties of the novel to incorporate becomings, it is (and to return to our discussion of control) *The Trial* – a novel – that Deleuze presents as constituting a good description of the transition between discipline and control in his 'Postscript'. This is interesting in the light of what we have just noted regarding the novel form and the way in which it is exactly at the breaking point that something happens. It is precisely because Kafka's novel takes shape – with the help of Josef K's wanderings between institutions – while at the same time resisting any division between the individual and the political that the control mechanisms that Deleuze describes become visible. This may be contrasted with the similar vacillation between power systems that Dimitris Vardoulakis notes in 'In the Penal Colony' – this time between three modalities of sovereignty – and the way in which the malfunctioning of the machine and the resultant premature death of the officer aborts the diffused workings of biopower (Vardoulakis 2016: 129–30). In *The Trial*, on the other hand, the control mechanisms become visible because Josef K, in accordance with Deleuze and Guattari's fourth point above, remain part of the process. In a similar way, Deleuze and Guattari underline how K, in *The Castle*, is 'nothing but desire: a single problem, to establish or maintain "contact" with the Castle, to establish or maintain a "liason"' (Deleuze and Guattari 1986: 58).

Earlier readings of Deleuze and Guattari's *Kafka* underline the ways in which *The Trial* consists of an open ended machinic desiring-machine. In this novel, Ronald Bogue notes, everyone is directly coupled up to an eroticised and all-encompassing social machine: the law. Josef K's journey goes 'from one assemblage of individuals, discourses, codes and objects to another' and through an 'open-ended series of connected components, all infused with an immanent desire' (Bogue 2003: 79). Bogue underlines how Deleuze and Guattari illuminate the immanent criticism in Kafka's work, a criticism that works 'by extracting "from social representations assemblages of enunciation and machinic assemblages and dismantling these assemblages"' (Bogue 2003: 80; also Deleuze and Guattari 1986: 46). As Bogue shows, Kafka's novel does not function primarily within an economy of representation, interpretation and meaning, but as an experimental machine (Bogue 2003: 80). Or, as Deleuze and Guattari themselves express it,

> [a] Kafka machine is thus constituted by contents and expressions that have been formalized to diverse degrees by unformed materials that enter into it, and leave by passing through all possible states. To enter or leave the machine, to be in the machine, to walk around it, to approach it – these are all still components of the machine itself: these are states of desire, free of all interpretation. (Deleuze and Guattari 1986: 7)

If we add to Deleuze's brief lines about Kafka in his control essay these more developed readings of how Kafka struggles to create lines of flight also within the format of the novel, we can see at least the beginnings of a way of tackling literature in control society. A Deleuzian and Guattarian perspective on literature in relation to control brings out how the emphasis on the individual in a major literature, as in civil society, can be seen as dependent on a disciplinary shadow life. At the same time, such a perspective underlines how a 'minor' reading can throw light on how everything is political and how the individual, to the extent we can still call it that, is directly coupled up with the political. Deleuze and Guattari cite Kafka:

> Even though something is often thought through calmly, one still does not reach the boundary where it connects up with similar things, one reaches the boundary soonest in politics, indeed, one even strives to see it before it is there, and often sees this limiting boundary everywhere. (Deleuze and Guattari 1986: 17)

Here, and sort of in passing, in a footnote, Deleuze and Guattari indicate a parallel between Foucault's theories of disciplinary society and Kafka's literary works. Foucault's method, as they note, is obviously quite different, but in its emphasis on the segmentarity and the immanent character of power, it is 'not without a certain Kafkaesque resonance' (Deleuze and Guattari 1986: 97, n3). Unlike a major literature, a minor literature comes before form and can, if necessary, break it up. When characters in minor literature are made up of desire and connections rather than individual subjects the formal limitations of the novel are challenged. Neither the individual nor the background remain the same. It is no longer possible to distinguish between what 'goes on down below' and what 'takes place in the full light of day' (Deleuze and Guattari 1986: 17). And with this opening, it also becomes easier to discern how tensions between discipline and control are expressed in literature.

In this way, the potential for minor literature to take on mechanisms of control society becomes visible, and it becomes equally visible that such possibilities do not exist in the same way in major literature. It seems evident that the emphasis on the individual in major literature makes it difficult for it to capture the more discreet mechanisms of control society. The parallel emergence of the modern novel and industrial society and the disciplinary power constructing its individuals on the one hand, and the liberal ideas of the subject influenced, as we have seen, by Descartes, Locke and Hobbes and thus with the two sides of civil society on the other, ties it to these strong but ambivalent traditions. But unlike a major literature, a minor literature does not have investments in conceptions of the individual and civil society and, therefore, such conceptions need not overshadow the desires and affect that, according to Deleuze and Guattari, constitute the dynamics of becoming. Quite on the contrary, it is exactly the movement away from the drama of the individual that is key. In a minor literature, becoming is deterritorialised; in a minor literature, everything is political; in a minor literature, everything has a collective value (Deleuze and Guattari 1986: 16–17). When they suggest that everything is political in a minor literature this is, as Réda Bensmaïa notes in his introduction to the English translation of the Kafka book, exactly because activity cannot be traced back to a unified and 'autonomous subjective substance that would be the *origin* of the choices we make, of the tastes we have, and of the life we lead' (Bensmaïa 1986: xviii). Deleuze and Guattari, as Bensmaïa underlines, want us to pay attention to the work done demolishing forms and categories that shape major literature (Bensmaïa 1986: xix). Instead of representing the individual subject, a minor literature notes connections and blockages of desire, it shows how the cogs of the machinery are different every time. This way, it also makes it easier to see when these cogs make up the tracks of a mole and when they follow the coils of the snake.

My point here is obviously not to suggest a direct equivalence between a minor literature and control society. Instead, what I have tried to illustrate is the many reasons to engage the former to better understand and analyse the latter. The mechanisms of control society and a minor literature both share a movement away from individuals and institutions, they both dissolve the borders between the upper and undersides of civil society, they are both interested in the permanent flows of desire. But in order to make a minor literature into the 'weapon' Deleuze asks for in his 'Postscript', it is also necessary, of course, to note how it contrasts with control society. To begin with, control is related to power, and its mechanisms are tied up with political and economic interests. The shifts towards control society constitute an effectivisation and intensification of control in accordance with the mechanisms of contemporary capitalism. Of course, a minor literature does not have any such interests and is not of the kind to be able to have interests to begin with. Second, control society has nothing to lose from a continued belief in the centrality of individuals and institutions to society – quite on the contrary, such beliefs constitute a convenient construction that hides the modulations of affect and desires that are harder to grasp. A minor literature, on the other hand, functions exactly to bring out that which constructions of individuals and institutions hide, 'the problem is not that of being free but of finding a way out, or even a way in, another side, a hallway, an adjacency' (Deleuze and Guattari 1986: 7–8), it wants to see 'how the map is modified if one enters by another point' (Deleuze and Guattari 1986: 3).

It seems, then, that Deleuze and Guattari's analysis of a minor literature can be useful in understanding literature in control society on two levels. To begin with, it can help us bring out and illuminate other forces and dynamics in the history of the novel. Because even if their reading of Kafka is heavily anchored in the specificities of Kafka's writing – his letters, his stories, his novels – its purpose is to bring out minor literature as a practice. In reality, and as Bogue points out, a minor literature is not so much a subcategory of literature but rather literature as it could (Bogue actually says 'should') work. This is the literature that Deleuze loves – full of becomings, stutterings, collective enunciations and 'a people to come' (Bogue 2003: 162). In reality, there is plenty of such literature – Deleuze himself tends to refer to authors such as Herman Melville, Antonin Artaud, Samuel Beckett and Lewis Carroll, to mention a few – and his and Guattari's readings can and have helped us find additional examples. This way, other established authors and texts can also be revisited and aspects that escape the disciplinary moulds of the established traditions of the novel may be illuminated. This reading practice is already well established within Deleuzian studies generally, but perhaps it is also possible to strengthen more specifically how a minor literature can illuminate or even challenge the biopolitical underpinnings of the modern novel.

Second, and this is a more specific but less developed dimension, Deleuze and Guattari's minor literature can provide us with the tools to analyse the relation between cultural expression and contemporary control mechanisms. The traditions of a major literature build, as we have seen, on the ambiguous grounds of individualism and disciplinarity that make up – or made up – civil society. As long as its narrative negotiations continue to mirror these grounds it remains hard for the novel to capture the spirit of control society, and it also, if involuntarily, risks hiding this spirit by reproducing ideas of the individual and its agency that are no longer completely tenable. A minor literature, on the other hand, brings out these smaller parts that control society has learned to play. By being open to dynamics outside the frameworks of the individual and institutions, it has the capacity to expose the mechanisms that now infuse every dimension of life. By resisting the impulse to interpret, find structures and organise into genres and forms (see for example Deleuze and Guattari 1986: 7) a minor literature also resists the traditions of representation and interpretation that enfold literature in disciplinary moulds. As Deleuze and Guattari make clear, it is not always literature itself but our readings of it that make the principles of a major literature overshadow those of a minor one. In other words, it might not be primarily a different kind of literature that we need to understand control society but a different way of reading literature. A work of art, Deleuze stresses in 'Having an Idea in Cinema' – and here we can add 'a literary reading' – must appeal to a people that does not yet exist (Deleuze 1998: 19). As Deleuze and Guattari note, a major language can open for an intensive use that discovers other lines, other openings (Deleuze and Guattari 1986: 26). I mentioned in my Introduction that Deleuze asks us in his 'Postscript' to seek 'new weapons' to deal with the challenges of control society. And as I have tried to show in this chapter, when it comes to literature, he and Guattari themselves provide great ammunition.

NOTES

1. For references to Kafka and Deleuze's concept of control, see for example Elmer (2012: 26) and O'Sullivan (2016: 209).
2. Max Brod disregarded Kafka's wish to have the novels and anything else not already published destroyed after his death.
3. Although they were indeed published eventually, it remains questionable whether Kafka's three novels really were complete – Brod's notes show Kafka himself saw *The Trial* as unfinished and Bogue underlines how all three novels can be seen as unfinished, but 'only unfinished in that they are machines that continue to operate without completely breaking down' (Bogue 2003: 78).

BIBLIOGRAPHY

Bakhtin, Mikhail (1981), *The Dialogic Imagination: Four Essays*, trans. Caryl Emerson and Michael Holquist, Austin: University of Texas Press.
Bensmaïa, Réda (1986), 'Foreword', in Gilles Deleuze and Félix Guattari, *Kafka: Toward a Minor Literature*, Minneapolis and London: University of Minnesota Press.
Bogue, Ronald (2003), *Deleuze on Literature*, New York: Routledge.
Deleuze, Gilles (1992), 'What is a Dispositif?', in *Michel Foucault Philosopher*, trans. Timothy J. Armstrong, New York and London: Harvester Wheatsheaf, pp. 159–66.
Deleuze, Gilles (1995a), 'Postscript on Control Societies', in *Negotiations*, trans. Martin Joughin, New York: Columbia University Press.
Deleuze, Gilles (1995b), 'Letter to Serge Daney: Optimism, Pessimism, and Travel', in *Negotiations*, trans. Martin Joughin, New York: Columbia University Press.
Deleuze, Gilles (1998), 'Having an Idea in Cinema (On the Cinema of Straub-Huillet)', trans. Eleanor Kaufman, in *Deleuze and Guattari: New Mappings in Politics, Philosophy, and Culture*, ed. Eleanor Kaufman and Kevin Jon Heller, Minneapolis: University of Minnesota Press, pp. 14–19.
Deleuze, Gilles (2003), *Francis Bacon: The Logic of Sensation*, trans. Daniel W. Smith, London: Continuum.
Deleuze, Gilles (2007), *Two Regimes of Madness, Texts and Interviews 1975–1995*, ed. David Lapoujade, trans. Ames Hodges and Mike Taormina, Cambridge: The MIT Press, pp. 312–24.
Deleuze, Gilles and Félix Guattari (1986), *Kafka: Toward a Minor Literature*, Minneapolis and London: University of Minnesota Press.
Deleuze Gilles and Claire Parnet (2007), *Dialogues II Revised Edition*, trans. Hugh Tomlinson and Barbara Habberjam, New York: Columbia University Press.
Elmer, Greg (2012), 'Panopticon–Discipline–Control', in *Routledge Handbook of Surveillance Studies*, ed. Kirstie Ball, Kevin D. Haggerty and David Lyon, New York: Routledge.
Foucault, Michel (2003), *'Society Must Be Defended': Lectures at the Collège de France, 1975–76*, trans. David Macey, New York: Picador.

Hardt, Michael (1995), 'The Withering of Civil Society', *Social Text* 45:14, pp. 27–44.
Kafka, Franz (2015), 'A Report for an Academy', in *Collected Works*, Herstellung und Verlag: BoD – Books on Demand Nordenstedt.
Land, Christopher (2005), 'Apomorphine Silence: Cutting-up Burroughs' Theory of Language and Control', *Ephemera: Theory & Politics in Organization* 5:3, pp. 450–71.
Lukács, György (1971), *The Theory of the Novel: A Historico-Philosophical Essay on the Forms of Great Epic Literature*, trans. Anna Bostock, Berlin: Merlin Press.
Mazzoni, Guido (2017), *Theory of the Novel*, trans. Zakiya Hanafi, Cambridge, MA: Harvard University Press.
Miller, D. A. (1988), *The Novel and the Police*, Berkley and Los Angeles: University of California Press.
Moore Nathan (2007), 'Nova Law: William S. Burroughs and the Logic of Control', *Law & Literature* 19:3, pp. 435–70.
Murphy, Timothy S. (1997), *Wising Up the Marks: The Amodern William Burroughs*, Berkeley: University of California Press.
O'Sullivan, Simon (2016), 'Deleuze against Control: Fictioning to Myth-Science', *Theory, Culture & Society* 33:7–8, pp. 205–20.
Tambling, Jeremy (1995), *Dickens, Violence and the Modern State: Dreams of the Scaffold*, Basingstoke: Macmillan Press.
Vardoulakis, Dimitris (2016), *Freedom from the Free Will: On Kafka's Laughter*, Albany: SUNY Press.
Watt, Ian (2000), *The Rise of the Novel: Studies in Defoe, Richardson and Fielding*, London: Pimlico.

CHAPTER 11

Philosophy and Control

Paul Patton

Deleuze's 'Postscript on Control Societies' is one of his most influential essays. As noted in the Introduction to this volume, it was published in French in *L'autre journal*, before it appeared alongside the 'Control and Becoming' interview with Antonio Negri in Deleuze's *Pourparlers* (see Introduction, p. 1). It first appeared in English in *October* in 1992 before the translation of *Negotiations* in 1995 (Deleuze 1995a: 169–76). Both English versions have been widely cited. The influence of this short essay is further amplified by references to it in highly cited works such as those by Nikolas Rose, Michael Hardt and Antonio Negri (Rose 1999: 233–5; Hardt and Negri 2000: 22–3).[1]

Deleuze's 'Postscript' is also one of his more enigmatic essays, giving rise to a variety of interpretations of what exactly is meant by control, along with multiple and sometimes conflicting accounts of its relationship to Foucault's concepts of disciplinary, biopolitical and modern liberal and neoliberal society. I begin with a brief discussion of the relationship to Foucault and the specific content of Deleuze's concept of control, before turning to the real focus of this chapter, namely the application of this concept to philosophy. I explore the institutional mechanisms of power in philosophy and how these have evolved in the context of control societies. Finally, I discuss the relevance of Deleuze and Guattari's experimental practice of philosophy and its associated rhizomatic image of thought to the discipline and practice of philosophy in control societies.

DELEUZE'S CONCEPT OF CONTROL

Deleuze argues in 'Postscript' that in the latter half of the twentieth century disciplinary society was being replaced by control society. He takes the term 'control' from William Burroughs, but the connection to Foucault is more important, locating control society in the lineage of sovereign and then disciplinary societies outlined in *Discipline and Punish*. This connection allows readers to assume that Deleuze is simply extending the analysis of technologies of power initiated by Foucault, even though they offer varying accounts of the relationship between Foucault's work and Deleuze's concept of control.[2] However, Deleuze takes the alignment with Foucault further by attributing to him his own diagnosis of the present as the period in which control societies are replacing disciplinary societies. In the 'Control and Becoming' interview with Negri, he suggests that Foucault 'was actually one of the first to say that we're moving away from disciplinary societies' (Deleuze 1995a: 174). In 'Postscript', he argues that, as the government of lives by means of disciplinary techniques deployed in closed institutions such as the family, school, barracks, factory, hospital and prison began to break down, 'we were no longer in disciplinary societies, we were leaving them behind' (Deleuze 1995a: 178). He then goes on to suggest that Foucault, like William Burroughs and Paul Virilio, saw that the new form of control society was 'fast approaching' (Deleuze 1995a: 178).

Foucault's interviews support Deleuze's first claim but not the second. For example, in a 1977 discussion of Bentham's *Panopticon* with historians, he noted that 'the procedures of power at work in modern societies are much more numerous, diverse and rich' than the principles of permanent visibility so important to Bentham and that it 'would be wrong to say that the principle of visibility governs all technologies of power used since the nineteenth century' (Gordon 1980: 148).[3] However, there is no support in interviews or anywhere else for the stronger claim that Foucault thought disciplinary societies were giving way to societies of control (Deleuze 1995a: 174). Further confusion about the relationship between Deleuze's thesis and Foucault's analysis of discipline is generated by the fact that Foucault made widespread use of the word 'control' with reference to the operation of disciplinary power. In *Discipline and Punish*, for example, he introduces the concept of disciplinary power by reference to its novel object (the body), scale ('an infinitesimal power over the active body') and objective ('the meticulous control of the operations of the body') (Foucault 1995: 136–7).[4] On this basis, Mark Kelly argues that Deleuze's thesis is 'partly redundant, inasmuch as he is talking about things already covered by Foucault's notion of discipline, and partly simply false, describing as changes things which are either not new or are not happening at all' (Kelly 2015: 151). The problem with this argument is that it takes the appearance of a word to imply the appearance of a concept, thereby overlooking the fact that Deleuze is advancing a quite specific concept of control.

Control in Deleuze's sense of the term does not have the same object, nor the same objective as disciplinary power. It does not employ the same techniques or modes of regulation of individual and group behaviour. It does not operate on the physiological, affective and intellectual capacities of human bodies to produce certain kinds of individuals, as Foucault famously argued that disciplinary power produces docile and obedient subjects. Control societies do not 'mould' individuals in the way that disciplinary societies do, but rather 'modulate' certain 'dividuals'. Dividuals are not whole subjects but partial subjects defined by certain functional aspects identified in relation to particular ends. The same biological person might correspond to a financial capacity to repay a bank loan, as defined by their age, income, lifestyle and existing level of debt; to an intellectual capacity to undertake a given programme of study, as defined by their prior education and levels of achievement; and to a physiological capacity to qualify for a certain insurance product based on their medical history, genetic make-up and lifestyle. Each of these financial, intellectual and physiological dividuals can be tabulated and recorded along with others of the same kind to form a data bank that can be analysed and exploited for commercial, governmental or other ends.

In contrast to discipline, control does not establish institutional spaces of confinement where the actions of individuals can be strictly ordered in space and time. Control does not confine people but operates through 'continuous control and instant communication' (Deleuze 1995a: 174). It operates in the open rather than in confined spaces, by means of various digital and electronic technologies. To take an example that has emerged since Deleuze wrote his 'Postscript', consider the manner in which GPS location has become endemic in a whole series of devices, from mobile phones to electronic watches and other tracking devices. These simultaneously serve the interests of the individual who voluntarily consents to using them and the interests of the providers or other agencies who are thereby able to monitor the individual in the course of his or her daily activities.[5]

Control establishes series of thresholds through which individuals can only pass with appropriate passwords, which Deleuze contrasts with the 'order-words' that accomplish the transition from one phase or state of life to the next in disciplinary societies: childhood to adulthood, failure to success, good health to ill-health, and so on. These are not the increasingly complex, everyday passwords that we carry about as individual members of control societies. Rather, Deleuze uses the term to refer to the various ways in which we are coded to indicate that we meet the criteria for access to particular services or environments.

At the level of the modality of action, control mechanisms do not impose particular moulds according to the nature of the institution in which they are employed, producing a certain kind of subject, body or relationships. Rather, they involve the continuous modulation of behaviours or performances in and by means of their relations to one another. Deleuze writes that 'enclosures are moulds, distinct mouldings, but controls are modulations, like an auto-deforming [self-transmuting] mould that would continuously change from one moment to the next' (Deleuze 1995a: 178–9). He takes the concept of modulation from Simondon. Before this essay, he used it in a variety of contexts, including his elaboration of a transcendental empiricism in *Difference and Repetition*.[6]

Deleuze associates the emergence of control with a mutation in the nature of capitalism. He describes this in terms that partly recall the transition from Fordist to post-Fordist techniques of production, but also the transition from economies of production to economies based on services and the marketing of products produced elsewhere. Capitalism in its present form, he argues, relies on metaproduction rather than production,

> It no longer buys raw materials and no longer sells finished products: it buys finished products or assembles them from parts. What it seeks to sell is services, and what it seeks to buy are activities. It's a capitalism no longer directed towards production but toward products, that is, toward sales or markets. (Deleuze 1995a: 181)

Whereas discipline was a long-term, infinite and discontinuous process, control is 'short-term and rapidly shifting, but at the same time continuous and unbounded' (Deleuze 1995a: 181). This is consistent with the replacement of manufacture by the sale of services or immaterial products in the economic sphere, the replacement of apparent acquittal by unlimited deferral of judgment in the judicial sphere, and the replacement of examinations by continuous assessment in the educational sphere. He imagines education becoming less and less a matter of confining students to closed sites, such as schools or universities that are separate from workplaces, hospitals, military establishments or prisons, and more and more a matter of continual training and monitoring of behaviours: 'In a control-based system nothing's left alone for long' (Deleuze 1995a: 175).

PHILOSOPHY AND CONTROL 1: CONTROL OVER OTHER ACTIVITIES

In his brief survey of the transition to societies of control, Deleuze mentions a variety of social institutions and milieus: the school, the hospital, the judiciary, business and finance. However, he only indirectly refers to the university and makes no specific mention of philosophy. Can we identify a similar transition in a field as recondite as that of philosophy? How could we begin to think about control in relation to philosophy?

Perhaps we should begin by specifying the kind of control we are talking about. We can distinguish control exercised over activities external to philosophy, such as the conduct of scientific enquiry, the defence of human rights or the treatment of morality and politics in literature, from the kinds of control exercised within philosophy, such as what counts as philosophical argument or what kinds of issue are appropriate subject matter for philosophy. The first kind of control might seem to be a non-issue. After all, it is a long time since anyone took seriously the idea that philosophy was entitled to legislate over other disciplines or social practices. When Deleuze and Guattari define philosophy in *What is Philosophy?* as the art of making concepts, where these are distinct from the intellectual products of art and science, they are careful to point out that there is no hierarchy between these different forms of intellectual production.[7] However, the fact that it is necessary even to assert that philosophy enjoys no privileged status in relation to science or art might be considered evidence that this remains a sensitive issue among philosophers and nonphilosophers alike.

The same sensitivity is apparent in a recent exchange between Samuel Moyn and John Tasioulas over the nature of human rights.[8] Moyn criticised an article by Tasioulas that took issue with the controlling gesture of many philosophers of human rights who see themselves as responding to the 'proliferation of rights discourse' by stating clearly what is required for something to be a human right (Tasioulas 2012: 5). Tasioulas did not disagree with their concern to 'instil greater clarity and rigour into the discourse of human rights' but rather with the way they did this (Tasioulas 2012: 6). He accuses the philosophers of being unduly restrictive in seeking to found human rights on a single principle such as fundamental human interests, or freedom, and offers his own more liberal conception of the basis of human rights that includes not only fundamental interests but also human dignity and, importantly, a historically variable 'threshold' of the feasibility of ensuring that the rights in question are available to people (Tasioulas 2012: 15–18).

As liberal and historically sensitive as this may be, Tasioulas' conception of what it is to be a human right remains an exercise in identifying normative foundations. Moyn regards this as a philosopher's project that distracts us from conceiving of human rights as 'the political enterprise they also clearly are' (Moyn 2018: 70). His fundamental objection is that the philosopher's project shifts the object of enquiry from the intellectual, institutional and political processes by means of which internationally recognised human rights became established to the abstract and ahistorical terrain of moral norms:

'human rights in heaven, so to speak' (Moyn 2018: 78). In this sense, it is a type of intervention that serves to draw the discussion of human rights back into the realm of normative debate that is the specialty of philosophers. In reply, Tasioulas insists that he shares Moyn's desire to engage with the everyday practice of human rights and denies that he begins with an abstract and atemporal concept of human rights. Rather, he begins with the 'rich and complex discourse of human rights' and asks whether this discourse involves some core concept of a human right (Tasioulas 2018: 89). Not unlike Deleuze, he argues that this is what philosophers are good at, making concepts. He defends the philosopher's approach to human rights as simply a matter of expertise rather than an attempt to exercise authority over other disciplines or human rights practitioners.

PHILOSOPHY AND CONTROL 2: CONTROL IN/OF PHILOSOPHY

The second kind of control exercised within the practice of philosophy raises a different series of questions about the nature of the activity and its institutional setting. Consider first the activity of philosophising. Deleuze devoted a central chapter of *Difference and Repetition* to analysing the image of thought that, in his view, dominated European philosophy from Aristotle to Kant. This was a 'dogmatic, orthodox or moral image' of thought as representation, as a natural faculty of human beings, as oriented towards truth and only forced into error by forces external to thought, as propositional rather than problem-oriented, and so on (Deleuze 2011: 167ff.). He argued that these 'postulates' or presuppositions about the nature of thought were not so much explicit propositions defended by philosophers as implicit themes that formed part of a pre-philosophical understanding of thinking. Together, they defined an image of thought that served a repressive function whereby its postulates served to 'crush thought under an image which is that of the Same and the Similar in representation, and which profoundly betrays what it means to think' (Deleuze 2011: 207).

However, if we ask how this dogmatic image of thought functions as an apparatus of power, then we are inevitably led from the implicit postulates to the institutional and other mechanisms by means of which they become embedded in the minds of professional philosophers. In *Dialogues* Deleuze suggested that the history of philosophy has always been an apparatus or 'agent of power' in philosophy:

> A formidable school of intimidation which manufactures specialists in thought – but which also makes those who stay outside conform all the

more to this specialism which they despise. An image of thought called philosophy has been formed historically and it effectively stops people from thinking. (Deleuze and Parnet 2002: 13)

Deleuze's reference to the 'image of thought' here speaks to the way in which the history of philosophy is used to impose and reinforce the dogmatic conception of what it is to think. In France, the history of philosophy was able to function as a school of intimidation in part through the system of competitive examinations and prescribed curricula associated with the *agrégation de philosophie*. This involved competitive written and oral examinations, for which students studied a prescribed curriculum. The curriculum changed from year to year but mainly focused on the classical and early modern history of philosophy. Relatively few nineteenth-century philosophers figured on the programme, and even fewer from the twentieth century. The primary function of the *agrégation* was to select those who became teachers of philosophy in secondary schools and universities. The manner in which it functioned explains why a thorough grounding in the history of philosophy has long been a distinguishing feature of philosophy in France. Students were expected to become familiar with the entire oeuvre of those figures selected for the written examination in a given year. In addition, the influence of this examination on the nature of French philosophy is further magnified by the manner in which university teaching at the leading institutions such as the Sorbonne and the École Normale Supérieure became geared to the *agrégation* programme.[9]

Putting together Deleuze's analysis of the dogmatic image of thought and the institutional mechanisms through which this image is maintained and reinforced gives us something like what Deleuze and Guattari called an assemblage (*agencement*) or what Foucault called an apparatus (*dispositif*). This is a complex series of institutional and discursive acts, a system of things people say alongside or in response to a system of material practices or things people do. In these terms, in France, the history of philosophy amounts to an apparatus of control of, or control over, philosophy. It is a specifically philosophical apparatus of power that functions in a manner analogous to the way in which the apparatuses described by Foucault control other human activities.[10] For example, the carceral apparatus that emerged in Europe in the nineteenth century serves to control criminality, by recycling and reproducing it and at the same time producing new subjects of criminal behaviour. In similar fashion, the modern apparatus of sexuality produces a uniquely modern subject of desire and sexual activity that controls the sexual behaviour of individuals. In the same way, the French apparatus of the history of philosophy controls the activity of philosophy, producing a certain kind of philosopher thoroughly imbued with a canon of philosophical thinkers and trained to think philosophically by way of commentary and critical analysis of canonical texts.

Deleuze's own philosophical trajectory is defined by the French dispositif of the history of philosophy. As he says in dialogue with Parnet, he began with the history of philosophy. Throughout the first period of his career he was drawn to those thinkers who 'seemed to be part of the history of philosophy, but who escaped from it in one respect, or altogether: Lucretius, Spinoza, Hume, Nietzsche, Bergson' (Deleuze and Parnet 2002: 14). In his later work with Guattari, he explicitly sought to present another image of thought, one that was pragmatic or interventionist rather than representational. Although it often made use of historical figures, this was not a thought that took the form of commentary on or dialogue with the canonical figures of the history of philosophy. It was a rhizomatic or nomadic thought that sought to engage with and transform itself in relation to a variety of other intellectual activities, literary, anthropological, scientific, mathematical, musical and so on. This kind of 'thought without image – nomadism, the war-machine, becomings, nuptials against nature, capture and thefts, interregnums, minor languages or the stammering of language, etc.' did not seek to control philosophical thought but to engage it in an endless series of becomings, alongside and with other activities (Deleuze and Parnet 2002: 14).

Needless to say, for many philosophers this kind of thinking was unrecognisable as philosophy. It was seen rather as something to be 'crushed and denounced as a nuisance' (Deleuze and Parnet 2002: 14). On Deleuze's own account, the large book co-written with Guattari that he regarded as his best work, *A Thousand Plateaus*, failed to resonate with the social milieu in which it appeared in 1980: 'The book was perhaps too big. And above all, the times had changed' (Deleuze 1995b: 51). This book remains largely outside the purview of serious philosophy around the world as it does in France.

Equally, the institution that made it possible to produce such a book, The University of Paris VIII at Vincennes, has been fully normalised and reintegrated into the French university system. After 1980 it was relocated to Saint-Denis and the demountable buildings of the old campus demolished. Deleuze took very seriously the experimental character of the original Vincennes that flourished for a few years as an extraordinary anomaly within the French university system. Founded in 1969, partly in response the demands of students in 1968, it was initially named the *Centre Universitaire Expérimental de Vincennes* before becoming the University of Paris VIII in 1971. In an essay that he contributed to a volume published in defence of the initial mandate, in the face of threats to the very existence of Paris VIII coming from the Ministry of Education, Deleuze drew attention to the distinctive features of the way teaching was conducted there (Deleuze 2007: 152–4).[11] There was no distinction between the level of courses, no progression from a first to second or third year, but simply a suite of courses that were open to all, whatever the student's level of prior education.[12] Second, the content of classes was constantly adjusted in response to the needs or the interests of those attending: there was no preordained programme of instruction in the discipline of the kind required for the *agrégation*.

For Deleuze, this institutional arrangement allowed for a very different practice of philosophy that faced outwards towards the interests of its students rather than inwards towards the history or the concerns of professional philosophers. As he explained, the students in a given class in philosophy at Vincennes might include mathematicians, musicians, psychologists or historians. In contrast to the usual manner in which students took courses in a subject outside their primary interest or major, the Vincennes students did not leave their other intellectual interests at the door to the philosophy classroom. They came in search of something that would be useful to them in the pursuit of those interests. In this manner, he suggested, philosophy mattered to them not in relation to their level of achievement in the discipline, but in direct relation to their other interests. In this way, the teaching of philosophy as Deleuze understood and practised it was oriented towards the question of knowing

> how it might be useful to mathematicians, or to musicians etc., even and especially when it does not speak about mathematics or music. This kind of teaching has nothing to do with general culture; it is practical and experimental, always outside itself, precisely because those attending are drawn to intervene in terms of their own needs or competences. (Deleuze 2007: 167; translation modified)

Deleuze defended the experimental teaching practised at Vincennes as a pathway towards pedagogic innovation and renewal, not only in philosophy but in all disciplines in the French university. In his short essay in defence of Vincennes, he does not reflect on the relationship between this experimental pedagogy and its institutional setting and the philosophy that he developed in collaboration with Guattari during this period. Years later, in a long interview on philosophy, he commented on the 'exceptional conditions' at Vincennes and how important the diverse audience attending his lectures was to the philosophical experiment he was engaged in at that time: 'It was there that I realized how much philosophy needs not only a philosophical understanding, through concepts, but a nonphilosophical understanding rooted in percepts and affects' (Deleuze 1995a: 139).

Deleuze's comments draw attention to the relationship between the institutional setting and the practice of philosophy. It is hard to imagine how his work with Guattari could have been produced in the mainstream French university. Even harder to imagine, and impossible to have foreseen at the time, is the way in which the novel rhizomatic image of thought that they produced has since come to appear as an appealing response to the crisis in philosophy brought about by the larger transformation of universities in societies of control.

THE NEOLIBERAL UNIVERSITY AND THE CRISIS IN PHILOSOPHY

Just as France has the *agrégation* to police entry into the profession, so other countries and other times have their own institutional mechanisms for the control of philosophy. Richard Rorty explained the differences between analytic and continental philosophy in North America by reference to the differences in professional formation of aspiring philosophers (Rorty 2003). He appealed to the different kinds of knowledge that would be expected of applicants for jobs in philosophy, such as the canon of leading philosophers, or the ways in which the discipline was organised into subfields (epistemology, metaphysics, ethics, aesthetics as opposed to ontology, phenomenology, critical theory, and so on). Aspiring philosophers would also need to know the central issues or problems that have defined the history of the relevant subdiscipline. In countries which do not have the kind of centralised system of qualification that operates in France via the *agrégation*, the formation of philosophical minds and entry to the profession is closely regulated by the system of graduate training. In the US the progression towards a PhD involves the completion of coursework, as well as a thesis written to the satisfaction of a committee of individual scholars who function both as supervisors and examiners of the work. The effect is a no less rigorous control of the philosophical skills, basic knowledge and attitudes of those who eventually become philosophers than that achieved by the French system of competitive examination. Only the contents of the canon and the images of thought associated with it vary from place to place. Analytic philosophy has one series of such images, from logical positivism to the Quinean conception of philosophy as continuous with natural science, from the later Wittgenstein to the varieties of 'ordinary language' philosophy, conceptual analysis, and so on. Continental philosophy has another series, from phenomenological reduction to deconstruction, historical reconstruction and genealogical enquiry.

Both the French system of competitive examination and the graduate school training of philosophers function against the background of a larger historical shift in the institutional form of philosophy, namely its incorporation into the modern university. In Britain this process began in the late nineteenth century but was not completed until the mid-twentieth century (Mander 2014). Philosophy in North America and other parts of the English-speaking world followed a similar trajectory with the result that, over the last hundred years or so, 'philosophers have formed a professional class whose main audience consisted of one another. In other words, philosophy has become a discipline' (Frodeman, Briggle and Holbrook 2012: 314). This new institutional setting has directly influenced the nature of the activity. Only certain people become qualified to speak as philosophers. The bulk of their professional activity is henceforth directed at other philosophers. Instead of being an activity directed at a broader educated public, philosophy has become 'an inside game': 'Philosophers specialize, and direct their attentions to other philosophers, just as chemists or biologists direct their attention to their disciplinary peers' (Frodeman, Briggle and Holbrook 2012: 314). For Frodeman and Briggle, this institutionalisation of philosophy represents 'the great unthought of contemporary philosophy' (Frodeman and Briggle 2016: 7).

For much of the twentieth century, philosophy and other humanities disciplines survived under the protection of the nineteenth-century ideal of the autonomous university. Some philosophers sought to model themselves on the natural sciences while others preferred to align themselves with the classical humanities, but in either case it was widely accepted that students and the broader public benefited from exposure to largely self-contained and self-governed forms of academic enquiry. Since the 1980s, the impact of neoliberal demands for a more market-sensitive and market-responsive university has undermined this consensus. Universities are increasingly held accountable for their use of public funds, even as the proportion of public funding of universities in many countries has declined sharply in favour of non-public funding sources such as student fees and targeted research. More recently, they are held accountable not only for the quality of their teaching and research but also for the degree to which their research engages with real-world problems and communities.[13] Universities are increasingly under pressure to transform themselves into more responsive and dynamic institutions that engage with economic actors and other 'end-users' outside the academic enclave.

This 'postmodern' or neoliberal university shares many of the characteristic features of social and economic institutions in Deleuze's societies of control. Universities are no longer expected to mould the intellect and character of students. They are viewed rather as service providers as well as centres of knowledge-production and knowledge-transfer that are supposed to be responsive above all to the economic needs of the community. Their role is not only to provide a skilled labour force but also to generate the knowledge bases of new technologies susceptible to commercialisation. In this context, philosophy and other liberal arts face a profound challenge. Only a few elite institutions sufficiently protected by their endowed wealth will be able to resist the pressure to become more accountable to society. The more enrolments decline, the greater the pressure to reinvent the curriculum in ways that will both appeal to students and reduce the cost to the university of running courses in philosophy. The old disciplinary conception of philosophy is increasingly at odds with the market-driven propensities of students and administrators alike: 'Philosophers thus find themselves in the peculiar position of being professionals whose institutional home is increasingly hostile to their profession' (Frodeman, Briggle and Holbrook 2012: 315).

Assuming the survival in some form of philosophical enquiry in the new university, the question arises how the changed institutional environment will affect its form and content. Frodeman, Briggle and Holbrook's diagnosis of the likely outcome of the changing nature of the university, along with the dissemination of sites of knowledge production outside the ivy-covered walls, points to the emergence of a more diverse and partly 'postdisciplinary' institutional setting with consequences for the nature of philosophical research and teaching. On their account, developments such as transdisciplinarity or the encouragement of various forms of applied philosophy appear to be little more than half-way measures. They amount to attempts to broaden the target audience and diversify the output, thereby addressing the call for greater social relevance, while retaining the disciplinary structure of knowledge production. Newly emergent fields of applied philosophy from the 1970s onwards, such as environmental or business ethics, failed to escape the gravitational pull of the home discipline. Applied philosophers in these and other fields still tended to write for their peers in the academy rather than for those directly engaged in real-world policy or political issues. They employed epistemic rather than occasional or contextual criteria of rigour in their analyses. So, for example, to the extent that environmental ethicists remain located in philosophy departments, still write for a professional philosophical audience and still attend conferences along with other environmental philosophers, they remain captured by their discipline of origin.

> One finds neither a practical (e.g. the development of internship programs at the National Park Service) nor theoretical (e.g. how does the nature of our arguments change when our audience is nonphilosophers?) questioning of the disciplinary model of knowledge production. (Frodeman, Briggle and Holbrook 2012: 317–18)

Bioethics appears to be an exception to disciplinary capture, perhaps because it was from the outset a multidisciplinary field that included practitioners from medicine, law, nursing, political science, sociology and theology as well as philosophy. It was practised across a variety of institutional sites, from hospital ethics committees to government advisory boards. Nonetheless, Frodeman et al. argue that it failed to become truly postdisciplinary because of the way in which it formalised the evaluation of particular issues. It quickly adopted a framework whereby issues were approached in terms of a limited set of principles (respect for persons, beneficence and justice) at the expense of a more profound reflection on the meaning of those ideas, or on the ways in which existing understandings of what it is to be a person, to be beneficent or to be just are challenged by technoscientific developments. Deleuze explicitly refuses the appeal to such expertise in relation to the problems posed by modern biosciences. He rejects the idea of a new code or body of laws to deal with bioethical or biopolitical problems, opting instead for a more democratic and postdisciplinary approach: 'We don't need an ethical committee of supposedly well-qualified wise men but user groups' (Deleuze 1995a: 170).

FIELD PHILOSOPHY, RHIZOMES AND NOMADIC THOUGHT

Frodeman and Briggle's response to the dilemma facing disciplinary philosophy is to embrace a postdisciplinary practice that they call 'field philosophy'. In part, this is a response to the fact that the production of knowledge is no longer the prerogative of academic institutions but increasingly carried out in privately funded research hubs, think tanks and public companies. Silicon Valley entrepreneurs engage directly with philosophical questions about the nature of consciousness, the boundaries of the human and how we should be governed. Field philosophy is offered as a response to this state of affairs that draws directly on Deleuze and Guattari's conception of the rhizomatic nature of social processes and institutions and their indirect or 'subterranean approach to problems' (Frodeman and Briggle 2016: 123). Field philosophers are envisaged as coexisting alongside those privileged few who remain in academic departments, and those who find employment in public and private sector positions. Field philosophers work in-between institutions and diverse constituencies, with a primary focus on problems faced by nonphilosophical actors in real-world settings. Their aim is not to extract idealised versions of problems and provide solutions of interest only to philosophers, but to contribute to solving practical problems in terms that are attractive to the nonphilosophers engaged in them. In sum, 'field philosophy begins with problems as defined by non-philosophic actors in real world settings and seeks to make contributions deemed successful according to more-than-disciplinary standards' (Frodeman and Briggle 2016: 124).

The central characteristics of field philosophy bear striking resemblance to the experimental practice of philosophy described by Deleuze. In the first place the initial audience for field philosophy consists of one or another specific group of nonphilosophers. It is these nonphilosophers who define what counts as a problem and what would constitute a satisfactory solution. Field philosophers may therefore have to spend time learning the historical, political, scientific, technological, economic, legal and cultural dimensions of a problem. Frodeman offers the examples of work carried out with the US

Geological Survey in relation to fracking regulation, work with stakeholders in relation to acid mine drainage, or the evaluation of peer-review practices at government research funding agencies (Frodeman and Briggle 2016: 125).

Consistent with this extra-disciplinary approach, field philosophy rejects the linear, disciplinary model of knowledge production according to which knowledge is produced in isolation from the context of use and then deposited in a reservoir of peer-reviewed publications where it can be accessed and drawn upon by potential end-users. Field philosophy is nomadic. Its practitioners engage in the co-production of knowledge with nonphilosophers, in relation to particular problems that in turn define the relevant domains of thought that might be drawn upon to construct solutions. Whereas traditional models of applied philosophy are essentially top down, field philosophy takes a bottom-up approach. It begins with a problem in the world that has philosophical dimensions and seeks to work with the parties involved 'on terms initially set by them but continually refined as the process of thinking-together ensues' (Frodeman, Briggle and Holbrook 2012: 324–5). As such, there is no single analytical method but rather a plurality of methods and research techniques appropriate for the problem.

Finally, while disciplinary philosophers continue to think that one can make progress in the discipline according to its own internal criteria of success, field philosophers embrace a different notion of progress that places more value on helping nonphilosophers to reimagine, to work through and to solve their own problems. Disciplinary philosophy continues to measure 'progress' in philosophy on the model of progress in the natural sciences, by the extent to which it increases our understanding of the world. By contrast, 'field philosophy measures progress by the extent to which it manages to change the world (but again, without pretending to know in advance of the actual field work what kind of change will be for the best)' (Frodeman, Briggle and Holbrook 2012: 325).

Field philosophy carries implications for both the institutional setting and the practice of philosophy. Proposed as a response to changes in the nature of knowledge production and the government of universities that are already underway, it is also a response to the widely perceived sterility of disciplinary philosophy and its disconnection from the problems that often lead people to philosophy in the first place. At the institutional level, it is an adaptation to the realities of control society, a strategy for the survival of philosophy in a world in which the old institutional borders and disciplinary techniques no longer hold sway. At the intellectual level, the question is whether field philosophy can also underwrite new forms of resistance to the rigours of control society. As Deleuze comments,

> It's not a question of asking whether the old or new system is harsher or more bearable, because there's a conflict in each between the ways they

free and enslave us . . . It's not a question of worrying or hoping for the best, but of finding new weapons. (Deleuze 1995a: 178)

It is at this point that Deleuze and Guattari's rhizomatic image of thought and their experimental practice of philosophy might be useful. They insist on both the creativity of philosophical thought and its collective character. But the collectivity required for creative thought is necessarily diverse, made up of different kinds of thinkers and practitioners: philosophers, artists or scientists. It is a patchwork, a bastard mixed race, such that creative thought always takes place in between these different constituents. That is why Deleuze insists on the need for mediators, which are fundamental to the process of creative thought: 'Without them nothing happens' (Deleuze 1995a: 125). Field philosophy also requires mediators, or allows the philosopher to serve as mediator between different intellectual or political constituencies. The institutional conditions of field philosophy provide at least some of the conditions for the possibility of creative thought. Deleuze and Guattari's rhizomatic image of thought provides a further condition. Together, they allow for an intellectually and institutionally nomadic thought that can produce creative responses to social, environmental or economic problems. There is no guarantee that the results will fuel resistance to the forms of control, but some form of creative thought is indispensable to evade or overcome the constraints of control society.

ACKNOWLEDGEMENT

I am grateful for helpful comments on an earlier draft by Frida Beckman and Gregg Lambert. This chapter has been improved as a result.

NOTES

1. The *October* version of 'Postscript' has over 3,100 citations on Google Scholar and the *Negotiations* version a further 700.
2. François Dosse suggests that Deleuze's concept of control encompasses the range of technologies of power that Foucault discussed under the heading of 'biopower' (Dosse 2010: 329). Jeff Nealon argues that Deleuze's term can stand as a cover-all for the 'lighter, more effective, and more diffuse methods of subject production' discussed in Foucault's work after *Discipline and Punish* (Nealon 2014: 84). Gilbert and Goffey, in their Introduction to the issue of *New Formations* devoted to 'Control Societies', suggest that the modality of power described in Foucault's analysis of security mechanisms 'can usefully be equated with' Deleuze's 'control' (Gilbert and Goffey 2015: 9). Frida Beckman suggests that the concept of control society 'does not break off from Foucault's analyses of biopower so much as it constitutes a continuation and elaboration of disciplinary and regulatory technologies that Foucault had already begun to theorise' (Beckman 2016: 3).

Thomas Nail suggests 'a clear equivalence between biopower and control in both content and form' (Nail 2016: 257).
3. He noted that 'disciplinary power was in fact already in Bentham's day being transcended by other and much more subtle mechanisms for the regulation of phenomena of population, controlling their fluctuations and compensating their irregularities' (Gordon 1980: 160). See also the 'Body/Power' interview from 1975, in which Foucault suggests that: 'From the eighteenth to the early twentieth century I think it was believed that the investment of the body by power had to be heavy, ponderous, meticulous and constant. Hence those formidable disciplinary regimes in the schools, hospitals, barracks, factories, cities, lodgings, families. And then, starting in the 1960s, it began to be realised that such a cumbersome form of power was no longer as indispensable as had been thought and that industrial societies could content themselves with a much looser form of power over the body' (Gordon 1980: 58).
4. A section of the chapter on discipline is entitled 'The Control of Activity' (Foucault 1995: 149–56). In the chapter on Panopticism, he refers to the tendency of disciplinary mechanisms to become 'de-institutionalized': 'the massive, compact disciplines are broken down into flexible methods of control, which may be transferred and adapted' (Foucault 1995: 211).
5. Olivier Razac comments that: 'GPS represents the final stage of this evolution [from discipline to control]. Even the electronic bracelet remains essentially disciplinary, transforming the home into a prison and trapping the condemned as though in his apartment burrow. By contrast, mobile technologies of surveillance in real time liberate the individual. They liberate his energy and his desire so that he can work at his own always ephemeral and perfectible integration' (Razac 2008: 61).
6. Simondon (2005). For helpful commentary on Deleuze's use of this concept, see Hui (2015).
7. 'The exclusive right of concept creation secures a function for philosophy, but it does not give it any preeminence or privilege since there are other ways of thinking and creating, other modes of ideation that, like scientific thought, do not have to pass through concepts' (Deleuze and Guattari 1994: 8).
8. See Tasioulas (2012, 2018) and Moyn (2018). Moyn is a historian and reader of Foucault and author of a very influential book, *The Last Utopia: Human Rights in History* (Moyn 2010). Tasioulas is a legal philosopher and author of a number of articles on human rights.
9. For this reason Alan Schrift argues that the content of the annual *agrégation* programmes reflects 'the foundational historical knowledge that philosophers educated in France will draw upon, and frequently write upon, early and sometimes throughout their careers' (Schrift 2008: 456). Schrift's article provides helpful detail on the history of the *agrégation*, how it works and the influence of its changing content on twentieth-century philosophy.
10. I am using 'control' here in its ordinary non-technical sense rather than the specific sense given to it by Deleuze in 'Postscript'.
11. Originally published in Jacqueline Brunet et al. (1979: 120–1).
12. Commenting on his teaching at Vincennes in an interview, Deleuze notes that: 'In philosophy we rejected the principle of "building up knowledge" progressively: there were the same courses for first-year and nth-year students, for students and nonstudents, philosophers and nonphilosophers, young and old, and many different nationalities. There were always young painters and musicians there, film-makers, architects, who showed great rigor in their thinking. They were long sessions, nobody took in everything, but everyone took what they needed or wanted, what they could use, even if it was far removed from their own discipline' (Deleuze 1995a: 139).

13. The UK's Research Excellence Framework was extended in 2014 to include case studies on the impact of research beyond academia. In 2018 an Engagement and Impact assessment will be added to the biannual Australian Excellence in Research assessment exercise. In both cases, the aim is to measure the extent to which universities' research is translated into economic, social and other benefits and the ways in which universities engage with industrial, community and other end-users of research.

REFERENCES

Beckman, Frida (2016), *Culture Control Critique: Allegories of Reading the Present*, London and New York: Rowman & Littlefield International.
Brunet, Jacqueline, Bernard Cassen, François Châtelet, Pierre Merlin and Madeleine Rebérioux (eds) (1979), *Vincennes ou le désir d'apprendre*, Paris: Editions Alain Moreau.
Deleuze, Gilles (1990), *Pourparlers*. Paris: Éditions de Minuit.
Deleuze, Gilles (1995a), *Negotiations 1972–1990*, trans. Martin Joughin, New York: Columbia University Press.
Deleuze, Gilles (1995b), 'Le "je me souviens" de Gilles Deleuze', *Le Nouvel Observateur* 1619, 16–22 novembre, pp. 50–1.
Deleuze, Gilles (2007), *Two Regimes of Madness: Texts and Interviews 1975–1995*, trans. Ames Hodges and Mike Taormina, New York: Semiotext(e). (Revised Edition.)
Deleuze, Gilles (2011 [1968]), *Difference and Repetition*, trans. Paul Patton, London: Continuum. (Corrected edition.)
Deleuze, Gilles and Félix Guattari (1994), *What Is Philosophy?*, trans. Hugh Tomlinson and Graham Burchell, New York: Columbia University Press.
Deleuze, Gilles and Claire Parnet (2002), *Dialogues II*, trans. Hugh Tomlinson and Barbara Habberjam; 'The Actual and the Virtual', trans. Eliot Ross Albert, London: Athlone Press.
Dosse, François (2010), *Gilles Deleuze and Félix Guattari: Intersecting Lives*, trans. Deborah Glassman, New York: Columbia University Press.
Foucault, Michel (1995), *Discipline and Punish*, trans. Alan Sheridan, New York: Vintage.
Frodeman, Robert and Adam Briggle (2016), *Socrates Tenured: The Institutions of 21st-Century Philosophy*, London: Rowman & Littlefield International.
Frodeman, Robert, Adam Briggle and J. Britt Holbrook (2012), 'Philosophy in the Age of Neoliberalism', *Social Epistemology* 26:3–4, pp. 311–30.
Gilbert, Jeremy and Andrew Goffey (2015), 'Control Societies: Notes for an Introduction', *New Formations* 84–5, pp. 5–19.
Gordon, Colin (ed.) (1980), *Michel Foucault: Power/Knowledge: Selected Interviews and Other Writings 1972–1977*, Hemel Hempstead: Harvester Wheatsheaf.
Hardt, Michael and Antonio Negri (2000), *Empire*, Cambridge, MA: Harvard University Press.
Hui, Yuk (2015), 'Modulation after Control', *New Formations* 84–5, pp. 74–91.
Kelly, Mark (2015), 'Discipline is Control: Foucault contra Deleuze', *New Formations* 84–5, pp. 148–62.
Mander, W. J. (2014), 'The Professionalization of British Philosophy', *Oxford Handbook of British Philosophy in the Nineteenth Century*, Oxford: Oxford Handbooks Online.
Moyn, Samuel (2010), *The Last Utopia: Human Rights in History*, Cambridge, MA: Harvard University Press.
Moyn, Samuel (2018), 'Human Rights in Heaven', in *Human Rights: Moral or Political?* ed. A. Etinson, Oxford: Oxford University Press.

Nail, Thomas (2016), 'Biopower and Control', in *Between Deleuze and Foucault*, ed. N. Morar, T. Nail and D. W. Smith, Edinburgh: Edinburgh University Press, pp. 247–63.

Nealon, Jeff (2014), 'Control', in *The Cambridge Foucault Lexicon*, ed. Leonard Lawlor and John Nale, Cambridge: Cambridge University Press, pp. 83–6.

Razac, Olivier (2008), *Avec Foucault, Après Foucault: Disséquer la société de contrôle*, Paris: L'Harmattan.

Rorty, Richard (2003), 'Analytic and Conversational Philosophy', in *A House Divided: Comparing Analytic and Continental Philosophy*, ed. C. G. Prado, Amherst: Humanity Books, pp. 17–32. (Reprinted in Rorty, Richard (2007), *Philosophy as Cultural Politics: Philosophical Papers, Volume 4*, Cambridge: Cambridge University Press, pp. 120–30.)

Rose, Nikolas (1999), *Powers of Freedom: Reframing Political Thought*, Cambridge: Cambridge University Press.

Schrift, Alan (2008), 'The Effects of the *Agrégation de Philosophie* on Twentieth-Century French Philosophy', *The Journal of the History of Philosophy* 46:3, pp. 449–73.

Simondon, Gilbert (2005), *L'individuation à la lumière des notion de forme et d'information*, Paris: Editions Jérôme Millon.

Tasioulas, John (2012), 'Towards a Philosophy of Human Rights', *Current Legal Problems* 65:1, pp. 1–30.

Tasioulas, John (2018), 'Philosophizing the Real World of Human Rights: A Reply to Samuel Moyn', in *Human Rights: Moral or Political?*, ed. A. Etinson, Oxford: Oxford University Press.

Index

Note: 'n' indicates chapter notes; 'coll.' denotes works by collaboration.

abstraction, 52, 58, 60
Abu Ghraib prison, 174–5
accumulation, 34, 45, 51, 53–5, 57, 58
action-images, 164
Adorno, Theodor, 112, 114–16
Aesop's *Fables*, 170
aestheticism, 67, 73, 78
Agamben, Giorgio, 30, 172–3
Ahmed, Sarah, 176
Ahuja, Neel, 5, 14
'algorithmic governmentality', 8–9, 12
Althusser, Louis, 9, 20, 22, 86–8, 91, 92
analytics *see* metadata
animal control, 166–78
animal imagery, military use of, 174–5
animal reason, 74–6
animal-becomings, 186
animals
    in literature, 74–8, 170, 185–6
    violence against, 170–1, 174–5
art, 1, 7, 13, 190
art of existence, 67–9, 78–9
assemblages, 20–3, 34, 40–2, 44, 51, 130, 137, 147, 155, 186–7, 199
Attali, Jacques, 111–12
attention economy, 115–17
authenticity, 102, 107–111, 115–17, 135
automata, 122–3, 136; *see also* cybernetics

Bakhtin, Mikhail, 181
Bateson, Gregory, 84–5
Baucom, Ian, 60
Beckett, Samuel, 143

Beckman, Frida, 5, 17, 178, 207n2
becoming-animal, 169, 171, 172, 178, 185–6
Beller, Jonathan, 115
Beniger, James R., 8
Benjamin, Walter, 116
Bensmaïa, Réda, 189
Bentham, Jeremy, 52, 60, 194, 208nn3–4; *see also* panopticon
Bergson, Henri, 6–7
Bernier, François, 75
Bhandar, Brenna, 60
bioethics, 204–5
biopolitics, 2, 5, 10–11, 13–14, 29–30, 40, 47–9, 52, 57, 101–19, 182–3, 190; *see also* Foucault, Michel: *The Birth of Biopolitics*
biopower
    and animal control, 168, 169, 172, 174, 176
    and literature, 187
    and 'minor' fascism, 144
    and the periodisation of control, 47–9, 52
    and popular music, 101–3, 105–7, 112, 117–18
    and state forms, 29, 31
biotechnology, 40, 41
black hole phenomenon, 156–8
black racism/anti-blackness, 36, 39, 41
'blind spots' of social observation, 95, 97–8, 99n9
Boggs, Colleen Glenney, 5, 17
Bogue, Ronald, 187, 190, 191n3
Boileau, Nicolas, 'The Art of Poetry', 64
Boulez, Pierre, 23

Bourdieu, Pierre, 107–8
Bourne film franchise, 124, 128–37
Bowie, David, 106
Bradbury, Ray, 'The Pedestrian', 20–2, 24–6, 32
Bratton, Benjamin H., 9, 12, 13
Briggle, Adam, 203–5
Brown, Wendy, 82–6, 90–4, 96–7, 99n9
Browne, Simon, 50, 53
bureaucracy, 8, 57
Burke, Kenneth, 95
Burke, Peter, 77
Burroughs, William S., 4, 7, 8, 34–7, 40, 41, 88, 183–4
Butler, Judith, 69

capital, 38, 39, 54–5, 60
capitalism, 6, 11
   and colonialism, 36–8
   and counterculture, 110–11
   and the novel, 180–1, 188, 189
   and periodisation of control, 48, 54
   and philosophy, 196, 208n3
   and popular music, 101–2, 105–6, 111, 115, 118
   real capitalist subsumption, 11, 54, 57
   and sovereignty, 64, 65
'capitalist supersystem', 10, 12
cartoon animals, 166–72, 178
Castiglione, Baldesar, *Il Cortegiano*, 68
Catholicism, 70–1, 77, 78
Chicago School, 86
childhood pedagogy, 170–1
China, 38
choice, 126
Chun, Wendy Hui Kyong, 12
cinema, 22–3, 45, 121–39
   Bourne film franchise, 124, 128–37
   Citizenfour (dir. Poitras), 138–9
   and the control-grid, 124–37, 138–9
   see also cartoon animals; Deleuze, Gilles: *Cinema I, Cinema II*; television
Citizenfour (dir. Poitras), 138–9
Citizens United v. FEC (2010), 83
citizenship, 42, 50, 153, 170–1
Citton, Yves, 116
civil society, 10, 27, 30, 39, 88, 90–1, 94, 170, 173, 181–2, 185, 188–90
class, 23, 47, 83, 110, 115, 147–54, 181–2, 202–3
classicism, 64–5, 69–73, 76, 78
cognitive mapping, 12, 113, 118
colonialism, 35, 39, 42, 55, 60
communication, 6–7, 39, 45, 74, 88, 126–31, 134, 184, 195
compassion, 171
concentration camp as state form, 29–30

confession, Christian, 70–1, 77
Control Revolution, 8
control-grid, 124–9, 138–9, 139n6
   Bourne film franchise, 124, 128–37
   going 'off the grid', 124, 128–9, 137, 138, 139n6
conversation, art of, 70–2, 74, 76
counterculture, 110–11
Counter-Reformation, 77
court societies, 63–4, 69, 71–2, 76, 79n1
   'court rationality', 64–5, 69, 73, 76, 77, 79
   honnêteté, 68–9, 73, 76
credit see debt
critical race theory, 34, 39–41
criticism, social, 94–5
critique, art of, 65, 68–70, 72–4, 76, 77
cybernetics, 8, 9, 36, 37, 38, 47–8, 123; see also automata; control-grid

Daney, Serge, 183
data, 47, 50, 57, 195; see also metadata
Dean, Mitchell, 26
debilitated populations, 46, 47, 49–50
Debord, Guy, 54
debt, 37, 38, 55, 60
deficiency, 13
Deleuze, Gilles, 1–6, 9
   and animal control, 168–9
   and cinema, 121, 122–7, 138
   diagram of control, 23–7, 31, 32n4
   and literature, 180, 182, 183–7
   and 'minor' fascism, 141–3, 153–4
   'new weapons' against control, 6, 16, 118, 139, 180, 189–91, 207
   and philosophy, 193–201, 205, 206–7, 207n2, 208n12
   and the political, 85, 88, 92, 96, 97
   and popular music, 101–2, 105, 106, 118
   and race, 34, 36–41
   and sovereignty, 63, 76
   and state forms, 27–30
   WORKS
   Anti-Oedipus (coll. Guattari), 27, 31, 147, 151, 155
   Cinema I: The Movement-Image, 22, 122–3
   Cinema II: The Time-Image, 1, 22, 122–4, 164
   'Control and Becoming' (coll. Negri), 1, 6, 45, 46–7, 183, 188–9, 194
   Dialogues (coll. Parnet), 143–4, 156–8, 160, 183, 198, 200
   Difference and Repetition, 198
   Foucault, 154
   Francis Bacon: The Logic of Sensation, 183

'Having an Idea in Cinema', 7, 44, 46, 190
Kafka: Toward A Minor Literature (coll. Guattari), 51, 184–90
'Postscript on Control Societies', 3–4, 6–7, 23–6, 31, 44, 46, 47, 50–1, 53, 55, 101–2, 105, 106, 118, 121, 125–7, 129, 139, 139n4, 161, 180, 183, 187, 189, 190–1, 193–6, 207n2
Pourparlers, 31–2
A Thousand Plateaus (coll. Guattari), 6, 20–3, 27, 30–1, 32n2, 155–6, 168–9, 184, 200–1
Two Regimes of Madness, 142
What is Philosophy? (coll. Guattari), 197
democracy, 82, 91, 96, 99n9, 150–1, 185; *see also* political, the
'depressive' position, 117
Derrida, Jacques, 75
Descartes, René, 64–6, 71, 73–5, 78
desire, 4, 12, 147–54, 159, 189; *see also* pleasure
determinism, 87
deterritorialisation, 27, 34, 143–4, 147, 151, 154, 156, 189
deviant populations, 46, 47, 49–50, 55–6
diagram of control, 5–6, 10, 23–7, 31, 32n4, 45, 49, 51, 53, 125–6
difference, racial, 34, 38, 40, 44, 56–7
digital media, 37, 39, 41, 56, 121–4, 126, 128, 130, 135
digital technologies, 2, 7–9, 11–12, 37, 55, 183, 195, 208n5
disability, 46–7, 50, 55, 56
disciplinary societies, 2–5, 10, 12, 45, 46–8, 47, 49, 51, 52, 57, 194
and cinema, 125–6
and the novel, 182, 183
and popular music, 101–7, 109, 111–12, 118
discipline, 5–6, 22–4, 37, 38, 39, 64, 145
and biopower, 101–6, 117
and the cinema, 125–7
and literature, 180–2, 184, 188, 190
and periodisation of control, 47, 48, 49, 52, 57
disposal, population, 49, 56
dispositif (apparatus), 2, 24, 26, 31, 144–7, 199–200
distraction, 115–17
dividuals, 4, 38, 47, 50, 105–6, 114, 161, 163–4, 183, 195
Dosse, François, 207n2
doubt, 71

ecology, 84, 87, 116
economy, the, 50–1, 53–6, 82–91, 96, 181, 196; *see also* capital; capitalism; debt; neoliberalism
ecosocialism, 84
education
childhood, 170–1
philosophy, 196, 199, 200–1, 208n12
see also universities
effectivity, 90, 93
Ehrenberg, Alain, 65
Elias, Norbert, 63, 64, 69, 71, 72, 78, 79n1
Elmer, Jonathan, 174
empire, 11, 12, 13, 30, 34–6, 38, 45, 48
enclosure, 21–4, 26, 49, 57
energy analysis, 84
England, Lindy, 175
Eno, Brian, 114
enslavement, 65, 68–70, 106, 117–18; *see also* machinic enslavement; slavery
entrepreneurship, 111
epic narratives, 180–2
Epicureanism, 68, 71, 75–6
equality, 91
Esposito, Roberto, 92–4
ethnonationalism, 34, 38
Europa '51 (The Greatest Love) (dir. Rossellini), 125–6
excess, 13
exploitation, 56, 57
'expository society', 12, 13

fables, 74–8, 170
Faret, Nicolas, *The Honest Man or the Art to Please in Court*, 68
fascism, 30, 34, 38, 42, 142, 151, 155–6
lines, 154–60
'minor' fascism, 143–7
velvet, 141–3
'fatigue of being oneself', 65, 67
fear, 141–3, 176–7
feminism, 40, 116
field philosophy, 205–7
films *see* cinema
Flaxman, Gregory, 5, 6, 16
flexibility, 10, 64–5, 69–70, 76
Foucault, Michel, 2–5, 9
and animal control, 168, 172
and the cinema, 125–7
diagrams of control, 23, 24, 27, 29, 31, 32n4
dispositif / apparatus, 143–7
and 'minor' fascism, 141, 144, 147–54
and the novel, 181–2
and the periodisation of control, 45, 46, 47–8, 57
and philosophy, 193–4, 199
and race, 39

Foucault, Michel (*cont.*)
    and sovereign societies, 64, 67–71, 76, 77
    WORKS
    The Birth of Biopolitics, 2, 27–8, 48, 64, 82, 85–92, 94, 95, 98, 98n5, 101, 102, 127, 141, 144, 182–3
    Discipline and Punish: The Birth of the Prison, 144, 168, 172, 182, 194, 207n2, 208nn3–4
    The Hermeneutics of the Subject, 67
    The History of Sexuality, Volume I, 48–9
    Security, Territory & Population, 144
    Society Must be Defended, 48, 182–3
    The Use of Pleasure, 67, 78–9
Frankfurt School, 11
Franklin, Seb, 5, 11–12, 14
Franzén, Carin, 5, 15
free will, 64, 71–2
freedom, 91, 102, 126–7
Frith, Simon, 104
Frodeman, Robert, 203–6
Furetière, Antoine, 70

Gaiman, Neil, 25
Galloway, Alexander R., 8, 9, 12, 13, 45, 53
Game, Jérôme, 162–3
Gardner, Colin, 5, 16–17
Gassendi, Pierre, 68, 75
gender, 46, 47, 50, 54–6, 72, 110, 118
genetics, 28–30, 85, 195
geopolitics, 37–8
Gilbert, Jeremy, 207n2
Gilmore, Ruth Wilson, 55
gnothi seauton (know thyself), 77
Godard, Jean-Luc, 164
Goffey, Andrew, 207
Goh, Irving, 169
governmentality, 8–9, 48, 56, 70, 71, 76–9, 172
governments, 90–1; *see also* democracy; political, the; state, the
GPS (Global Positioning System), 24, 130–1, 195, 208n5
Gramsci, Antonio, 185
Grateful Dead, The (band), 104–6, 108, 110
grid *see* control-grid
Gritz, James (Bo), 139n6
Grossberg, Lawrence, 109, 119n3
Grove, Jairus, 40
Guattari, Félix
    Anti-Oedipus (coll. Deleuze), 27, 31, 147, 151, 155
    Kafka: Toward A Minor Literature (coll. Deleuze), 51, 184–90
    A Thousand Plateaus (coll. Deleuze), 6, 20–3, 27, 30–1, 32n2, 155–6, 168–9, 184, 200–1
    What is Philosophy? (coll. Deleuze), 197

Haraway, Donna, 84, 178
Harcourt, Bernard E., 12, 13
Hardt, Michael, 10–11, 12, 13, 29, 45, 48, 54, 182, 185
Heath, Joseph, 110–11
heredity, 28–9
Hesmondhalgh, David, 103
higher education *see* universities
highways, 45
hippiedom, 104–7
Hobbes, Thomas, 181
Holbrook, J. Britt, 204–5
homo oeconomicus, 83–5, 91
homo politicus, 92–4, 96
Hong, Grace Kyungwon, 49
honnêteté, 68–9, 73, 76, 77
Huillet, Danièle, 45
human rights, 197–8
humanism, 40, 91–5, 103
humour, 13
Husserl, Edmund, 90

Ibbett, Katherine, 77
ideology, 20, 22, 39–40, 64, 86, 92–3, 95, 110–11, 147
India, 38
individualism, 104–5, 110, 114, 180–5, 188–90
information, 7, 9, 45–6, 50, 121–4, 126–8, 130–4, 137, 161, 184
institutions, 4, 11, 39, 45, 125–6, 182–3, 189, 197–8
integration, 49–50
Islamophobia, 36, 38, 41, 42
Israel, 38

Jameson, Fredric, 11–12, 44

Kafka, Franz, 26, 37, 51, 57, 143, 180, 184–90, 191nn2–3
Kassabian, Anahid, 114
Kelly, Mark G. E., 5, 32n5, 194
Kittler, Friedrich, 121
Klay, Phil, *Redeployment*, 169–78
Klein, Melanie, 117

La Fontaine, Jean de
    'Discourse to Madame de la Sablière', 74–9, 79n4
    Fables, 74–6
labour, 13, 35, 37–9, 54–6
Lacan, Jacques, 116
laissez-faire economics, 90

Lambert, Gregg, 5, 13–14, 98n5
Land, Christopher, 184
Laruelle, François, 53
Lazzarato, Maurizio, 106
Le Rochefoucauld, François de, *Maxims*, 69, 71, 73
Leibniz, Gottfried Wilhelm, 76
Lenclos, Ninon de, 72–3, 79n2
letters, 72–3, 79n2
Lévi-Strauss, Claude, 66–7, 79n5
liberalism, 88, 89
libertinism, 64–5, 67–73, 76–9
lifestyle, 67–8, 70, 72–3, 102, 104, 105, 195
lines of flight, 6, 154–60, 188
literature *see* animals: in literature; epic narratives; major literature; minor literature; novels
Locke, John, *Some Thoughts Concerning Education*, 170–4, 181
Louis XIV of France, 63, 64, 77
love, 71–3
Lowe, Lisa, 56, 57
Luhmann, Niklas, 85, 87–90, 92–5, 97, 98–9nn6–7
Lukács, György, 181
Luxemburg, Rosa, 54

machines, 4, 24–5, 30, 50, 52–4, 57; *see also* technology; war machines
machinic enslavement, 20–8, 30–1, 32n2, 106, 113, 118
Macpherson, C. P., 181
macro-fascisms, 150, 158–60
major literature, 184–6, 188, 190
Malabou, Catherine, 40, 65, 69–70, 76
Malebranche, Nicolas, 75
management, 45–7, 49–52, 54, 57, 61
Marx, Karl, 29, 54, 92
Marxism, 11, 53–5, 57, 86–8, 90, 91, 94, 95, 147–8
mass culture, 112–13, 116
mass media, 25–6, 40–2; *see also* communication; digital technology
Massumi, Brian, 10, 12–13
Maya civilisation, 35, 36
Mazzoni, Guido, 181
Mbembe, Achille, 50
media *see* communication; digital technology; mass media; social media
mega-machine, 28, 32n2
metadata, 127, 137–8; *see also* data
metaproduction, 196
micro-fascism, 141–3, 145, 149–50, 156–8, 160–4
migration, 41, 96
militarisation, 36, 38, 39, 41
military, the, 168–74; *see also* state security; United States of America: military; war machines
Military Balance, The (journal), 173
Miller, D. A., 181, 182
'minor' fascism, 143–7, 151, 159, 164
minor literature, 143–4, 180–91
mobile phones *see* smartphones
modulations, 3, 4, 5, 13, 34, 37, 41–2, 55, 60, 105, 126–7, 196
Moeller, Hans-Georg, 87, 94, 95
molar structures, 145, 154, 156, 159–60, 184–5
molecular line, 154–60
Montaigne, Michel de, *Essays*, 65–71, 74–6
Moore, Nathan, 184
moralists, French, 64–5, 67, 69, 72, 74, 76
Moriarty, Michael, 68–9
Morris, Meaghan, 116–17
Moyn, Samuel, 197–8, 208n8
Mumford, Lewis, 32n2
Murphy, Timothy D., 184
music *see* popular music

Nail, Thomas, 208n2
narcissism, 72
national security *see* state security
Nealon, Jeffrey T., 5, 16, 98n4, 207n2
Negri, Antonio, 1, 11, 12, 13, 29, 45, 46–7, 48, 54, 102
'Control and Becoming' (coll. Deleuze), 1, 6, 45, 46–7, 183, 188–9, 194
neoliberalism, 5
and the control-grid, 127, 137
and the diagram of control, 20, 30–1
and periodisation of control, 49–50, 54
and the political, 82–6, 88, 91, 92, 97, 98n5
and popular music, 101–2, 105–12, 117–19
reason, 82–4
and sovereignty, 63, 65, 69–70, 79
subjectivity, 106–9, 111, 114
and universities, 199–205, 209n13
networks, 8, 9, 12, 13, 34, 41, 122, 126, 130, 137, 149; *see also* control grid; cybernetics
'new weapons' against control, 6, 16, 118, 139, 180, 189–91, 207
norms, 10, 107, 181–2
novels, 180–2, 184–6, 188–90

Obama, Barack, 39
obedience, 64, 77, 195
ordoliberalism, German, 86, 90, 96
orientalism, 36, 41
O'Sullivan, Simon, 7

panopticon, 2, 50, 52, 53, 57, 141, 142, 162, 194, 208nn3–4

paranoia, 24, 40–1, 128, 138, 155
    paranoid position, 117–18
    paranoid state form, 30, 34, 36
    paranoid style, 13, 27, 117
Parisi, Luciana, 9
Parker-Starbuck, Jennifer, 173
Parnet, Claire, *Dialogues* (coll. Deleuze), 143–4, 156–8, 160, 183, 198, 200
Pascal, Blaise, 69
passions, 70–3, 76
Patton, Paul, 5, 18
Penguins of Madagascar (film), 166
periodisation of control, 44–61
    and economy, 53–6
    and power, 46–50
    and representation, 56–60
    and technology, 50–3
Pettman, Dominic, 115
Philip, M. NourbeSe, *ZONG!*, 57–60
Philippines, 38
philosophy, 193–207
    control in/of philosophy, 198–202, 208n7
    field philosophy, 205–7
    and neoliberal universities, 199–205, 209n13
    and other disciplines, 196–7
plasticity, 34, 36, 40, 41, 69–70, 76
pleasing (*plaire*), 71, 76, 78
pleasure, 12, 67, 74, 78, 117–18; *see also* desire
Poe, Edgar Allen, 57
Poitras, Laura, 138
political, the, 82–98
    and neoliberalism, 82–6, 88, 91, 92, 97, 98n5
    see also biopolitics; geopolitics; governments; *homo politicus*; state, the
political steering, 95–6
popular music, 101–19
    listening practices, 113–19
populism, 96–7
'possessive individualism', 181
'postcivil' society, 10, 12, 185
Poster, Mark, 8, 9, 12, 13
Potter, Andrew, 110–11
power, 4, 5, 9, 12
    geometry of, 126
    and the novel, 181–3, 185, 188, 189
    and periodisation of control, 46–54, 57
    and philosophy, 198–9
    and popular music, 102–3, 116
    racial, 34
    sovereign, 39, 64, 68, 70, 74, 77
    see also biopower
primitivism, 36; *see also* racism; 'savages'
Prince (musician), 106
production, 35, 37–8, 40–1, 54, 56, 196

'productive interference patterns', 13
property, 58–9, 60, 181
'prosumption', 112
protocol, 8, 12, 13, 45, 53
Puar, Jasbir, 40

queer theory, 40

race, 23, 34–42, 47, 57, 100
    critical race theory, 34, 39–41
racial difference, 34, 38, 40, 44, 56–7
racialisation, 37, 46, 47, 49–50, 56, 57, 60
racism, 36, 40–1, 49
Rasch, William, 97
Razac, Olivier, 208n5
Reagan, Ronald, 105
real capitalist subsumption, 11, 54, 57
reason, 64–7, 70–2, 79
    animal, 74–6
    neoliberal, 82–4
    rational submission, 76–8
Reasoner, Harry, 104
Reformation, 77
religion, 84; *see also* Catholicism; confession
'reparative' engagement, 117–18
resistance, 6–7, 12–13
    and popular music, 102, 111, 114–15
    and race, 39–40
    and sovereignty, 63–4, 68–70, 72–3, 77, 79
Rheinberger, Hans-Jörg, 51
Rodriguez Delgado, José Manuel, 36
Rorty, Richard, 202
Rosnay, Joël de, 84
Rouvroy, Antoinette, 8–9, 12
Russia, 38, 41

Saint-Évremond, Charles de, 67–8, 72, 73
Saint-Simon, Louis de Rouvroy, 72
Saldanha, Arun, 40
salon culture, 69, 72–4, 76, 78, 79n4
satellite navigation *see* GPS
'savages', 27, 60, 75, 79n5; *see also* primitivism
scepticism, 66–9, 71, 72, 74, 75
Schachter, Marc, 70
Schmitt, Carl, 89, 97
Schrift, Alan, 208n9
science fiction, 6, 20–1, 24–6, 31, 123, 128, 129, 138
Scooby-Doo (TV series), 167, 171, 172
Secret Life of Pets, The (film), 166
security, 29–30, 36, 38–9, 142–6, 154, 207n2
    hierarchies, 146, 149–50
    spending, 38, 173
    state, 36, 38, 39, 41, 129, 131, 137, 143–4, 149–50
Sedgwick, Eve Kosofsky, 117–18

self, 13, 65–6, 67, 70–3, 79, 105–6, 171, 185
  'fatigue of being oneself', 65, 67
  'return to the self', 68, 69
self-control, 70–3, 178
self-mastery, 65–6, 67, 73, 76
self-technology, 70–1, 77
semantics, 94–6
services, 46, 54–5, 196
sex, 46, 50, 55–6
Sexton, Jared, 39, 41
sexuality, 47, 48, 95, 103, 199
Shadow of Angels (film), 142
Shapiro, Michael J., 162
'shared materiality', 75–6
shareware, 108
Shaviro, Steven, 7
Siegert, Bernhard, 51–3, 57
slavery, 35, 36, 42, 49, 50, 58–60
smartphones, 2, 113, 122, 124, 127, 130, 195, 208n5
Smith, Daniel W., 143–4
Snowden, Edward, 138
social complexity, 85–92, 95, 97–8
social media, 2, 41, 72
social systems, 87–93, 95–8
social welfare *see* welfare state
'soft machines', 24
sovereignty, 63–79
  and animal reason, 74–6
  and the art of existence, 67–9, 78–9
  and biopower, 172–3
  and the *dispositif* / apparatus, 144–7
  forms of subjectivity, 65–7
  and literature, 187
  and periodisation of control, 44, 45, 47, 50, 55
  popular, 91, 96–8, 99n9
  and race, 38, 39
  and reason (*raison d'état*), 64–7, 70–2, 76–9
  and style, 68, 69–73, 77
species, companion, 167, 170–1, 174, 176, 178
speculation, financial, 58–9
Spooks (TV series), 141–2, 144–52, 155–64
Stack model, 12, 13
Stanton, Domna C., 73
state, the, 5, 9, 27–30, 34–6, 38–9, 168–72; *see also* state security; surveillance; violence: state; welfare state
state security, 36, 38, 39, 41, 129, 131, 137, 143–4, 149–50; *see also* terrorism; war machines
steering, political, 95–6
Still, Judith, 75
Stoicism, 71
Straub, Jean-Marie, 45
'structural causality', 86

style, 68, 69–73, 77
subjectivity, 8–9
  forms of, 25–6
  in literature, 180–1
  neoliberal, 106–9, 111, 114
  sovereign, 63–7, 70, 73, 77, 79
submission, rational, 76–8
suicidal line, 154–60
superpanopticon, 12, 13
surplus, 54–7
surveillance, 12, 50, 128–31, 137, 138, 142–3, 160–4, 208n5
  state, 36, 38, 41, 42, 124, 127
  see also GPS

Tadiar, Neferti X. M., 55
Tambling, Jeremy, 181, 182
Tasioulas, John, 197–8, 208n8
taste, 107, 114; *see also* value
technology, 7–9, 34–6, 40, 45, 47, 50–3, 58–60; *see also* digital technology; machines
television, 23–5, 160–4; *see also* cartoon animals; cinema; *Spooks* (TV series)
Terranova, Tiziana, 9, 13
terrorism, 39, 41, 142, 146, 149, 157, 159, 169; *see also* state security
Thacker, Eugene, 7, 8
Thatcher, Margaret, 105
thinking-feelings, 73
Third World, 4, 37–8
thought, 198–201, 203, 206–7
time, 35–6, 42
time–image, 164
torture, 36, 39, 41, 174–5; *see also* violence
totalitarianism, 28, 30, 96, 155–6
truth, 66, 70–1, 77, 155, 198
Turkey, 38, 142

United States of America, 35–6, 38–9, 41, 169, 173
  military, 131–2, 173–5
universities, 83, 98n4, 199–205, 209n13; *see also* education
Urstaat, 28, 30
utopias, 95–6

value, 53–6, 60, 82–3, 111
  'attention theory of value', 115
  collective, 143, 189
  extraction, 53, 56, 59
  imaginary, 60
  scientific, 28
  surplus, 22, 46
values, 10, 54, 67–8, 82–3, 95, 110–12
Vardoulakis, Dimitris, 187
velvet fascism, 141–3, 149, 164

Villadsen, Kaspar, 26
violence
    against animals, 170–1, 174–5
    economic, 55–6
    racial, 38–41, 58–9
    state, 29, 30, 38–42, 50, 57, 97
    see also torture
Virilio, Paul, 4, 29–30
virtue, 69–70, 79
Vora, Kalindi, 55

war, 30, 38, 40, 41
war machines, 3, 6, 30, 155–6, 160, 168–9, 174
War on Terror, 169, 174–6

Watt, Ian, 181
'weapons, new' against control, 6, 16, 118, 139, 180, 189–91, 207
Weber, Max, 8, 9
Weheliye, Alexander G., 49
Weiss, Philip, 139n6
welfare state, 95–6, 126, 139n4
West, Kanye, 109
Wiener, Norbert, 8
Wolfe, Cary, 5, 15, 174

Yu, Timothy, 36

Zootopia (film, *Zootropolis* in UK), 166
Zylinka, Joanna, 75

CPSIA information can be obtained
at www.ICGtesting.com
Printed in the USA
JSHW050446090920
7725JS00002B/44